9.00

LUTHERAN QUARTERLY BOOKS

Editor

Paul Rorem, Princeton Theological Seminary

Associate Editors

Timothy J. Wengert, The Lutheran Theological Seminary at Philadelphia and Steven Paulson, Luther Seminary, St. Paul

Lutheran Quarterly Books will advance the same aims as *Lutheran Quarterly* itself, aims repeated by Theodore G. Tappert when he was editor fifty years ago and renewed by Oliver K. Olson when he revived the publication in 1987. The original four aims continue to grace the front matter and to guide the contents of every issue, and can now also indicate the goals of *Lutheran Quarterly Books*: "to provide a forum (1) for the discussion of Christian faith and life on the basis of the Lutheran confession; (2) for the application of the principles of the Lutheran church to the changing problems of religion and society; (3) for the fostering of world Lutheranism; and (4) for the promotion of understanding between Lutherans and other Christians."

For further information, see www.lutheranquarterly.com.

The symbol and motto of *Lutheran Quarterly*, VDMA for *Verbum Domini Manet in Aeternum* (1 Peter 1:25), was adopted as a motto by Luther's sovereign, Frederick the Wise, and his successors. The original "Protestant" princes walking out of the imperial Diet of Speyer 1529, unruly peasants following Thomas Muentzer, and from 1531 to 1547 the coins, medals, flags, and guns of the Smalcaldic League all bore the most famous Reformation slogan, the first Evangelical confession: the Word of the Lord remains forever.

TITLES

Living by Faith: Justification and Sanctification by Oswald Bayer (2003).

Harvesting Martin Luther's Reflections on Theology, Ethics, and the Church, essays from *Lutheran Quarterly* edited by Timothy J. Wengert, with foreword by David C. Steinmetz (2003).

FORTHCOMING

A More Radical Gospel: Essays on Eschatology, Authority, Atonement, and Ecumenism by Gerhard O. Forde, edited by Mark Mattes and Steven Paulson (spring 2004).

Harvesting Martin Luther's Reflections on Theology, Ethics, and the Church

Edited by

Timothy J. Wengert

with a Foreword by

David C. Steinmetz

WILLIAM B. EERDMANS PUBLISHING COMPANY

GRAND RAPIDS, MICHIGAN / CAMBRIDGE, U.K.

© 2004 Wm. B. Eerdmans Publishing Co.

Wm. B. Eerdmans Publishing Co.
255 Jefferson Ave. S.E., Grand Rapids, Michigan 49503 /
P.O. Box 163, Cambridge CB3 9PU U.K.

Printed in the United States of America

08 07 06 05 04   7 6 5 4 3 2 1

Library of Congress Cataloging-in-Publication Data

Harvesting Martin Luther's reflections on theology, ethics,
and the church / edited by Timothy J. Wengert;
with a foreword by David C. Steinmetz.
p.   cm. — (Lutheran quarterly books)
Includes bibliographical references and index.
ISBN 0-8028-2486-2 (pbk.: alk.paper)
1. Luther, Martin, 1483-1546. 2. Theology, Doctrinal — History —
16th century. 3. Christian ethics — History — 16th century.
4. Church — History of doctrines — 16th century.
5. Lutheran Church — Doctrines — History —16th century.
I. Wengert, Timothy J. II. Series.
BR332.5.H37 2004
230'.41'092 — dc22

2003049484

www.eerdmans.com

This volume of essays, originally published
in *Lutheran Quarterly*, n.s., from 1999-2002
is dedicated to all those who supported
the reestablishment of that journal,
especially Mr. David Hardy, esq., treasurer.

Contents

Foreword

In a famous sixteenth-century caricature Luther is portrayed as a monster with seven heads. Johannes Cochlaeus, on whose treatise the caricature appeared as a frontispiece in 1529, certainly looked upon Luther as a despicable monster, and it must have seemed to him on more than one occasion that he faced, not a single Luther, but an untamed herd of them, all bearing the same name and trampling underfoot the old order Cochlaeus loved. Although Luther was not the seven-headed monster of the Apocalypse against whom Cochlaeus warned his readers, he did nevertheless present more than one face to his contemporaries. On the one hand, Luther made an indelible impression on his contemporaries as a man of unbending principle who would not compromise with pope and emperor, even though his stubborn persistence in what he thought was right placed his life in jeopardy. On the other hand, some of Luther's contemporaries charged that he was far too eager to compromise with the powers that be. Thomas Müntzer called him *Doktor Leisetritt* ("Dr. Pussyfoot"). It is certainly true that Luther was prepared to compromise when he thought compromise was appropriate. The last journey of his life to Eisleben, where he died in 1546 away from home and family, is a case in point. Although he was mortally ill, he nevertheless demonstrated his considerable negotiating skills by successfully mediating a tax dispute between the quarreling counts of Mansfeld. Cochlaeus was therefore correct to suggest that Luther was no simple personality, quickly summed up and as quickly dismissed.

Historians have in their turn identified various images of Luther that were dominant in Protestant and Catholic circles from Luther's death until the present. From the first, Luther was admired by his friends as the prophet who had inaugurated a new evangelical age and reviled by his enemies as a morally corrupt and theologically ignorant arch-heretic. Later generations added their own images. The Lutheran orthodox saw Luther as a teacher of true doctrine, the Pietists as a model of conversion and the life of faith, the German Nationalists as a defender of German identity and culture, and the Enlightenment as an early proponent of freedom of conscience. Luther has been claimed by theologians — and not just Lutheran theologians — as an inspiration for a wide variety of theological positions from Ritschlian liberalism to confessional orthodoxy. All of these images (except the slanderous charge that Luther was morally corrupt) have some basis in the historical Luther and are not merely alien impositions on his life and thought.

Compounding the difficulties of understanding Luther's thought is the sheer quantity of what he wrote. Even before the one-hundredth volume of the Weimar edition of Luther's works had been published, scholars were already busily engaged in reediting earlier volumes. Melanchthon once labeled Caspar Schwenckfeld as a *centimanus,* a man with a hundred hands, but the label seems to fit Luther even better. In the hectic early years of his reforming career Luther could be found in his study struggling to finish treatises whose first pages were already in the press. Even as an old man, when he complained that age and infirmity had slowed him down, Luther managed to maintain a pace that would have been thought rigorous by a much younger man. It could be said of Luther throughout his life what G. K. Chesterton once said of H. G. Wells, that you could hear him growing in the night. No one who has ever stood before the shelves of Luther's collected works can keep from marveling at the enormous productivity they represent.

In the end, all of this means that interpreting Luther is a corporate enterprise. No one scholar has ever succeeded in mastering all the works in the Weimar edition or in charting all the twists and turns in Luther's thought. There is for most scholars not "world enough and time" for such a monumental enterprise. It is therefore a pleasure to greet and commend the present collaborative volume of essays on Lu-

ther by experts in the various aspects of his thought. Their work is a
gift to Luther research and an important aid for the general reader who
wants a reliable guide to Luther, a figure who has an undiminished capacity after nearly five hundred years to surprise and instruct us.

DAVID C. STEINMETZ
Duke University

Abbreviations

BC-T   *The Book of Concord.* Edited by Theodore E. Tappert. Philadelphia: Fortress, 1959.

BC   *The Book of Concord.* Edited by Robert Kolb and Timothy J. Wengert. Minneapolis: Augsburg Fortress, 2000.

BSLK   *Die Bekenntnisschriften der evangelisch-lutherischen Kirche.* 12th printing. Göttingen: Vandenhoeck & Ruprecht, 1998.

LC   Large Catechism

LW   *Luther's Works* [American edition]. 55 vols. Philadelphia: Fortress and St. Louis: Concordia, 1955-1986.

MLStA   *Martin Luther: Studienausgabe.* Edited by Hans-Ulrich Delius. 6 vols. Berlin: Evangelische Verlagsanstalt, 1979-1999.

SC   Small Catechism

WA   *Luthers Werke: Kritische Gesamtausgabe* [*Schriften*]. 65+ vols. Weimar: H. Böhlau, 1883- .

WA DB   *Luthers Werke: Kritische Gesamtausgabe: Bibel.* 12 vols. Weimar: H. Böhlau, 1906-1961.

WA Br   *Luthers Werke: Kritische Gesamtausgabe: Briefwechsel.* 18 vols. Weimar: H. Böhlau, 1930-1985.

WA TR   *Luthers Werke: Kritische Gesamtausgabe: Tischreden.* 6 vols. Weimar: H. Böhlau, 1912-1921.

Contributors

Carl Axel Aurelius is currently Church Secretary for the Church of Sweden.

Karlfried Froehlich is currently the B. B. Warfield Professor of Ecclesiastical History Emeritus at Princeton Theological Seminary.

Scott Hendrix is currently James Hastings Nichols Professor of Reformation History and Doctrine at Princeton Theological Seminary.

Helmar Junghans is Professor of Theology Emeritus at the University of Leipzig.

Robert Kolb is Mission Professor of Systematic Theology and Director of the Institute for Mission Studies at Concordia Seminary, St. Louis.

Dietrich Korsch is currently on the faculty of the University of Marburg.

Carter Lindberg is now Professor Emeritus at Boston University.

Gregory J. Miller is Associate Professor of History at Malone College, Canton, Ohio.

Ricardo Willy Rieth teaches at the Universidade Luterana do Brasil and at the Escola Superior de Teologia (IECLB) in São Leopoldo, Brazil.

Gerhard Sauter is Professor on the Evangelical Faculty of Theology at the University of Bonn.

Johannes Schwanke is currently an assistant for Prof. Oswald Bayer in the Theological Faculty of the University of Tübingen.

David C. Steinmetz is the Amos Ragan Kearnes Professor of Religion, Church History, and Doctrine for the Divinity School and Graduate Faculty of Duke University.

Mark D. Tranvik is currently teaching at Augsburg College in Minneapolis, Minnesota.

Timothy J. Wengert is the Ministerium of Pennsylvania Professor of the History of Christianity at The Lutheran Theological Seminary at Philadelphia.

Introduction

TIMOTHY J. WENGERT

This collection of essays provides perspectives on essential elements of Martin Luther's theology and writings. Given the flood of books on the subject since World War II, even in English alone, an introduction to such a work must immediately convince potential readers of the importance of yet another volume on Luther. In the case of the studies contained in this volume — first published in *Lutheran Quarterly* in a series entitled "Luther on . . ." — the authors themselves have made the job easy. Their contributions, representing a cross-section of scholars from this continent and abroad, combine the most recent historical scholarship with personal engagement in prominent theological and ethical issues of today. They cover a wide range of topics and thus serve as a useful introduction to the breadth of Luther's life and thought, under three headings: theology, ethics, and the church.[1] The essays reap a harvest from Luther's catechetical theology, from his encounter with the world of his day, and from his love for the living church.

---

1. This follows in the footsteps of other historians of ideas, David C. Steinmetz, *Luther in Context* (Bloomington: Indiana University Press, 1986); Gerhard Ebeling, *Luther: An Introduction to His Thought*, trans. R. A. Wilson (Philadelphia: Fortress, 1970); Eric W. Gritsch, *Martin — God's Court Jester: Luther in Retrospect* (Philadelphia: Fortress, 1983). This work differs from those in that here various authors, from differing perspectives, have collaborated by producing essays that represent their particular area of expertise.

Luther on Luther

This does not mean, however, that what these researchers present would have pleased Luther. He did not want his writings published for posterity or his name necessarily connected with a theological movement, let alone whole denominations. His own ornery words put the reader on notice that when we study Luther, we are always at least one or two steps away from what Luther considered most important: confession of the gospel of Jesus Christ, crucified and risen.

Luther on His Writings

Regarding [the plan] to collect my writings in volumes, I am quite cool and not at all eager about it because, roused by a Saturnian hunger, I would rather see them all devoured. For I acknowledge none of them to be really a book of mine, except perhaps the one *On the Bound Will* and the *Catechism*.[2]

So much for Luther scholarship in Luther's mind. Despite his suggestion, in 1883 German linguists and Reformation scholars began producing the critical edition of Luther's work — a task they hoped to complete in twenty years. Only now is the end of the so-called *Weimar Ausgabe* (Weimar edition) — well over one hundred volumes of Luther's works — coming into view. In the English-speaking world, not only is the fifty-five-volume American edition in print, but other portions of his writing are also still being translated and published.[3] It is clear that Luther scholars have paid no attention to his request.[4]

---

2. In a letter to Wolfgang Capito, dated 9 July 1537, LW 50:172-73 (WA Br 8:99-100).

3. See LW; *The 1529 Holy Week and Easter Sermons of Dr. Martin Luther,* trans. Irving L. Sandberg (St. Louis: Concordia, 1999) and *Sermons of Martin Luther: The House Postils,* ed. Eugene F. A. Klug, 3 vols. (Grand Rapids: Baker, 1996).

4. See Ulrich Köpf, "Kurze Geschichte der Weimarer Luther-Ausgabe," in *D. Martin Luthers Werke: Sonderedition der kritischen Weimarer Ausgabe: Begleitheft zu den Tischreden* (Weimar: Hermann Böhlaus Nachfolger, 2000), pp. 1-24.

Luther on His Theology

In the first place, I ask that people make no reference to my name; let them call themselves Christians, not Lutherans. What is Luther? After all, the teaching is not mine. Neither was I crucified for anyone. St. Paul, in 1 Corinthians 3, would not allow the Christians to call themselves Pauline or Petrine, but Christian. How then should I — poor stinking maggot-fodder that I am — come to have people call the children of Christ by my wretched name?[5]

Although Luther may have gotten his wish in Europe, where many churches associated with his message call themselves "evangelical," in the English-speaking world, such Christians are stuck with the name "Lutheran."[6] Moreover, ubiquitous terms such as "Luther scholar," "Luther Congress," "Lutheran confessions," and "Lutheran World Federation" prove that in this regard, too, Luther's ecclesiastical descendants have largely ignored his advice and found ample reason to attach themselves to this "food for worms."

The Catechetical Luther

The German scholar, Georg Hoffmann, has noted that Luther's catechisms offer the basics of Luther's theology.[7] Our first set of essays proves his observation in reverse: Luther's theology is fundamentally catechetical in shape and intent.[8] Especially when shorn of its polemi-

---

5. Martin Luther, *A Sincere Admonition . . . to All Christians to Guard against Insurrection and Rebellion* (1522), LW 45:70 (WA 8:685). See also LW 36:265 (WA 10/2:39-40).

6. See the struggles over naming the Evangelical Lutheran Church in America at the time of its inception in 1987.

7. Georg Hoffmann, "Der Kleine Katechismus als Abriß der Theologie Martin Luther," *Luther: Mitteilungen der Luthergesellschaft* 30 (1959): 49-63.

8. This implies a criticism of the still useful book by Paul Althaus, *The Theology of Martin Luther*, trans. Robert C. Schultz (Philadelphia: Fortress, 1966). Althaus divides Luther's theology into the theological *loci communes* more appropriately associated with Luther's colleague, Philip Melanchthon. In so doing, he disturbs the coherence of Luther's own work. More successful is the work of Bernhard Lohse, *Martin Luther's Theology: Its Historical and Systematic Development*, trans. Roy A. Harrisville (Minneapolis: Fortress, 1999).

cal edge, his theology is pre-eminently catechesis in the richest sense of that term. No wonder that several of the articles in this volume reflect the contents of the catechism and, hence, the core of Luther's theology: baptism, righteousness, creation, and resurrection — all summarized in Luther's coat-of-arms. The catechism forms the canvas upon which he sketched the Christian message.

Luther on Baptism

> Therefore baptism remains forever. Even though someone falls from it and sins, we always have access to it so that we may again subdue the old creature. . . . I say this to correct the opinion, which has long prevailed among us, that baptism is something past that we can no longer use after falling back into sin. This idea comes from looking only at the act that took place a single time. Indeed, St. Jerome is responsible for this view, for he wrote, "Penance is the second plank on which we must swim ashore after the ship founders," [the ship] in which we embarked when we entered the Christian community. . . . It is incorrect to say this. The ship does not break up because, as we said, it is God's ordinance and not something that is ours. But it does happen that we slip and fall out of the ship. However, those who do fall out should immediately see to it that they swim to the ship and hold fast to it, until they can climb aboard again and sail on it as before.[9]

Excavations under the cathedral in Geneva, Switzerland, depict graphically the decline in the centrality of Holy Baptism from the ancient church into the Middle Ages. An original, enormous baptistery with elaborately decorated tiled floors was slowly replaced by ever smaller, simpler fonts until the entire building was demolished and covered over by the present, medieval cathedral. What had been the central event of the Christian life had gradually become a *rite du passage* for medieval infants.

Martin Luther single-handedly rescued baptism from obscurity to place it again at the center of Christian life and thought. Medieval

9. *The Large Catechism* (1529), trans. James Schaaf, Baptism, par. 77-82, in BC 466; BSLK 706-7.

4

theology had reduced baptism to powerful magic for children. Anabaptists and some followers of Ulrich Zwingli had twisted it into a
badge of commitment. Luther, on the contrary, rediscovered God's
promise of grace at baptism's center and the faith that clings to that
baptismal promise throughout life. Based upon the extensive research of a doctoral dissertation, Mark D. Tranvik traces the development of Luther's theology of baptism and how it contrasts with both
medieval and Anabaptist alternatives. In an age when churches and
theologians conspire to obscure baptism with introductory rites or
conversion experiences, Luther's surprisingly fresh approach to this
sacrament may help both to recover the centrality of God's action
and also to trust it.

Luther on the Two Kinds of Righteousness

Not only does faith bestow so much that the soul becomes equal to
the divine Word — full of grace, free, and holy — but also it unites the
soul with Christ as a bride is united with her bridegroom. From this
marriage comes, as St. Paul says [Eph. 5:30], that Christ and the soul
become one body, so that they share both fortune and misfortune
and all things in common. Accordingly, whatever Christ has is the
property of the believing soul, and whatever the soul has becomes
the property of Christ. Christ has all goodness and blessings that are
the soul's property. The soul has in it all vices and sin; they become
Christ's property. Here now arises the joyous exchange and struggle.
For Christ is God and Human Being, who has never sinned. Moreover, his righteousness is unassailable, eternal, and almighty. Thus,
when he through the wedding band, which is faith, then makes the
sins of the believing soul his own and behaves in no other way than
as if he had committed them, then sin must be devoured and
drowned. For his unassailable righteousness is too strong for all sins.
Thus, the soul, simply by virtue of its engagement ring[10] (that is, because of faith), becomes unencumbered, free and endowed with the
eternal righteousness of its bridegroom, Christ. Is this not a joyous

10. German: Malschatzts — the traditional gift of the bridegroom to the bride
guaranteeing his faithfulness.

marriage feast where the rich, pure, upright Bridegroom, Christ, takes in marriage the poor, despised, evil maid and releases her from all evil while adorning her with all good things?[11]

Over the past one hundred years, scholars have developed two different ways of describing Luther's understanding of justification. Some, including Gerhard Ebeling and Werner Elert, have emphasized the distinction between law and gospel.[12] Others, often relying on traditional Lutheran orthodox constructions of Luther's theology, emphasize the forensic declaration of righteousness.[13] Gerhard Forde, while championing the former position, goes to great lengths to demonstrate how the two principles work together in Lutheran theology.[14] In this volume, Robert Kolb performs a similar task in his analysis of the two kinds of righteousness. He shows both the theological and anthropological consequences of this distinction and how Luther connected it to all aspects of his thought.

Luther's Seal

Dear Christians, one and all, rejoice, With exaltation springing, And with united heart and voice And holy rapture singing, Proclaim the wonders God has done, How his right arm the vict'ry won, What price our ransom cost him! . . . For God had seen my wretched state Before the world's foundation, And, mindful of his mercies great, He planned for my salvation. He turned to me a father's heart; He did not choose the easy part, But gave his dearest treasure.[15]

11. Martin Luther, *Von der Freiheit eines Christenmenschen* (1520), WA 7:25 (translating the text in MLStA 2:275-77). Cf. the translation of the Latin version, *The Freedom of a Christian* in LW 31:351 (WA 7:54-55).

12. Gerhard Ebeling, *Luther: An Introduction to His Thought* and Werner Elert, *The Structure of Lutheranism,* trans. Walter A. Hansen (St. Louis: Concordia, 1962).

13. See, especially, Paul Althaus, *The Theology of Martin Luther.* This construal also touches on the question of the relation between Luther and Melanchthon. For a review of this issue, see Timothy J. Wengert, "Melanchthon and Luther/Luther and Melanchthon," *Luther-Jahrbuch* 66 (1999): 68-70.

14. Gerhard Forde, *Justification: A Matter of Death and Life* (Philadelphia: Fortress, 1982).

15. Martin Luther, "Dear Christians, One and All Rejoice" (1523), *Lutheran Book of Worship* (Minneapolis: Augsburg and Philadelphia: Board of Publication, 1978), no. 299.

Luther used any and all means to spread his witness to Christ's gospel. A papal legate wrote back to Rome that the cause was lost because "Luther's hymns are on the lips of all the people." He could as easily have said that they were also whistling his tunes, memorizing his catechisms, purchasing woodcuts designed under Wittenberg's direction, and reading his sermons aloud. His was a multimedia gospel in a world of organ, printing press, folk song, and illustration.

No wonder that, as Dietrich Korsch demonstrates, Luther was so particular about his seal — a seal that 450 years later continues to bear the message of his theology! "God is for us and we are in God on the basis of being in the likeness of Christ," Korsch writes in summarizing this remarkable visible compendium of Luther's theology. Moreover, this compendium was not a private message but something open to the entire community of believers, so that even today Lutherans the world over still use this "rose" to express their faith. Like the poet in the Song of Solomon (8:6), Luther through his seal could well have gushed about his God. "Set me as a seal upon your heart, as a seal upon your arm; for love is strong as death, passion fierce as the grave. Its flashes are flashes of fire, a raging flame."

Luther on Creation

But for the young pupils it is now enough to indicate the most necessary points, namely, as we have said, that this [first] article [of the Creed] deals with creation. We should emphasize the words "creator of heaven and earth." What is meant by these words or what do you mean when you say, "I believe in God, the Father almighty, creator," etc.? Answer: I hold and believe that I am God's creature, that is, that he has given me and constantly sustains my body, soul, and life, my members great and small, all my senses, my reason and understanding, and the like; my food and drink, clothing, nourishment, spouse and children, servants, house and farm, etc. Besides, he makes all creation help provide the benefits and necessities of life — sun, moon, and stars in the heavens; day and night; air, fire, water, the earth and all that it yields and brings forth; birds, fish, animals, grain, and all sorts of produce. Moreover, he gives all physical and temporal blessings — good government, peace, security. Thus we learn from this article that none of us has life — or anything else that has been mentioned here or can be mentioned — from ourselves, nor can we by ourselves preserve any of them, however small and unimportant. All this is comprehended in the word "Creator."[16]

For Luther, teaching about the first article of the Creed meant neither speculating about the nature of God nor returning to the beginning of time for a glimpse at our cosmic origins. Instead, as Johannes Schwanke of the University of Tübingen points out, Luther focused on the creation of each individual and upon the way in which God's creation through the Word continues into the present. Creation itself is a profound act of God's communication with the creature that arises from grace alone. God's Word institutes a world of nature and relationships that makes all of life in its varying domains holy. Armed with the mandate of God, all activities that serve this world and its creatures become the locus of human "dominion."

Luther on the Resurrection

You have heard in the Passion how Christ let himself be crucified and buried and how sin and death trampled him underfoot. Satan and the sins of the world lie on him in the tomb. Sin, death and the devil are his lord. Therefore you must look into his tomb and realize that my sins and my death tear him apart and oppress him. There the devil regards himself as secure, and the chief priests boast and rejoice: He is gone and will not return. But in the instant when they believe him destroyed, the Lion tears himself away from sin, death, hell, and the jaws of the devil and rips them to shreds with his teeth. This is our comfort, that Christ comes forth: Death, sin, and the devil cannot hold him. The sin of the entire world is powerless. When he appears to Mary Magdalene, one sees in him neither death nor sin nor sadness but sheer life and joy. There I see that the Lord is mine and treads on the devil. Then I find my sins, torment, and devil where I ought to find them. There is the seed of the woman, who has

---

16. Martin Luther, *The Large Catechism* (1529), The Creed, par. 12-16, in BC 432-33; BSLK 648.

struck the head of the serpent [Gen. 3:15], and says: Death, you shall die; Hell, you are defeated! Here is the victor.[17]

Luther, known the world over for his theology of the cross, was, catechetically speaking, a theologian of the cross and resurrection. His sermons during Holy Week and Easter stressed repeatedly the intimate connection between these two events in Christ's life. The centrality of baptism and Paul's explanation of it in Romans 6 for Luther also tied both Christ's death and his resurrection to the central event in the Christian life. Gerhard Sauter takes Luther's lifelong proclamation of Christ's resurrection one step further by joining it to the resurrection of the dead. In this essay, we see most clearly how Luther's catechetical theology dominates his thinking. Sauter uncovers the practical Luther, who realized that preaching itself leads the hearers from this valley of tears into eternal life. By examining Luther's sermons on 1 Corinthians 15, Sauter demonstrates just how Luther's proclamation served his theology (and vice versa) to provide consolation for the conscience under attack *(Anfechtung)*.

Luther and God's World

A second side of Luther's theology is its celebrated practicality. Luther was no "ivory tower" theologian, or, rather, adapting Heiko Oberman's provocative phrase, he turned the ivory tower into a watchtower.[18] Here, our essayists have managed to touch upon some of the most important social and political issues of Luther's day. Each author reveals that the heart of Luther's ethics was his ability to separate works-righteousness from love of neighbor and to generate a completely different way to envision the Christian life.

17. Martin Luther, "Sermon on Easter Sunday Morning" (1529), in *The 1529 Holy Week and Easter Sermons of Dr. Martin Luther,* 124 (cf. WA 29:263-64).
18. Heiko A. Oberman, *Werden und Wertung der Reformation: Vom Wegestreit zum Glaubenskampf,* 2nd edition (Tübingen: Mohr/Siebeck, 1979), p. 4.

Luther on Vocation

> Nothing but good fruit can come from the station that God has cre-
> ated and ordained, and from the person who works and lives in this
> station on the basis of the Word of God. . . . Learn to look at your sta-
> tion on the basis of this statement ["Good trees bear good fruit"
> (Matthew 7:17)], and draw this conclusion from it: "Thank God, I
> know now that I am in a good and blessed station, one that pleases
> God. Though it may be annoying to my flesh and contain a great
> deal that is troubling and disgusting, I shall cheerfully put up with
> all that. Here I have the comfort that Christ says: 'A good tree bears
> good fruit.'" . . . When an upright hired man is hauling a wagonload
> of manure to the field, he is actually hauling a wagonload of pre-
> cious figs and grapes — but in the sight of God, not in our own sight,
> since we do not believe, so that everyone gets tired of his [or her] sta-
> tion and goes staring at another one.[19]

Especially in the English-speaking world, the best-kept secret of
Luther's practical theology is his insight that the everyday life of the
Christian is the Christian life. The allure of a higher, special "Christian" ethic continues to seduce Christians of all sorts into dividing the
Christian household of faith into carnal Christians and spiritual
ones.[20] Luther, on the contrary, had a completely different understanding of the Christian life. If we are clothed in Christ's righteousness alone, then all walks of life, all human activities that serve the
neighbor and creation, have worth and qualify as "callings" before
God.

As a result, Luther's sermons are filled with righteous haulers of
manure, brewers of beer, and changers of diapers. This insight reveals a
startling character of Luther's ethic: It has little to do with works (after
all, everyone, even unbelievers, do these menial tasks) and everything to
do with faith. For who believes that such works are "holy and precious"? In this light, for Luther the law is far less a guide to what we
ought to do (the legalist's "third use" of the law) than a guideline de-

19. Martin Luther, *Matthew 5–7: Preached and Interpreted* (1532), in LW 21:265-66 (WA
32:519-20).

20. See, for example, the plea of James Gustafson, *Can Ethics Be Christian?* (Chicago:
University of Chicago Press, 1975), especially pp. 169-79.

claring as righteous what we are already doing — or, rather, what God is doing with us in the world.[21]

With direct simplicity, Karlfried Froehlich's essay — first delivered to seminarians (among whom the temptation to find a higher ethic remains particularly strong) — sketches the contours of Luther's understanding of vocation and then applies it to the present. Not only does Froehlich explain Luther's doctrine of vocation, but he also resists using that doctrine to denigrate or to eliminate the special vocation of pastor and seminary in the life of the church.

Luther on Poverty

The second virtue of a prince is to help the poor, the orphans, and the widows to justice, and to further their cause. But, again, who can tell all the virtues that follow from this one? For this virtue includes all the works of justice: as when a prince or lord or city has good laws and customs; when everything is regulated in an orderly way; and when order is kept by people in all ranks, occupations, trades, businesses, services, and works, so that it is not said: "the people are without laws." For where there are no laws, the poor, the widows, and the orphans are oppressed. Then there is no peasant so low that he cannot practice extortion. And this is equally true of buying, selling, inheriting, lending, paying, borrowing, and the like. It is only a matter of one getting the better of another, robbing him, stealing from him, and cheating him. This happens most of all to the poor, the widows, and the orphans. . . . See now what a hospital such a prince can build! He needs no stone, no wood, no builders; and he need give neither endowment nor income. To endow hospitals and help poor people is, indeed, a precious good work in itself. But when such a hospital becomes so great that a whole land, and especially the really poor people of that land, enjoy it, then it is a general, true, princely, indeed, a heavenly and divine hospital. For only a few enjoy the first kind of hospital, and sometimes they are false knaves masquerading as beggars. But the second kind of hospital comes to the

---

21. For the origins of the third use of the law in Melanchthon's thought, see Timothy J. Wengert, *Law and Gospel: Philip Melanchthon's Debate with John Agricola of Eisleben over Poenitentia* (Grand Rapids: Baker, 1997), pp. 177-210.

aid only of the really poor, widows, orphans, travelers, and other for-lorn folk.[22]

In many quarters, Luther's theology and ethics are associated with blessing the "status quo." For Luther himself, however, it meant em-powering Christians in government and in the society as a whole to ful-fill their God-given calling by taking care of the weak and poor. No one has done more to investigate the radical nature of Luther's approach to poverty than Carter Lindberg, whose books and articles on the subject have helped to restore Luther's pioneering efforts in this aspect of Christian thought and life.[23]

In this essay, Lindberg carefully debunks theories that either dis-miss theology as causing changes in views of the poor or else glorify theologians for influencing social movements that arose centuries later. Instead, he demarcates the real differences between the attitudes toward poverty and almsgiving that characterized the Middle Ages and Luther's theology. Once having destroyed the "self-chosen spirituality" (Col. 2:23) of monastic poverty, Luther turned the full attention of his society to-ward the real poor and what individuals and governments needed to do for them. He focused on the idolatry of greed and the use of wealth (not simply the having of it) and the social structures that "daily defraud the poor." Here is an approach to poverty, grounded in Luther's own time, that still speaks a word of judgment upon later generations.

Luther on Greed

But beware of how you deal with the poor — there are many of them now — who must live from hand to mouth. If you act as if everyone has to live by your favor, if you skin and scrape them right down to the bone, if you arrogantly turn away those who need your aid, they will go away wretched and dejected, and, because they can complain to no one else, they will cry out to heaven. Beware of this, I repeat, as if it were the devil himself. Such sighs and cries are no laughing mat-ter, but will have an effect too great for you and all the world to bear.

22. Martin Luther, *An Exposition of the 82nd Psalm* (1530), in LW 13:53 (WA 31/1:200).
23. See especially his *Beyond Charity: Reformation Initiatives for the Poor* (Minneapolis: Fortress, 1993).

For they will reach God, who watches over poor, troubled hearts, and he will not leave them unavenged. But if you despise and defy this, see whom you have brought upon yourself. If you succeed and prosper, however, you may call God and me liars before the whole world.[24]

As the author of this essay, Ricardo Willy Rieth, admits, this topic is actually a subset of the previous one on poverty. By focusing on Luther's interpretation of a variety of biblical texts, Rieth demonstrates Luther's consistency in excoriating greed and its consequences for the poor throughout his life. Greed was for Luther a particularly devious form of idolatry, often downplayed by his contemporaries. Against those who argue that Luther's thinking about the economy is useless, out-of-date, and even reactionary, Rieth demonstrates both here and in his book on the same subject just how profoundly Luther struggled with the social injustices of his time.

Luther on Marriage

Now observe that when that clever harlot, our natural reason, . . . takes a look at married life, she turns up her nose and says, "Alas, must I rock the baby, wash its diapers, make its bed, smell its stench, stay up nights with it, take care of it when it cries, heal its rashes and sores, and on top of that care for my wife, provide for her, labor at my trade, take care of this and take care of that, do this and do that, endure this and endure that, and whatever else of bitterness and drudgery married life involves? What, should I make such a prisoner of myself? O you poor, wretched fellow, have you taken a wife? Fie, fie upon such wretchedness and bitterness! It is better to remain free and lead a peaceful, carefree life; I will become a priest or a nun and compel my children to do likewise."

What then does Christian Faith say to this? It opens its eyes, looks upon all these insignificant, distasteful, and despised duties in the Spirit, and is aware that they are all adorned with divine approval as with the costliest gold and jewels. It says, "O God, because I

24. Martin Luther, *The Large Catechism*, Ten Commandments, par. 247, in BC 419; BSLK 622.

13

am certain that thou has created me as a man and hast from my body begotten this child, I also know for a certainty that it meets with thy perfect pleasure. I confess to thee that I am not worthy to rock the little babe or wash its diapers, or to be entrusted with the care of the child and its mother. How is it that I, without any merit, have come to this distinction of being certain that I am serving thy creature and thy most precious will? O how gladly will I do so, though the duties should be even more insignificant and despised. . . . Now you tell me, when a father goes ahead and washes diapers or performs some other mean task for his child, and someone ridicules him as an effeminate fool — though that father is acting in the spirit just described and in Christian faith — my dear fellow you tell me, which of the two is most keenly ridiculing the other? God, with all his angels and creatures, is smiling — not because that father is washing diapers, but because he is doing so in Christian faith.[25]

Luther's theological revolution drove him to rethink the basic building blocks of medieval society: monastery, prince, poverty, and even marriage. For Luther, these considerations were never peripheral to the Reformation but close to its center. Far from denigrating marriage by refusing to call it a sacrament, Luther redefined and revitalized it. The Christian no longer had first to "christianize" marriage in order to enjoy its benefits. Instead, it ranked for Luther among the most glorious of God's gifts to creation. As Scott Hendrix points out in his essay, Luther even praised the very physicality of marriage, in language later Puritan and even Victorian ages could scarcely imagine. For him, God speaks to each believer's heart in the face of the spouse.

Luther on the Turks and Islam

And, finally, I strongly urge that the children be taught the catechism. Should they be taken captive in the invasion, they will at least take something of the Christian faith with them. Who knows what God might be able to accomplish through them. Joseph as a seventeen-year-old youth was sold into slavery into Egypt, but he had

---

25. Martin Luther, *The Estate of Marriage* (1522), in LW 45:39-40 (WA 10/2:295-96).

God's word and knew what he believed. And he converted all Egypt. The same is true of Daniel and his companions.[26]

Luther dealt with "the other" in his world in ways that, while consonant with the cultural constraints of his day, sometimes cause his followers to be ashamed in ours. While his views of the Jews are well known and reported,[27] those regarding the other major "alien" force in his world, the Turkish invaders of Europe in the sixteenth century, are not. To help fill this lacuna, Gregory Miller takes the reader through the basic contours of Luther's thought on the subject. We learn how much Luther knew of the Turks and Islam, and what his sources were. We discover his role in the publication of a new and improved Latin translation of the Qur'an. We find how he, like his contemporaries, caricatured the Muslim invaders. However, unlike some, Luther refused to advocate a crusade against them, despite the role he thought they were playing in the immanent endtimes.

Luther and Christ's Church

Finally, Luther's theology was not merely reflections for his scholarly world. Instead, it retained, at a very deep level, a churchly element. Here, however, we must carefully delineate what Luther meant by "church." It was not, in the first instance, a building or a hierarchy; it certainly was never a place of power — although the church may have buildings, possess hierarchy, and wield power. For Luther, the church was an event — the Holy Spirit's act of gathering believers around Word and sacrament.

Luther on the Reform of Worship

In short, I will preach it, teach it, write it, but I will constrain no one by force, for faith must come freely without compulsion. Take myself as an example. I opposed indulgences and all the papists, but never

26. Martin Luther, *Appeal for Prayer against the Turks* (1541), in LW 43:239 (WA 51:621).
27. See, for example, Heiko Oberman, *The Roots of Anti-Semitism,* trans. James I. Porter (Philadelphia: Fortress, 1984).

with force. I simply taught, preached, and wrote God's Word; otherwise I did nothing. And while I slept [cf. Mark 4:26-29], or drank Wittenberg beer with my friends Philip [Melanchthon] and [Nicholas von] Amsdorf, the Word so greatly weakened the papacy that no prince or emperor ever inflicted such losses upon it. I did nothing; the Word did everything.[28]

Luther's so-called conservative streak in liturgical matters, which first came to light during his 1522 struggle with Andreas Bodenstein von Karlstadt over worship practices in Wittenberg, has often prevented modern liturgical scholars from fully appreciating his perspective. To remedy that deficiency, Helmar Junghans provides a look at the heart of Luther's liturgical reform. This was no fly-by-night, provisional reform of the liturgy, waiting for Strasbourg or Geneva to finish the task. Instead, Luther based his approach to liturgy on his convictions about the centrality of the Word and sacraments for the Christian community. Luther refused to reduce the Word and the sacraments to something human beings did for God. They were far more God's means of making believers and sustaining their life with him and each other. The variety of worship in Wittenberg bespeaks the reformer's deep conviction to include all people under God's Word and sacraments.

Luther on the Psalter

Moreover, I want to point out to you a correct way of studying theology, for I have had practice in that. . . . This is the way taught by holy King David (and doubtlessly used also by all the patriarchs and prophets) in the one hundred nineteenth Psalm. There you will find three rules, amply presented throughout the whole Psalm. They are *Oratio, Meditatio, Tentatio*.[29]

Firstly, you should know that the Holy Scriptures constitute a book which turns the wisdom of all other books into foolishness because

28. Martin Luther, *Eight Sermons at Wittenberg* (1522), "The Second Sermon, March 10, 1522, Monday after Invocavit," in LW 51:77 (WA 10/3:18-19).
29. Prayer, meditation, struggle [*Anfechtung*].

not one teaches about eternal life except this one alone. Therefore you should straightway despair of your reason and understanding. With them you will not attain eternal life, but, on the contrary, your presumptuousness will plunge you and others with you out of heaven (as happened to Lucifer) into the abyss of hell. But kneel down in your little room and pray to God with real humility and earnestness, that he through his dear Son may give you his Holy Spirit, who will enlighten you, lead you, and give you understanding. Thus you see how David keeps praying in the above-mentioned Psalm, "Teach me, Lord, instruct me, lead me, show me" and many more words like these.[30]

From his time in the monastery on, Martin Luther lived in the Psalms. No wonder, when asked to provide a preface to his German works in 1539, he went immediately to the Psalms to describe the work of a theologian! No wonder that in the Large Catechism he argued not only that the first commandment with its call to faith encapsulated the entire message of Scripture but also that the Psalms were a fitting commentary on that very commandment![31] By juxtaposing Luther's life in the Psalms with comments of an eighteenth-century Swedish soldier in exile and Dietrich Bonhoeffer, Carl Axel Aurelius demonstrates the broad appeal of the Psalms and Luther's work with them. Here we discover the grand contours of the Reformer's thought in miniature — finding the words believers may pray to God in the midst of struggle and, hence, finding the heart and life of the church itself, for which Christ died.

Martin Luther's Reformation of Spirituality

In these matters, which concern the spoken, external Word, it must be firmly maintained that God gives no one his Spirit or grace apart from the external Word which goes before. We say this to protect ourselves from the enthusiasts, that is the "spirits," who boast that they have the Spirit apart from and before contact with

30. Martin Luther, *Preface to the Wittenberg Edition of Luther's German Writings* (1539), in LW 34:285-86 (WA 50:659).

31. *The Large Catechism* (1529), Ten Commandments, par. 325, in BC 430; BSLK 643.

the Word.[32] On this basis, they judge, interpret, and twist the Scripture or oral Word according to their pleasure. Müntzer did this, and there are still many doing this today, who set themselves up as shrewd judges between the spirit and the letter without knowing what they say or teach. The papacy is also purely religious raving in that the pope boasts that "all laws are in the shrine of his heart" and that what he decides and commands in his churches is supposed to be Spirit and law — even when it is above or contrary to the Scriptures or the spoken Word. This is all the old devil and old snake, who also turned Adam and Eve into enthusiasts and led them from the external Word of God to "spirituality" and their own presumption — although he even accomplished this by means of other, external words. In the same way, our enthusiasts also condemn the external Word, and yet they themselves do not keep silent. Instead, they fill the world with their chattering and scribbling — as if the Spirit could not come through the Scriptures or the spoken word of the apostles, but the Spirit must come through their own writings and words. Why do they not abstain from their preaching and writing until the Spirit himself comes into the people apart from and in advance of their writings? After all, they boast that the Spirit has come into them without the preaching of the Scripture.[33]

In the version of the Smalcald Articles printed in 1538, Martin Luther added this criticism of the regnant spirituality. It concluded his discussion of the gospel and sacraments and mapped out a very different approach to *spiritualitas,* one that rejects any self-chosen worship of the God within *(enthusiasmus)* in favor of the external Word. Whether practiced by Müntzer or the pope, this claim to the Holy Spirit apart from God's Word simply went back to the Garden, and the temptation to "be like gods, knowing good and evil." The article by Scott Hendrix of Princeton Theological Seminary, "Martin Luther's Reformation of Spirituality," was not originally a part of *Lutheran Quarterly's* "Luther on . . ." series. However, it examines a topic so central to Luther's theol-

32. Lutherans in the sixteenth century labeled any group that denigrated the efficacy of the external word of the gospel "enthusiasts," after certain ancient heresies that worshiped the "God within" *(en theou).*

33. Martin Luther, *The Smalcald Articles* (1536/1538), III.8.3-6, in BC 322; BSLK 453-55.

ogy that it deserves a place here. In contrast to the spirituality of Ignatius of Loyola, which reaffirmed late medieval devotion, Luther discovers a piety connected to Christ alone in the spiritual realm but available to all Christians in all walks of life. In Hendrix's own words, Luther believes the Christian lives "in the world bravely, yet provisionally" and thus develops a "guestly spirituality," which nonetheless is not simply a metaphor for dressing up religious business-as-usual but a new reality.

Martin Luther may have wished that his writings would disappear and that his name would be soon forgotten. Instead, over 500 years after his birth, believers continue to pour over his witness to the gospel and to find important insights into their own struggles of faith. It is that ongoing task of enriching faith today that constitutes Luther's most lasting gift to the church of Jesus Christ.

The Catechetical Luther

Luther on Baptism

MARK D. TRANVIK

Martin Luther extols the benefits of baptism in his Large Catechism, barely able to contain his delight:

> In Baptism every Christian has enough to study and to practice all his life. He always has enough to do to believe firmly what Baptism promises and brings — victory over death and the devil, forgiveness of sin, God's grace, the entire Christ, and the Holy Spirit with his gifts. In short the blessings of Baptism are so boundless that if timid nature considers them, it may well doubt whether they could all be true.[1]

Halting the sacrament's gradual slide into obscurity in the Middle Ages, Luther injected a vitality into baptism missing since the early days of the church. No longer was this merely the sacrament of infancy. Luther saw baptism's significance extending far beyond the momentary rite at the font. Baptism permeates the entire life of the believer,

---

1. LC, Baptism, 41-43: BSLK 699; BC-T 441-42. Luther's main writings on baptism are "The Holy and Blessed Sacrament of Baptism" (1519), WA 2:727-37; LW 35:29-43; "The Babylonian Captivity of the Church" (1520), WA 6:497-573; LW 36:11-126; "The Large Catechism" (1528), BSLK 691-707; BC-T 436-46; "The Small Catechism" (1528), BSLK 515-17; BC-T 348-49; "Concerning Rebaptism" (1528), WA 26:144-74; LW 40:229-62; "Sermon at the Baptism of Bernhard of Anhalt" (1540), WA 49:124-35; LW 51:315-29.

This article first appeared in *Lutheran Quarterly* 13 (1999): 75-90, under the same title.

and therefore plays a large role in Luther's theology. References to the sacrament are found not only in predictable places such as catechisms and treatises but also in surprising sources such as the *Lectures on Genesis*. Further, Luther relied on baptism in the midst of his intense spiritual assaults *(Anfechtungen)*, as has often been noted.[2]

Two factors shape Luther's theology of baptism.[3] One is the internal necessity of coordinating baptism with the central tenet of the reforming movement, the doctrine of justification. After his recovery of the gospel, Luther viewed all of theology through the lens of justification by faith alone. That is, church structure and doctrine are reshaped so that the eschatological message of Christ crucified and risen is clearly proclaimed. In his writings on baptism it is Luther's intention to reform the understanding of the sacrament so that it signifies, as he puts it, "full and complete justification."[4]

The other factor is the external context. No thinker is unaffected by the institutional and intellectual currents of his age. Hence, commentators on Luther must keep one eye on the historical surroundings. While Luther's views on baptism do not fundamentally change, they are shaded and nuanced in certain ways depending on the context.

Luther and the Middle Ages

The importance of baptism in the Middle Ages had decreased compared with the early church. Whereas the church fathers saw baptism as a light that illumined the entire life of the Christian pilgrim, for the church of Luther's time the sacrament was but a single point on the

2. See Roland Bainton, *Here I Stand* (Nashville: Abingdon, 1950), p. 287 and Heiko Oberman, *Luther: Man Between God and the Devil,* trans. Eileen Walliser-Schwarzbart (New Haven and London: Yale, 1989), pp. 226-31.

3. Among the book-length treatments of Luther on baptism are the following: Edmund Schlink, *The Doctrine of Baptism,* trans. J. A. Bouman (St. Louis: Concordia, 1972); Jonathan D. Trigg, *Baptism in the Theology of Martin Luther* (Leiden: Brill, 1994); Albrecht Peters, *Kommentar zu Luthers Katechismen,* Band 4, *Die Taufe, Das Abendmahl,* ed. Gottfried Seebass (Göttingen: Vandenhoeck & Ruprecht, 1993); Lorenz Grönvik, *Der Taufe in der Theologie Martin Luthers* (Abo: Abo Akademi, 1968). An expanded version of this essay can be found in Mark D. Tranvik, *The Other Sacrament: The Doctrine of Baptism in the Late Lutheran Reformation* (Th.D. thesis, Luther Seminary, 1992), pp. 6-42.

4. "Babylonian Captivity," LW 36:67; WA 6:534.

sacramental spectrum, important to be sure, but superseded by penance and eucharist. This happened for two reasons.

First, the notion that a sacrament worked *ex opere operato* tended to ritualize and desiccate baptism. In essence this Latin formula meant that the sacraments infused grace simply from the use of them, apart from any act of the soul. As long as the recipient posed no obstacle (such as being in a state of mortal sin) the sacrament effected the transmission of grace. Given this background, one can begin to understand Luther's charge that the Scholastics "had reduced the power of baptism to such small and slender dimensions that . . . it had now become entirely useless."[5]

Second, in the development of the medieval sacramental system, baptism tended to be associated only with the beginning of life, its chief role being to wash away the guilt of original sin. Its link with ensuing Christian pilgrimage was largely supplanted by the sacrament of penance. Once a person reached the age of reason and was guilty of mortal sin, he sought restoration via the penitential system.

For Luther the medieval understanding of the sacraments and the concept of *ex opere operato* had diluted baptism's transformative power because they virtually eliminated the need for faith. While the necessity of baptism was acknowledged, the sacrament itself was often viewed in a mechanical manner, which allowed it to become infected by nomism. As Luther recognized, the vacuum created by the absence of faith is filled by works:

> For if the sacrament confers grace on me because I receive it, then indeed I receive grace by virtue of my work, and not by faith; and I gain not the promise in the sacrament but only the sign instituted and commanded by God.[6]

Against the sacramentalism of the medieval church Luther emphasizes the necessity of faith: "Thus it is not baptism that justifies or benefits anyone, but it is faith in that word of promise to which baptism is added. This faith justifies and fulfills that which baptism signifies."[7] The sign by itself remains empty. Nor does the water contain any magi-

---

5. LW 36:69; WA 6:536.
6. LW 36:67; WA 6:534.
7. LW 36:66; WA 6:532-33.

cal power. Unless faith be present (not understood merely as intellectual belief but as a trusting relationship with the living God), the sacrament is "vanity of vanities and vexation of Spirit."[8]

Faith plays a crucial role in baptism, but Luther never imagines that faith "makes" the sacrament. In other words, the recipients do not gather together their crumbs of belief and offer them to God who in turn makes their baptism efficacious. This grossly distorts Luther's understanding of how God's promises work and is fundamentally as legalistic as the Scholastic understanding.

Rather, Luther's sacramental theology turns on his dynamic understanding of God's word as *promise*. In the medieval tradition the word "consecrated" conferred a power upon the substance of the sacrament. For Luther the Word is directed not to the element itself but to the recipient of the sacrament. Moreover, this Word is not a dead letter but something powerful, active and creative, working faith itself in the believer.

The God who created the world through his Word is also able to create faith in those receiving the sacrament. In a sermon from 1537, Luther makes this connection between the creative and sacramental Word:

> How does this (creation) happen? Through the words "Let it come into being." Through this word everything was created and conceived. Even humanity was created by this word. If you or I were to speak thusly nothing would happen. But when God says, "Let it come into being," the world is full of people, children and animals. . . . Thus you can reason: If God is able by the word to create heaven and earth and fill the world, that is, everything we see with our eyes, why is it not possible to take water and baptize, saying "In the name . . ." and so be washed from all sins in body and soul?[9]

If the Word spoken in baptism is understood only as a human word, it conveys essentially nothing. But because God himself is speaking through his human instrument, the same God who by speaking created heaven and earth, the Word achieves its soteriological goal, namely cleansing from sin in body and soul.

---

8. LW 36:61; WA 6:529.

9. "Predigt am Freitag nach Dionisii in der Schlosskirche" (1537), WA 45:172. Translation mine.

Consequently, the Word of promise always precedes faith. The promise awakens and nourishes faith. A sacrament can be said to "depend" on faith only in the sense that a promise has no effect apart from belief. Luther asserts that the meeting of promise and faith gives a "real and most certain efficacy to the sacraments."[10]

Luther's concern to highlight faith separates his understanding of baptism from a medieval one. But faith is never an autonomous act of the believer, but rather the trust engendered by hearing God's promises. It is no accident that in his definitive attack on the medieval sacramental system, *The Babylonian Captivity of the Church,* Luther gives priority to the promise in his understanding of baptism:

> Now, the first thing to be considered about baptism is the divine promise. . . . This promise must be set far above all the glitter of works, vows, religious orders and whatever else man has introduced, for on it all our salvation depends.[11]

With the notion of the Word as promise, Luther reshapes baptism under the dynamic rubric of Word and faith.

In his early writings on baptism, Luther latches onto a "family" of words well suited to his new understanding of justification. It becomes clear that nothing less than the language of baptism, the language of death and life, can aptly describe the transformation wrought on one who trusts in God's promises.

For example, when one is baptized, says Luther, one should not understand this "allegorically" as the death of sin and the life of grace but as "actual death and resurrection . . . for baptism is not a false sign." Similarly, he disdains those who speak of baptism as a "washing" away of sin for that is "too meek and mild." Rather, "the sinner needs to die, in order to be wholly renewed and made into another creature."[12] Following Paul in Romans 6:4, Luther sees baptism as the way the cross and resurrection become contemporaneous with the believer.[13] Baptism effects the "joyous exchange" (*fröhliche Wechsel*), a term Luther

---

10. "Babylonian Captivity," LW 36:67; WA 6:533.

11. LW 36:58-59; WA 6:527.

12. LW 36:68; WA 6:534.

13. See Robert Kolb, "God Kills to Make Alive: Romans 6 and Luther's Understanding of Justification (1535)," *Lutheran Quarterly,* n.s., 12 (1998): 33-56.

used frequently to express his understanding of the atonement. As Ulrich Asendorf has made clear, this "exchange" is not merely an intellectual construct but rather effects a *real* transformation in the believer.[14]

Furthermore, Luther's claim that "baptism is full and complete justification" represents another protest against the late medieval church. Rejecting any understanding of the salvation that envisions cooperation between the human and divine wills, baptism for Luther effects a death and resurrection, which rules out a segmented or progressive understanding of justification. Neither the Thomist nor nominalist conceptions of justification, both of which allow for the incremental cooperation of the human subject with grace, can possibly serve as paradigms for Luther's new understanding of the God-human relationship. However, baptism goes to the heart of justification — God's slaying of the sinner and God's resurrection of a completely new creature.

Luther's early writings on baptism not only highlight the role of God's promise and baptism's close link with justification, they also reveal his concern to merge baptism with the sacrament of penance. Medieval theologians divided penance into the categories of contrition, confession, and satisfaction. It was especially subject to abuse in Luther's day, most notoriously in the indulgence controversy. Luther complained that penance, which had its foundation in baptism and whose function was to point to baptism, had degenerated into the "external pomp of works" and the "deceits of man-made ordinances."[15]

A specific target for Luther is Jerome, who said that penance is the "second plank after the shipwreck" and thereby inferring that the power of baptism is broken because of sin. Luther, concerned to stress baptism's lifelong significance, turns this image on its head:

> The ship remains one, solid, and invincible; it will never be broken up into separate "planks." In it are carried all those who are brought to the harbor of salvation, for it is the truth of God giving us his promise in the sacraments. Of course, it often happens that many rashly leap overboard into the sea and perish; these are those who

14. Ulrich Asendorf, *Die Theologie Martin Luthers nach seinen Predigten* (Göttingen: Vandenhoeck & Ruprecht, 1988), pp. 366-70.

15. "Babylonian Captivity," LW 36:62; WA 6:530.

abandon faith in the promise and plunge into sin. But the ship itself remains intact and holds its course unimpaired. If any one is able somehow by grace to return to the ship, it is not on any plank, but in the solid ship itself that he is borne to life.[16]

Concerned to combat the tendency to emphasize penance over baptism, by the end of *The Babylonian Captivity of the Church* he coalesces the two sacraments. Penance becomes a return to baptism. Consequently, baptism is no longer just the sacrament of infancy or merely an "initiation rite" into the church. Now baptism spans the earthly life of the believer.

This emphasis on the permanence of baptism is necessary because of sin. Although we are "pure and guiltless" at the moment of our baptism, sin continues to adhere to our nature, since we are "at once justified and a sinner." However, sin cannot harm the one who has been baptized. Since baptism was his "actual death," the believer is comforted in already knowing the result of God's future judgment. Moreover, in the daily return to baptism one has the assurance that God does not impute sins; he "winks" at them because of the pledge he has made in the sacrament.[17]

Finally, in his early writings on baptism Luther links baptism, Christian freedom, and the priesthood of all believers. The reform unleashed by Luther was not limited to the realm of doctrine. His new understanding of the gospel propelled him to criticize the institutional church because he believed it had undermined Christian liberty. As Luther saw it, traditional distinctions between temporal and spiritual orders or between clergy and laity did nothing but obfuscate the freedom bestowed in justification.

In *To the Christian Nobility of the German Nation Concerning the Reform of the Christian Estate*, Luther disputes on the grounds of baptism the arrogation of rights, privileges, and status by the clergy:

> Since those who exercise secular authority have been baptized with the same baptism, and have the same faith and the same gospel as the rest of us, we must admit that they are priests and bishops and we must regard their office as one which has a proper and useful

16. LW 36:61; WA 6:529.
17. "Blessed Sacrament," LW 35:34; WA 2:731.

place in the Christian community. For whoever comes out of the water of baptism can boast that he is already consecrated priest, bishop, and pope. . . .[18]

In the new evangelical understanding, baptism supplants the *character indelibilis*. Luther's view of the sacrament results in an "ontological leveling" of the church, eliminating the notion of a "higher" clerical estate.

The section on baptism in the *Babylonian Captivity* evidences a similar theme, particularly in the call for the abolition of all vows and religious orders. The latter are diametrically opposed to the sacrament because they hobble Christian liberty:

> By what right, I ask you, does the pope impose his laws upon us? . . . Who gave him the power to deprive us of this liberty of ours, granted to us in baptism? One thing only, as I have said, has been enjoined upon us to do all the days of our lives — to be baptized, that is, to be put to death and to live again through faith in Christ. . . . But now faith is passed over in silence, and the church is smothered with endless laws concerning works and ceremonies. . . .[19]

Luther views baptism as a forceful weapon in his battle against the Roman hierarchy. Because the sacrament bestows all that a Christian needs, namely full and complete justification, it becomes an explicit challenge to Rome's multitudinous additions to the gospel. Under the banner of baptism, and in the name of liberating bound consciences, Luther launches a wide-ranging assault on church tradition and canon law.

Luther and Enthusiasm

However, the Lutheran reformation witnessed the rise of other movements, including those referred to by Luther as the "enthusiasts," which included a wide spectrum of figures, from Thomas Müntzer to

18. "To the Christian Nobility of the German Nation Concerning the Reform of the Christian Estate" (1520), LW 44:129; WA 6:408.
19. "Babylonian Captivity," LW 36:70; WA 6:535-36.

Ulrich Zwingli.[20] This group, no less than Rome, challenged Luther's views on justification and the sacraments. In many of Luther's later writings on baptism it is evident that he often has the enthusiasts in mind. From his catechisms, letters, and sermons the following ideas are particularly prominent: (1) baptism as salvific; (2) the necessity of the earthly sign; (3) a strong advocacy of infant baptism.

Despite the considerable differences among them, the enthusiasts all denied the direct mediation of grace in the sacraments. With regard to baptism, they saw the sacrament as subsequent to conversion or to the experience of faith and therefore limited it to adults or "believers."

Luther, however, is quite explicit that baptism involves the real presence of the Triune God who acts in history through the administrator of the sacrament to save the one being baptized. Salvation does not occur in an experience of subjective ecstasy; it happens at the moment the baptized is washed with water in the name of the Father, Son, and Holy Spirit.

In both of his catechisms Luther makes the point clearly. The Small Catechism states: "What gifts or benefits does Baptism bestow? It effects the forgiveness of sins, delivers from death and the devil, and grants eternal salvation to all who believe. . . ."[21] The Large Catechism also says that baptism is the *locus* of salvation: "To put it most simply, the power, effect, benefit and fruit of baptism is to save."[22]

It is completely foreign to Luther's sacramental theology to make baptism depend upon human initiative or experience. He sees baptism occurring at the instigation of the Holy Trinity itself. Even the traditional description of baptism as a "means of grace" is a less than felicitous phrase because it suggests the presence of something other than God himself.

In his preaching on Jesus' baptism this accent on the divine presence is especially clear:

> But here everything is living, the Son and also the Father and the Holy Spirit in their own persons are truly and bodily present. . . .

20. The difficulties of translating the word "Schwärmer" are well known. Though some consider it be tendentious, this essay will use the term "enthusiasm" since is seems to best preserve Luther's concerns about this movement.

21. SC, Baptism, 6 in BC-T 348-49; BSLK 515-16.

22. LC, Baptism, 24 in BC-T 439; BSLK 695.

Therefore Christ ought to be depicted as the Son who shed his own blood for me, who died and was resurrected. Therefore he is in baptism with his own blood, death and life. . . .[23]

Enthusiasm attempted to make baptism secondary by seeing it as a human ceremony that confirms a prior experience of conversion or decision to believe. Luther, however, with his strong emphasis on the sacrament as God's work, sees baptism as the place where the Triune God in all his power makes himself concretely present and brings the person being baptized into his kingdom.

Second, in his later writings on baptism, Luther stressed the necessity of the earthly sign. While there were only a few on the fringe of the Reformation who denied the need for baptism altogether (Caspar Schwenkfeld was perhaps the most prominent), implicit in enthusiasm's belief that "the Spirit must do it" is a denigration of the material element. The sign is relegated to the realm of "external things," clearly inferior to the "spiritual reality" of faith. Luther could not countenance this position. He refused to minimize the outward sign for two reasons. First, baptism is commanded by God and second, the very nature of faith demands an objective referent.

Drawing from Matthew 28:19 and Mark 16:16, Luther meets the challenge that baptism is merely an "external thing" with the observation that God commands us to be baptized: "Baptism is no human plaything but is instituted by God himself. . . . We are not to regard it as an indifferent matter, then, like putting on a new red coat."[24] When God commands something it is not our prerogative to question it. No matter what the world may think, because God has instituted baptism it cannot be useless. Therefore, what is "mere water" to the outsider becomes "divine, heavenly, holy and blessed" when God's Word and commandment are added.[25]

Luther also underscored the importance of the external sign because of faith's fragility. He likens faith to "butter in the sunshine."[26] While Luther will always maintain that trust in the promise makes baptism efficacious, he is wary of focusing on faith: "One must believe,

23. "Predigt am Sonntag Septuagesima" (1534), WA 37:272. Translation mine.
24. LC, Baptism, 6 in BC-T 437; BSLK 691-92.
25. LC Baptism, 17 in BC-T 438; BSLK 694.
26. "Concerning Rebaptism" (1528), LW 40:252; WA 26:164,26.

but we neither should nor can know it for certain."[27] Therefore, one dare not base his baptism on his faith. For who can be sure if he really believes? The Enthusiasts' stress on subjectivity, like the late medieval view of penance and monasticism, troubles Luther because it put the question of salvation back into the hands of a frail and doubting humanity. God, however, is merciful. He comes to us via outward means — water, bread, and wine. He pledges himself to us in these visible and tangible signs, for "faith must have something to believe — something to which it may cling and upon which it may stand."[28]

From Luther's perspective, the dispute with the Enthusiasts is not merely about the nature of material things and whether or not they can be mediums of the divine. Rather, the gospel itself is at stake. Whenever God's promises are obscured or ignored, works inevitably fill the gap. In opposing Rome, Luther saw a ritualism divorced from the Word and therefore devoid of faith. In his conflict with enthusiasm, Luther suspects that faith itself is being idolized, the very faith that is subject to the vagaries of human moods and emotions. Faith simply cannot bear that burden and remain salvific. Again, as was the case with Rome, Luther believes the enthusiasts are shrouding the life-giving promise. God must move from the external to the internal. To reverse the order is to make faith a work and set up a pernicious *ordo salutis* based on law. What Luther did was expose the essential nomism of the Enthusiasts.

Finally, the question of infant baptism must be examined. While the church had been baptizing children for well over a millennium, Luther's emphasis on promise and faith inevitably made this practice problematic. If the efficacy of the sacrament is dependent upon faith then some kind of infant belief must be postulated. This was not a major issue for Rome because its *ex opere operato* theory of the sacraments tended to make the question of infant faith secondary. Thus in his early treatises Luther does not dwell on the issue at length. However, his inclusion of a section on infant baptism at the end of *The Babylonian Captivity* suggest that he is aware of the implications of his position. At this point he adopts the traditional arguments for infant faith, namely that children were aided by the faith of parents and

27. LW 40:241; WA 26:155.
28. LC Baptism, 29 in BC-T 440; BSLK 696.

sponsors as well as by the prayers of the church. He also says that infant baptism was less troublesome than that of adults because the faith of children was "simple" and less likely to be tainted by "greed and superstition."[29]

But in his clash with those Enthusiasts who were Anabaptists Luther is forced to develop his thoughts on this question more fully. In his treatise *Concerning Rebaptism* (1528) he gives three reasons for baptizing infants: (1) He cites the traditional biblical texts that suggest children can have faith; (2) he claims the weight of church tradition; (3) he emphasizes the covenantal nature of baptism.[30]

In making an argument for infant faith Luther proceeds cautiously. He conceded that Scripture does not prove this unequivocally; there are no passages that explicitly state: "You are to baptize children because they also believe."[31] But his method in general is to cast the burden of proof on the Anabaptists. He asks: Since the Bible nowhere denies infant faith how can they be sure children cannot believe? Then he proceeds to cite texts suggestive of infant faith such as Herod's murder of the holy innocents (how could they be innocent if they did not believe in Christ?) in Matthew 2 and John the Baptist's leaping in the womb at the greeting of Mary (Luke 1:14). He also notes Christ's admonition to become like children for "of such is the kingdom of heaven" (Matthew 19:14). Luther wonders why Jesus would speak thusly if children could not believe.[32]

While Luther believes he has established a solid exegetical defense of infant faith, this in itself would not justify infant baptism. For, as already mentioned, Luther is not content to make baptism contingent upon the faith of the recipient:

> Yet even if they could establish that children are without faith when they are baptized, it would make no difference to me . . . for faith doesn't exist for the sake of baptism, but baptism for the sake of faith. When faith comes, baptism is complete.[33]

29. "Babylonian Captivity," LW 36:72-73; WA 6:538.
30. See Jaroslav Pelikan, *Spirit Versus Structure: Luther and the Institutions of the Church* (New York: Harper and Row, 1968), pp. 82-83.
31. "Concerning Rebaptism," LW 40:254; WA 26:166.
32. LW 40:242-43; WA 26:156.
33. LW 40:246; WA 26:160.

In other words, faith in and of itself is not sufficient. Luther must buttress his position with other arguments.

Luther also favors the baptism of children because it "derives from the apostles and has been practiced since the days of the apostles."[34] He wonders how Anabaptism can so blithely ignore the tradition. If infant baptism were false there would have been no church for the last one thousand years (for without a "correct" baptism there cannot be Christianity). Not only is Luther incredulous at such a proposition because of all that it implies about God's mercy, he also wonders how one is to understand the gifts the Holy Spirit has showered on some of the great figures of the church (Huss, Gerson, St. Bernard) if they were not rightly baptized as infants.[35]

But the most significant warrant for infant baptism is its foundation in the objective command of God. God has made a covenant with all people, and baptism is the sign of that bond. Since the gospel is intended for the whole world, the church is to baptize everyone, including children. God will take care of faith. Christians have done enough when they preach and baptize.[36]

Here again we touch upon Luther's dynamic understanding of the biblical promises, so central to his baptismal theology. Decisive for his opponents was the child's lack of reason; because infants have no reason they cannot believe. However, Luther was less sanguine about reason's powers in matters theological. He saw it as an instrument of the flesh, deeply enmeshed in the logic of the law. The point for him is that God is able to create faith in human hearts in spite of reason. Thus infant baptism can even be called the surest and most certain baptism.[37] To exclude anyone from baptism on the basis of their age would not only challenge an ordinance of God; it would also suggest that the divine promises were dependent upon human activity.

34. LW 40:254; WA 26:166.
35. LW 40:256; WA 26:168.
36. LW 40:258; WA 26:169.
37. Gronvik, *Taufe,* p. 167.

Summary

This survey of Luther's baptismal theology can be summarized under the following themes:

(1) *Baptism is efficacious only in faith, which is awakened by God's word of promise.* Luther's constant concern was to highlight the pro me character of salvation and the stress in his theology falls on the believer's passionate involvement in his relationship with God. He believed the late medieval church had made baptism routine and lifeless, burying it in the mists of infancy. This understanding of the sacrament was aided by a theology that saw the word as conferring a special power upon the water. Luther redirects the word to the recipient of baptism. Because it is a word of promise, it achieves God's salvific purpose, namely the drowning of the old person and raising of a believer who trusts in Christ. Faith is never a human accomplishment but rather the result of being addressed by a gracious God.

(2) *In baptism, the word and the water are inseparable.* In the conflict with enthusiasm, Luther saw his opponents stressing belief (in some cases referred to as "spirit baptism") as the primary basis of salvation. Baptism was relegated to the secondary role of witnessing to a prior act of conversion, often restricted to adults and sometimes not practiced at all. Luther is disturbed by these trends because Scripture gives a clear mandate to baptize and he is wary of grounding salvation in human subjectivity. The water and the word mutually reinforce salvation's external derivation.

(3) *In baptism God grants salvation.* Luther assents to a long tradition in the church which asserted that baptism was necessary for salvation. (Like the tradition, he also granted certain extreme cases when this did not apply.) By making baptism a human act, the enthusiasts denied the causal link between salvation and the sacrament. Luther, however, sees baptism as God's act, stressing the real presence of the Holy Trinity in the performance of the sacrament. Because God himself is present and doing the baptizing through his appointed ministers, baptism is the moment when a person is made a member of the kingdom of God.

(4) *The power of baptism shapes the entire life of the believer.* In his attack on the Roman sacramental system Luther moved baptism from the periphery to the center of Christian life. By merging penance with baptism, all of life becomes a continual dying and rising with Christ. Long after the completion of the rite, the full power of baptism is effective in

the daily life of the Christian, continually turning him from idolatry to the living God. Baptism finally ends at death when its "work" is accomplished and we are fully united with Christ.

(5) *Baptism is the earthly means by which the believer participates in justification.* In declaring that "baptism is full and complete justification," Luther is making two significant claims. First, he is opposing the late medieval understanding of justification which saw it as a "process" by which one is transformed, with the aid of free will, to a state of righteousness. His understanding of justification is much more vital and forceful — an event of death and resurrection. Second, baptism "grounds" the reformer's new understanding of justification. God's declaration of the sinner's righteousness in Christ can never be understood as an external announcement that leaves hearers untouched but rather returns them to an earthly font where they were drowned and raised to new life.

(6) *In baptism God anchors the believer in the freedom of the gospel.* The church in sixteenth-century Germany was entangled in an intricate web of vows and regulations that oppressed consciences and in many cases created a large cleavage between clergy and lay. The source of much of this division was a theological structure that not only made religious consolation an arduous task but also legitimated a highly stratified society. Luther's theological revolution, centered on justification by faith and its corollary, the priesthood of all believers, severed the ecclesiastical cords that encumbered consciences and the polis. The all-sufficient sign of the "brave new man" of the Reformation was baptism. Baptism assured him of his status before God and propelled him (through the doctrine of the priesthood of all believers) to "desacralize" the civil realm.[38]

(7) *Infants are to be baptized.* Luther refused to break with church tradition on the baptism of infants. But tradition itself would not warrant his position on this question. The enthusiasts' insistence on a confession of belief prior to baptism could undermine confidence in the gospel. If Christ himself is baptizing, the same Christ who pointed to children as the model for his kingdom and who also commanded the church to baptize, then this will be sufficient to create faith in the child.

---

38. Steven E. Ozment, *The Reformation in the Cities* (New Haven and London: Yale University Press, 1975), p. 34. Ozment notes that the "Protestant movement was an unprecedented flattering of secular life." He sees the theological impetus for the civil realm's new esteem as rooted in the doctrine of the priesthood of all believers, which is inseparable from Luther's new understanding of baptism.

Luther on the Two Kinds of Righteousness

ROBERT KOLB

"Our theology," Martin Luther claimed as he wrote the preface to his commentary on Galatians in 1535, consisted of the distinction between two kinds of righteousness:

> This is our theology, by which we teach a precise distinction between these two kinds of righteousness, the active and the passive, so that morality and faith, works and grace, secular society and religion may not be confused. Both are necessary, but both must be kept within their limits.[1]

In making this observation Luther was referring to two kinds of human righteousness, both necessary for the whole and good human life that God had made human creatures to live.

---

1. WA 40,I:45,24-27; LW 26:7. For a summary of Luther's definition of "righteousness," and bibliography, see Bengt Hagglund, "Gerechtigkeit. VI. Reformations- und Neuzeit," *Theologische Realenzyklopadie XII* (Berlin: de Gruyter, 1984), pp. 432-34, 440. See also the December 1998 Beiheft issue of *Zeitschrift für Theologie und Kirche* 95, on Luther's understanding of righteousness and justification, particularly as it pertains to the "Joint Declaration on the Doctrine of Justification" (which ignores Luther's distinction of the two kinds of righteousness); see especially in that issue Reinhard Schwartz, "Luthers Rechtfertigungslehre als Eckstein der christlichen Theologie und Kirche," 15-46.

This article first appeared in *Lutheran Quarterly* 13 (1999): 449-66, under the title "Luther on the Two Kinds of Righteousness: Reflections on His Two-Dimensional Definition of Humanity at the Heart of His Theology."

Two Kinds of Divine Righteousness

Luther's theology also rested on a presupposition that there were two definitions for the term "the righteousness of God" as it referred to God's essence. But the Reformer believed that only one of those definitions corresponded to Paul's usage and to that of the Old Testament in general. Luther dismissed the predominant medieval understanding of what makes God righteous, or what makes God God, as he had learned it.[2] God's righteousness has usually been understood as distributive justice, according to the model of a Greek judge, who makes the system work by executing the law and executing human beings — when necessary (or just) — in order to preserve law and order. Luther indeed had grown up with this image of God, often depicted in altar pieces that displayed Christ as judge, with sword in hand. This vision of God's righteousness is alien to God's true nature and terrified Luther until he discovered that what makes God God — his most fundamental characteristic — is not his justice or wrath but rather his steadfast love and mercy. "To know God aright is to recognize that with him there is nothing but kindness and mercy. But those who feel that God is angry and unmerciful do not know him aright."[3] God's righteousness is that which bestows righteousness upon fallen human creatures.[4] In his exposition of Psalm 51:14, delivered in Wittenberg in 1532, Luther commented:

> This term "righteousness" really caused me much trouble. They [the scholastic theologians whose works Luther had read as a student] generally explained that righteousness is the truth by which God deservedly condemns or judges those who have merited evil. In opposition to righteousness they set mercy by which believers are saved. This explanation is most dangerous, besides being vain, because it arouses a secret hate against God and his righteousness. Who can love him if he wants to deal with sinners according to righteousness? Therefore remember that the righteousness of God is that by which

2. On nominalist covenant conceptions of the relationship between God and the human creature, see Alister E. McGrath, *Luther's Theology of the Cross: Martin Luther's Theological Breakthrough* (Oxford: Blackwell, 1985), pp. 100-13.

3. Comments on Psalm 130:7, 1525 (1517), WA 18:520,27-30; LW 14:193-94.

4. Comments on Psalm 51:14, 1525 (1517), WA 18:505,28-30; LW 14:173.

we are justified, or the gift of the forgiveness of sins. This righteous-ness in God is wonderful because it makes of God not a righteous Judge but a forgiving Father, who wants to use his righteousness not to judge but to justify and absolve sinners.[5]

This discovery, that God's righteousness or essence is steadfast love and mercy, played a key role in the formation of Luther's understand-ing of the biblical message.

Two Kinds of Human Righteousness

Also central to Luther's "evangelical breakthrough" was his discovery of what makes the human creature "righteous" or right, that is, truly human. This involves the distinction emphasized in the preface to the 1535 Galatians commentary cited above. In recalling how he came to understand the entire biblical message Luther focused on his finding a new definition for human righteousness. This distinction was not a new development in the Reformer's thought at this time. A decade later he would reflect on his coming to an understanding of the gospel in the 1510s. At that time his attempt to please God by living the holiest way of life the medieval church knew, the monastic way, had failed. It left him only with "an extremely disturbed conscience." He had come to hate the righteous God who punishes sinners; a secret, perhaps blas-phemous anger against God possessed him, and he "raged with a fierce and troubled conscience."

> At last, by the mercy of God, meditating day and night, I gave heed to the context of the words, namely, "In it the righteousness of God is revealed, as it is written, 'He who through faith is righteous shall live.'" There I began to understand that the righteousness of God is that by which the righteous lives by a gift of God, namely by faith. And this is the meaning: the righteousness of God is revealed by the gospel, namely, the passive righteousness with which merciful God justifies us by faith. . . . Here I felt that I was altogether born again and had entered paradise itself through open gates. There a totally other face of the entire Scripture showed itself to me. Thereupon I

5. Comments on Psalm 51:14, 1532, WA 40/II:444,36–445,29; LW 12:392.

ran through the Scriptures from memory. I also found in other terms an analogy, as the work of God, that is, what God does in us, the power of God, with which he makes us strong, the wisdom of God, with which he makes us wise, the strength of God, the salvation of God, the glory of God. And I treasured the word that had become the sweetest of all words for me with a love as great as the hatred with which I had previously hated the word "righteousness of God." Thus that passage in Paul was for me truly the gate to paradise.[6]

Luther realized, however, that what made him genuinely right in God's sight had to be distinguished from what made him truly human — genuinely right — in relationship to other creatures of God. This distinction is what he labeled "our theology" in 1535. By differentiating the two dimensions in which human creatures were created to be human, or righteous, Luther was establishing as his fundamental hermeneutical principle what Jesus was referring to when he divided the law into two parts: loving the Lord our God with all heart, soul, and mind, and loving our neighbors as ourselves (Matt. 22:37, 39). When the reformer introduced his readers to comments he had made on the Epistle to the Galatians in 1531 (as he edited them four years later), he began by sketching the "argument," that is, the central concerns, of the apostle Paul in writing to the Galatians. According to Luther, Paul's fundamental consideration in the letter was establishing God's message regarding "faith, grace, the forgiveness of sins or Christian righteousness." He noted that there are a variety of definitions for the word righteousness: "righteousness is of many kinds." Luther listed political righteousness, ceremonial righteousness, the moral righteousness of the decalogue, all of which, he pointed out, are genuine forms of righteousness. "Over and above there is the righteousness of faith."[7] Luther defined "this most excellent righteousness, the righteousness of faith, which God imputes to us through Christ without works" as a "merely passive righteousness." "For here we work nothing, render nothing to God; we only receive and permit someone else to work in us, namely, God. Therefore it is appropriate to call the righteousness of faith or

6. "Preface to the Complete Edition of Luther's Latin Writings," 1545, WA 54:186,3-16; LW 34:337.
7. WA 40/I:40,16-27; LW 26:4.

Christian righteousness 'passive.' This is the righteousness hidden in a mystery, which the world does not understand. In fact, Christians themselves do not adequately understand it or grasp it in the midst of their temptations."[8]

Righteousness in the Two Dimensions or Relationships of Human Life

In developing this contrast between passive righteousness — which expresses itself in faith — and active righteousness — which expresses itself in performing the deeds of God's plan for human life — Luther was bringing to light a fundamental distinction that had escaped articulation by most theologians since the time of the apostles. This distinction recognizes and rests upon Christ's observation that human life consists of two kinds of relationship, one with the author and creator of life, the other with all other creatures (Matt. 22:37-39).

Just as the relationship of child to parents differs from the relationship between children and all else that belongs to the family, so the relationship between Creator and creatures is fundamentally not the same kind of relationship as that among his creatures. Parents establish the essential identity of their children; God has made them "responsible" for these children in ways that no sibling or other caretaker — by definition — can be. Parents give the gift of life and determine the genetic identity of their progeny. They shape and form the life of these offspring through their loving care in ways that psychologists perceive to be unique. Siblings, friends, and acquaintances relate to each other in quite different ways than children relate to their parents. These two different spheres of relationship issue from — and express themselves in — God's design for our humanity. Likewise, as our Creator he alone is responsible for our identity. From that identity as his creatures and children proceeds the performance of activities which reflect that identity. Human creatures identify themselves as God's creatures when they live according to that identity which God has given them. This means that human life exists on two planes of dependence and interdependence, in two spheres of relationship. They may be described as vertical

8. WA 40/I:41,15-26; LW 26:4-5.

and horizontal so long as the vertical relationship is delineated with God both above us (because he is lord and author of the life of his children) and beneath us (because he is the loving Father who lifts us up and cuddles us to himself in Christ). The horizontal relationship has bound us to the rest of creation as people who are held accountable for exercising God-given responsibilities in an adult manner toward other creatures, human but also animal, mineral, and vegetable. God's human creatures are right — really human — in their vertical relationship because their faith embraces the God who loves them through Jesus Christ with the reckless trust of total dependence and reliance on him that constitutes their identity. They are right — really human — in their horizontal relationship with God's other creatures when they live a life that is active in reflecting his love through the deeds that deliver his care and concern. Two spheres and kinds of relationship demand two different ways of being right or righteous.

The Righteousness of Identity and the Righteousness of Performance

Thus, Luther's theology found its orientation in this distinction between the identity that God as creator gives to his creatures and the performance or activities with which that identity expresses itself within the relationships God has fashioned for human life. Luther compared the righteousness of our identity to the earth as it receives the blessing of rain.

> As the earth itself does not produce rain and is unable to acquire it by its own strength, worship, and power but receives it only by a heavenly gift from above, so this heavenly righteousness is given to us by God without our work or merit. As much as the dry earth of itself is able to accomplish and obtain the right and blessed rain, that much can we human creatures accomplish by our own strength and works to obtain that divine, heavenly, and eternal righteousness. Thus we can obtain it only through the free imputation and indescribable gift of God.[9]

9. WA 40/I:43,18-25; LW 26:6.

That leads the Christian conscience to say,

> I do not seek active righteousness. I ought to have and perform it; but I declare that even if I did have and perform it, I cannot trust in it or stand up before the judgment of God on the basis of it. Thus I put myself beyond all active righteousness, all righteousness of my own or of the divine law, and I embrace only the passive righteousness which is the righteousness of grace, mercy, and the forgiveness of sins.[10]

A simple theological parable may clarify the point. Although by the definition of his own theology Thomas Aquinas had sufficient merit to proceed directly to heaven, without having to work off temporal punishment in purgatory, the Dominican saint dallied along the way, visiting old friends and doing research among those who still had purgatorial satisfactions to discharge there. He arrived at Saint Peter's gate some 272 years after his death, on February 18, 1546. After ascertaining his name, Saint Peter asked Thomas, "Why should I let you into my heaven?" "Because of the grace of God," Thomas answered, ready to explain the concept of prevenient grace should it be necessary. Peter asked instead, "How do I know you have God's grace?" Thomas, who had brought a sack of his good deeds with him, was ready with the proof. "Here are the good works of a lifetime," he explained. "I could have done none of them without God's grace, but in my worship and observation of monastic rules, in my obedience to parents, governors, and superiors, in my concern for the physical well-being and property of others, in my chastity and continence, you can see my righteousness — grace-assisted as it may be." Since a line was forming behind Thomas, Peter waved him in, certain that Thomas would soon receive a clearer understanding of his own righteousness. The next person in line stepped up. "Name?" "Martin Luther." "Why should I let you into my heaven?" "Because of the grace of God." Peter was in a playful mood, so he went on, "How do I know you have God's grace? Thomas had his works to prove his righteousness, but I don't see that you have brought any proof along that you are righteous." "Works?" Luther exclaimed. "Works? I didn't know I was supposed to bring my works with

---

10. WA 40/I:42,26–43,15; LW 26:6.

me! I thought they belonged on earth, with my neighbors. I left them down there." "Well," said Gatekeeper Peter, "how then am I supposed to know that you really have God's grace?" Luther pulled a little, well-worn, oft-read scrap of paper out of his pocket and showed it to Peter. On it were the words, "Martin Luther, baptized, November 11, in the year of our Lord 1483." "You check with Jesus," Luther said. "He will tell you that he has given me the gift of righteousness through his own blood and his own resurrection."

Martin Luther knew *how* he was righteous *where;* he knew *where* he was truly human *in what manner.* That is, he recognized that being human in God's sight means receiving the unconditional love of God. It means childlike dependence, expressed in the absolute trust of complete love. Furthermore, Luther recognized that being human in relationship to the creatures of God meant the exercise of adult responsibility as God designed it for human creatures, expressed in the care and concern of deeds of complete love for others.

Two Kinds of Righteousness: Inseparable but Distinct

Luther did see these two kinds of righteousness as inseparable. Human life is of one piece, not divided into separate or separable spheres of sacred and profane. Human life is cruciform — eyes lifted to focus on God, feet firmly planted on his earth, arms stretched out in mutual support of those God has placed around us. Having the focus of our lives directed toward Christ inevitably extends our arms to our neighbors. Human beings are truly human, that is, right or functioning properly (according to the design for human righteousness that God made) when their identity does express itself in the activities that flow from that identity. Luther gave his students a critical word of caution:

> The weak, who are not malicious or slanderous but good, are offended when they hear that the law and good works do not have to be done for justification. One must go to their aid and explain to them how it is that works do not justify, how works should be done, and how they should not be done. They should be done as fruits of righteousness, not in order to bring righteousness into being. Having been made righteous, we must do them; but it is not the other

way around: that when we are unrighteous, we become righteous by
doing them. The tree produces fruit; the fruit does not produce the
tree.[11]

For, as Luther never tired of pointing out, our identity determines the
validity of the activities it produces.

> The righteousness of the law is earthly and deals with earthly things;
> by it we perform good works. But as the earth does not bring forth
> fruit unless it has been first watered and made fruitful from above —
> for the earth cannot judge, renew, and rule the heavens, but the heav-
> ens judge, renew, rule, and fortify the earth, so that it may do what
> the earth has commanded — so also by the righteousness of the law
> we do nothing even when we do much; we do not fulfill the law even
> when we fulfill it. Without any merit or any work of our own, we
> must first become righteous by Christian righteousness, which has
> nothing to do with the righteousness of the law or with earthly and
> active righteousness. This righteousness is heavenly and passive. We
> do not have it of ourselves; we receive it from heaven. We do not per-
> form it; we accept it by faith through which we ascend beyond all
> laws and works . . . for this righteousness means to do nothing, to
> share nothing, and to know nothing about the law or about works
> but to know and believe only this: that Christ has gone to the Father
> and is now invisible; . . . that he is our high priest, interceding for us
> and reigning over us and in us through grace.[12]

Shortly after he presented such ideas in lectures before his students in
1531, Luther proclaimed them to the congregation in Wittenberg. In
treating John 6:37 from the pulpit of the town church in 1532, he reminded his hearers that

> In order to retain the purity of the doctrine of justification by faith
> it is necessary to distinguish clearly between justification by faith
> and justification by good works. The performance of good works is
> not forbidden here. If I live according to the law, do good works,
> keep the commandments of the second table of the Ten Command-

11. WA 40/I:287,17-23; LW 26:169.
12. WA 40/I:46,20–47,21; LW 26:8.

ments, honor my government, abstain from theft, murder, and adultery, I am conducting myself properly; and such works are not condemned here. It is work-righteousness, however, when the papists propose to do good works before acknowledging the Lord Christ and believing in him. They lay claim to their salvation by virtue of their good works, and they abandon the article of faith in Christ. But those who come to faith and know that Christ is not a taskmaster, and then begin to lead a good life and do acceptable and upright works, do not call these works, performed either before or after accepting Christ, holy or righteous, as is the wont of the papists. Only faith in Christ is our righteousness.[13]

In the end this more fundamental righteousness grasped by faith, God's gift of our identity as his children, reveals itself as that upon which human existence depends:

When this life ends and death is at hand, the rules of earthly justice [righteousness] also expire. Christ declares here: This earth's justice does not apply here; it does not endure. You must rise above what you have done and come before God with a different righteousness; you must despair of your own works and rely on, and believe in, Christ's words: "Truly, truly, your food is indeed my flesh given for you and my blood shed for you" [John 6:55]. Then you hear that your sins and mine cannot be atoned and paid for by you or by me, but solely by him who shed his blood for me.[14]

The Roots of the Distinction

Luther's insight into the distinct dimensions of what it means to be human was an idea that was born in the struggle for his evangelical breakthrough in 1518 and 1519. After having composed a tract on three kinds of righteousness in 1518,[15] he went on to preach a sermon at the end of that year or early in 1519 on two kinds of righteousness. "There

---

13. On John 6:37, WA 33:85,23–86,17; LW 23:58.

14. WA 33:281,13-15; LW 23:178. Cf. his comments on John 6:54, WA 33:219,13–220,15; LW 23:140-41.

15. WA 2:41,43-47.

are two kinds of Christian righteousness, just as human sin is of two kinds. The first is alien righteousness, that is, the righteousness of another, instilled from without. This is the righteousness of Christ by which he justifies through faith."[16] This alien righteousness [from the Latin, "belonging to another"], which is bestowed from outside the human creature, belongs to the Christian "through faith in Christ; therefore, Christ's righteousness becomes our righteousness and all that he has becomes ours . . . this righteousness is primary; it is the basis, the cause, the source of all our own actual righteousness. For this is the righteousness given in place of the original righteousness lost in Adam. It accomplishes the same as that original righteousness would accomplish; rather it accomplishes more."[17]

Although Luther would continue to refine his definition of this alien righteousness, already in 1519 its basic elements were in place. This alien righteousness "instilled in us without our works by grace alone — while the Father, to be sure, inwardly draws us to Christ — is set opposite original sin, likewise alien, which we acquire without our works by birth alone." Luther went on to describe the active righteousness or "proper" [from the Latin "one's own"] righteousness as "the product of the righteousness of the first type, actually its fruit and consequence." Luther continued, "Therefore through the first righteousness arises the voice of the bridegroom who says to the soul 'I am yours,' but through the second comes the voice of the bride who answers, 'I am yours.'" God gives us the identity as his bride by choosing us and bringing us to himself. The active righteousness of response takes form in the things we do that respond to his goodness.[18]

That Luther employed a double focus on human righteousness can be seen in his understanding that the righteousness God gives "is not instilled all at once, but it begins, makes progress, and is finally perfected at the end through death."[19] This "partly righteous, partly sinful" view of the believer remained a part of Luther's discussion of the struggle of the Christian life for at least another decade. It describes the progress (or lack of it) experienced in the practice of actual righ-

16. WA 2:145,7-10; LW 31:297.
17. WA 2:146,12-19; LW 31:298-99.
18. WA 2:147,7-18; LW 31:300.
19. WA 2:146,32-35; LW 31:299.

teousness, in the performance of God's will within the horizontal sphere of life. However, the logic of the distinction between the two kinds of righteousness, combined with his belief that God's Word creates reality, had already led him to define the situation of believers in another, clearer fashion. He recognized that God's children are also completely righteous and completely sinful at the same time. His mature understanding of the righteousness of God's chosen children, reflected in the later Galatians commentary, could label them righteous "in fact" — in God's sight — in spite of their experience of sinfulness, because they had been re-created in Christ through faith by the power of the Word. For the Word has worked the forgiveness — the abolition — of sin by bringing the benefits of Christ's death and resurrection to believers. God removes the sinners from their sin.

> For believers in Christ are not sinners and are not sentenced to death but are altogether holy and righteous, lords over sin and death who live eternally. Only faith can discern that, but the trust believers place in Christ diverts their eyes and ears away from their own sins. According to the theology of Paul, there is no more sin, no more death, and no more curse in the world, but only in Christ, who is the Lamb of God that takes away the sins of the world and who became a curse in order to set us free from the curse. . . . True theology teaches that there is no more sin in the world, because Christ, on whom, according to Isaiah 53:6, the Father has laid the sins of the entire world, has conquered, destroyed and killed it in his own body. Having died to sin once, he has truly been raised from the dead and will not die any more (Rom. 6:9). Therefore wherever there is faith in Christ, there sin has in fact been abolished, put to death, and buried.[20]

Luther's ontology recognized that reality springs from and rests upon what God says. This ontology of the Word convinced him that when God declares, "forgiven," he restores the original humanity of his chosen children.

---

20. WA 40/I:444,34–445,33; LW 26:285-86.

ROBERT KOLB

Original Righteousness and Original Sin

The Word of forgiveness and life — fashioned through Christ's death and resurrection — has restored the original relationship between God and the human creature. In lecturing on Genesis 2 Luther revealed his presupposition that human creatures are totally dependent upon their Creator, products of his hand and breath, given their human identity purely out of his sovereign grace and favor. Adam and Eve had no time of probation in which to perform deeds that would make them eligible for and worthy of their humanity. They were created truly human.

> We are vessels of God, formed by God himself, and he himself is our potter, but we his clay, as Isaiah 64[:8] says. And this holds good not only for our origin but throughout our whole life; until our death and in the grave we remain the clay of this potter . . . in a state of merely passive potentiality, not active potentiality. For there we do not choose, we do not do anything; but we are chosen, we are equipped, we are born again, we accept, as Isaiah says: "Thou art the potter, we thy clay."[21]

The Wittenberg professor rejected the scholastic traditions that interpreted the original righteousness of Adam and Eve as a quality implanted in them. God had created them as his children, made them "righteous, truthful, and upright not only in body but especially in soul." They knew God and obeyed him with the utmost joy and understood the works of God even without prompting. The peace of Eden was God's gift to his human creatures. "It is part of this original righteousness that Adam loved God and his works with an outstanding and very pure attachment, that he lived among the creatures of God in peace, without fear of death and without any fear of sickness, and that he had a very obedient body, without evil inclinations and the hideous lust which we now experience."[22] The gift of human life had established Adam and Eve's existence and identity. The activities that flowed from that identity expressed who they were. At the center of their beings was their knowledge and trust of their Creator.

21. WA 42:64,22-26; LW 1:84.
22. WA 42:86,11-16; LW 1:113.

50

Luther formulated the negative side of this definition of the original human righteousness by defining original sin:

> . . . human nature has completely fallen; . . . the intellect has become darkened, so that we no longer know God and his will and no longer perceive the works of God; furthermore, the will is extraordinarily depraved, so that we do not trust the mercy of God and do not fear God but are unconcerned, disregard the Word and will of God, and follow the desire and the impulses of the flesh, likewise, our conscience is no longer quiet but, when it thinks of God's judgment despairs and adopts illicit defenses and remedies. . . . the knowledge of God has been lost; we do not everywhere and always give thanks to him; we do not delight in his works and deeds; we do not trust him; when he inflicts deserved punishments, we begin to hate God and blaspheme him.

From the broken relationship with God come broken relationships with others. Luther continued his definition of sinfulness with a focus on the actual sins that flow from original sin, the doubt and defiance of God: "when we must deal with our neighbor we yield to our desires and are robbers, thieves, adulterers, murderers, cruel, inhuman, merciless, etc. The passion of lust is indeed some part of original sin. But greater are the defects of the soul: unbelief, ignorance of God, despair, hate, blasphemy."[23] The root of sin is this doubt of the Word of God that created and shaped the relationship of love and trust between God and his human creatures. Breaking the contact, going deaf on God, destroyed the relationship that stood at the heart of what it meant to be human.

Righteousness in and through Christ

Luther knew that his definition of righteousness deviated from the commonly understood meaning of the word. In preaching on John 16:10 in 1537 he observed to his hearers that the righteousness Christ bestows upon believers, "the righteousness which abolishes sin and unrighteousness and makes human creatures righteous and acceptable before God," is "completely concealed, not only from the world but also

23. WA 42:86,17-41; LW 1:114.

from the saints. It is not a thought, a word, or a work in ourselves, as the scholastics fantasized about grace when they said that it is something poured into our hearts. No, it is entirely outside and above us; it is Christ's going to the Father, that is, his suffering, resurrection, and ascension."[24] Luther further commented,

> This is a peculiar righteousness; it is strange indeed that we are to be called righteous or to possess a righteousness which is really no work, no thought, in short, nothing whatever in us but is entirely outside us in Christ and yet becomes truly ours by reason of his grace and gift, and becomes our very own, as though we ourselves had achieved and earned it. Reason, of course, cannot comprehend this way of speaking, which says that our righteousness is something which involves nothing active or passive on our part, yes, something in which I do not participate with my thoughts, perception, and senses; that nothing at all in me makes me so pleasing to God and saves me; but that I leave myself and all human thoughts and ability out of account and cling to Christ. . . .[25]

Luther could not speak of restored human righteousness in God's sight apart from Christ. For sin had indeed destroyed that righteousness which consisted in trust in the Creator. Christ took sin into himself and substituted himself for sinners before the law's tribunal. Christ took the punishment for sin, its wage of death, into himself and satisfied the law's condemnation of human creatures who fail to be and behave like the creatures they were designed to be. No cheap atonement was possible from Luther's point of view. The Lamb had to die. Luther employed the Pauline baptismal model of dying and rising in Romans 6:3-11 and Colossians 2:11-15 to speak not only of God's saving action in baptism but also of his action of justifying.[26] The sinner's sin kills Christ. Christ buries the sinner's sin. Christ raises the sinner to new life — to a new identity and a new way of practicing that identity.

24. WA 46:44,23-28; LW 24:346-47.
25. WA 46:44,34–45,3; LW 24:347.
26. See Robert Kolb, "God Kills to Make Alive: Romans 6 and Luther's Understanding of Justification (1535)," *Lutheran Quarterly*, n.s., 12 (1998): 33-56, on the use of the baptismal enactment of the death of the sinner and the resurrection of the believer in Christ, as Luther developed the idea in the Galatians commentary of 1535.

Therefore Luther can state quite simply, "The work of Christ, properly speaking, is this: to embrace the one whom the law has made a sinner and pronounced guilty, and to absolve that person from his sins if he believes the gospel. 'For Christ is the end of the law, that everyone who has faith may be justified' (Rom. 10:4); he is 'the Lamb of God, who takes away the sin of the world' (John 1:29)."[27]

> We cannot deny that Christ died for our sins in order that we might be justified. For he did not die to make the righteous righteous; he died to make sinners into righteous people, the friends and children of God, and heirs of all heavenly gifts. Therefore since I feel and confess that I am a sinner on account of the transgression of Adam, why should I not say that I am righteous on account of the righteousness of Christ, especially when I hear that he loved me and gave himself for me?[28]

Luther followed the apostolic dictum regarding the source of that new life in righteousness, as Paul expressed it in Romans 4:25. Paul "refers to the resurrection of Christ, who rose again for our justification. His victory is a victory over the law, sin, our flesh, the world, the devil, death, hell, and all evils; and this victory of his life he has given to us. Even though these tyrants, our enemies, accuse us and terrify us, they cannot drive us into despair or condemn us. For Christ, whom God the Father raised from the dead, is the Victor over them, and he is our righteousness."[29]

> We must turn our eyes completely to that bronze serpent Christ nailed to the cross (John 3:14). With our gaze fastened firmly to him, we must declare with assurance that he is our righteousness and life and care nothing about the threats and terrors of the law, sin, death, wrath, and the judgment of God. For the Christ on whom our gaze is fixed, in whom we exist, and who also lives in us, is the Victor and the Lord over the law, sin, death, and every evil. In him a sure comfort has been set forth for us, and the victory has been granted.[30]

27. WA 40/I:250,10-13; LW 26:143.
28. WA 40/I:300,15-22; LW 26:179.
29. WA 40/I:65,10-17; LW 26:21-22.
30. WA 40/I:282,35–283,17; LW 26:166-67.

For "he alone makes us paupers rich with his superabundance, expunges our sins with his righteousness, devours our death with his life, and transforms us from children of wrath, tainted with sin, hypocrisy, lies, and deceit, into children of grace and truth."[31]

Christ is our righteousness not in his obedience to the law but rather in his obedience to the Father, not merely in his death or solely in his resurrection. What makes Christ the righteousness given to sinners that makes them human once again? "It is Christ's going to the Father, that is, his suffering, resurrection, and ascension."[32]

Adam and Eve, Luther believed, had also possessed only this passive righteousness. They were human in God's sight not because they had proved their humanity through specific activities that had won God's favor. Instead, they had been created by his breath and hand because he wanted them as his children. His love and mercy expressed themselves by forming his creatures as right and righteous in his sight. He formed them with the expectation that they would perform as his children in relationship to the rest of his creation as they trusted in him and showed him their love.

"Faith" or "trust" is the operative word. Trust defines the new creature's identity as child of God. Passive righteousness is the trust that embraces the loving Father and throws itself upon him. Just as that was true in the garden, until doubt broke in and broke down the relationship of trust in God, so it becomes true as Christ's word of love draws trust back to God in the human creatures that word recreates.

For fallen sinners the gift of this passive righteousness, which expresses itself first of all in trust toward the loving Father, comes through Christ's obedience to the Father as he took the sinfulness of fallen creatures into death with himself and as he reclaimed life for them in his resurrection. Christ promises forgiveness and life through his death and resurrection, and thus he elicits trust from those sinners whom the Holy Spirit has turned back to himself. That trust, directed toward the crucified and risen God, is the righteousness of Eden, restored and revivified, ready to advertise its identity in the performance of activities suitable for God's children.

---

31. WA 46:649,36–650,2; LW 22:131.
32. WA 46:44,26-27; LW 24:347.

Conclusion

The concept of the two kinds of human righteousness had sprung upon Luther as he was engaged in the study of the biblical text. In his exegetical studies, as he ran through the passages of Scripture, he found this concept to be a true and accurate description of what it means to be human. The concept also rang true in the midst of his own struggles against doubt about his own identity in God's sight and as he helped others with the pastoral care he was called to give them. He believed that the biblical message was given to the church for pastoral purposes, and this connection of biblical confession and pastoral practice stands at the heart of the Lutheran enterprise.

In the midst of societies around the world, in which new technologies, new economic forces, new political constellations, and new social structures join with the age-old sinfulness of individuals to unsettle life and deprive human beings of their humanity, Lutheran churches need to witness to Christ using the distinction of identity and performance, the distinction of passive and active righteousness. This insight into humanity enriches our ability to make the gospel of Jesus Christ meet individual human needs as we draw those outside the faith into the company of Christ's people. It also is one of the chief gifts Lutherans have to offer within the ecumenical conversation about how best to express the biblical message. For the distinction of the two dimensions in which we relate to God and his world, the two aspects that constitute our humanity, is "our theology"; and it is impossible to understand the Lutheran tradition without recognizing and employing it.

Luther's Seal as an Elementary Interpretation of His Theology

DIETRICH KORSCH

Martin Luther's seal, the so-called "Luther rose," has become the primary symbol of Lutheran Christianity. As a result, the "Luther rose" is often the object of historical inquiry and a starting point for spiritual inspiration.[1] However, many of the historical problems about the origin and appropriation of the seal have yet to be clarified. Even more astonishing is that no one has explained in detail the one aspect of the content of the seal, which makes it a characteristic sign of the Lutheran understanding of Christianity. Luther himself prepared this basis with his own interpretation: namely, that the seal is a compendium of his theology. Thus it is the goal of this article, first, to exegete the seal, interpreting it as a key to an elementary understanding of Luther's theology, for which he alone is responsible. Secondly, I include a historical hypothesis about the seal's formation.

I begin with Luther's explicit explanation from his own letter, and examine it in the light of today's requirements for an elementary theology. Then I inquire into the historical circumstances under which the

---

1. Oskar Thulin, "Vom bleibenden Sinn der Lutherrose," *Luther* 39 (1968): 41-42. Michael Freund, "Zur Geschichte der Lutherrose," *Luther* 42 (1971): 39-47.

For Bernd Moeller on his 65th Birthday. Originally from a guest lecture at the Faculty of Theology, University of Erlangen, February 8, 1993. Translated by Amy Marga from "Luthers Siegel: Eine elementare Deutung seiner Theologie," in *Luther* 67 (1996): 66-87. This article first appeared in English in *Lutheran Quarterly* 14 (2000): 409-31, under the same title.

sign became Luther's seal and under which his famous interpretation arose. Finally, following Luther, I give an exposition of *his* interpretation as my *own* attempt to produce an elementary theology, for which I alone am responsible.

Luther's Letter to Lazarus Spengler

On July 8, 1530, Martin Luther wrote from the Castle Coburg to the city clerk of Nuremberg, Lazarus Spengler:

> Grace and peace from the Lord. As you desire to know whether my painted shield, which you sent to me, has hit the mark, I shall answer most amiably and tell you my original thoughts and reasons about why my seal is a symbol of my theology.

> The first should be a black cross in a heart, which retains its natural color, so that I myself would be reminded that faith in the Crucified saves us. "For one who believes from the heart will be justified" (Rom. 10:10).

> Although it is indeed a black cross, which mortifies and which should also cause pain, it leaves the heart in its natural color. It does not corrupt nature, that is, it does not kill but keeps one alive. "The just shall live by faith" (Rom 1:17) but by faith in the crucified.

> Such a heart should stand in the middle of a white rose, to show that faith gives joy, comfort, and peace. In other words, it places the believer into a white, joyous rose, for this faith does not give peace and joy like the world gives (John 14:27). That is why the rose should be white and not red, for white is the color of spirits and angels (cf. Matt. 28:3; John 20:12).

> Such a rose should stand in a sky-blue field, symbolizing that such joy in spirit and faith is a beginning of the heavenly future joy, which begins already, but is grasped in hope, not yet revealed.

> And around this field is a golden ring, symbolizing that such blessedness in Heaven lasts forever and has no end. Such blessedness is ex-

57

quisite, beyond all joy and goods, just as gold is the most valuable, most precious and best metal.

This is my *compendium theologiae*. I have wanted to show it to you in good friendship, hoping for your appreciation. May Christ, our beloved Lord, be with your spirit until the life hereafter. Amen. From the wilderness Grubok [anagram of Coburg, used here for the first time] on July 8, 1530.[2]

The Seal as Elementary Theology

A short letter as a compendium of Luther's theology: what a promise! The concentration of an entire theology is contained in the tersest of spaces. This promise was particularly appealing back then, when reliable guidance was sought after on all sides, like today. It promises basics in the face of new uncertainties today, which are also characteristic of postmodern indifference.

However, it is characteristic of our spiritual condition that the tools that would normally reduce such variety and make it more manageable, cannot grasp this new form of plurality. It does not do any good to let lofty, general concepts rise above diverse differences. Not even the building-up of structures, which are to be filled with life, is able to bring together the divergences. The opposing powers are too strong.

These facts, I think, are a new challenge to theology. Can a conclusion about the constitution of Christianity be reached that possesses structures but also allows justifiable individual interpretations? Can Christianity be flexible, depending on the situation, without losing its certainty?

I think yes. And I would like to make an attempt using Luther's seal and his interpretation in the famous letter given above. It seems to me that the letter is especially appropriate for such a task on three grounds.

2. WA Br 5:444f.; LW 49:356-59. The edition for our text is from Johannes Schilling, *Briefe. Auswahl, Übersetzung und Erläuterungen* in vol. 6, *Ausgewählte Schriften/Martin Luther,* ed. Karin Bornkamm and Gerhard Ebeling, with Oswald Bayer (Frankfurt am Main: Insel-Luther, 1982), pp. 122f.

First, a highly concentrated and reliable sign lies in the seal. The seal and its contents, through their iconographic boundaries and certainty, call for understanding, interpretation, and consensus. The image of the seal vouches for its own reliability. It indicates that the letter comes from the true sender, and guarantees privacy for the receiver. Further, the receiver can rely on its contents. From the other perspective, the sealing of the letter is an action of the author by which he symbolically confirms his own authorship. The one who pressed the seal onto the letter can really and truly be heard here. Thus, content and relationship mingle together in the seal. Subject and person coincide.[3]

Second, we have in Luther's writing to Lazarus Spengler the unique case where (in a sealed letter!) the meaning of the seal is interpreted by the author himself. These lines deserve special attention because in them the author elucidates how he finds himself expressed and interpreted through his seal and its contents. This concerns the contents, which are encoded in the seal. If we want to understand this movement from the interpretation of the seal to the interpretation of the actual person, we ourselves become active interpreters, and are responsible for our interpretation.

Third, with this, we stand before the question of whether the interpretation, which is encoded in the seal, also points to an interpretation of ourselves. But exactly then — and only then — when an interpretation of the subject merges into the interpretation of one's own self, does the elementary emerge. Elementary theology is therefore in no way the mere learning and making use of basic concepts, which are normally unsatisfying procedures since they do not allow us to reach the layer of self-interpretation. Theology is elementary when the features of the content are written into the features of one's own self; and exactly then, in this individual expression, the real thing is expressed.

Luther's seal as compendium of his theology promises to introduce us comprehensively to such an elementary theology.

---

3. For the relationship between person and subject in the seal, cf. Kristin Bühler-Oppenheim, *Zeichen, Marken, Zinken — Signs, Brands, Marks* (Teufen/Schweiz and New York: Hastings House, n.d.), pp. 46-47.

On the History of the Seal and
the Circumstances of Its Interpretation

Before I begin with an interpretation of the seal itself, I want to share what I can about the history of the seal.[4]

Luther's use of the well-known seal is traceable at least to December 11, 1517;[5] perhaps as far back as July 22, 1516.[6] In 1519 it surfaced for the first time in Leipzig as a sign of authenticity in the press.[7] In Wittenberg it became the trademark of the reliable imprints of Luther's works until the 1530s.[8] Later it turned from this function into an ornamental image.

4. I rely, especially, upon the following older works: Julius Köstlin, "Geschichtliche Untersuchungen über Luthers Leben vor dem Ablasstreite," *Theologische Studien und Kritiken* 45 (1871): 7-45; J. K. F. Knaake, "Stoffsichtung zur kritischen Behandlung des Lebens Luthers," and "Name und Herkommen," *Zeitschrift für die gesammte Lutherische Theologie und Kirche* 33 (1872): 462-90; Knaake, "Luthers Wappen," *Zeitschrift für kirchliche Wissenschaft und kirchliches Leben* 1 (1880): 50-54; Gotthilf Hermann, *Die Lutherrose. Martin Luthers Wappen* (Zwickau: Hermann, 1932); Johannes Ficker, "Luthers Siegel" in *450 Jahre Luther,* ed. Oskar Thulin, a special edition of the *Illustrierten Zeitung,* (Leipzig 1933): 13-15.

5. Knaake, "Luthers Wappen," pp. 54f.

6. If the seal of the letter in WA Br 1 Nr. 17 is the same (cf. WA Br 13:6, Nr. 1-Nr. 17), it must be checked against the original letter found in the Biblioteca Vaticana. On the one microfilm found in the Institut für Spätmittelalter und Reformation in Tübingen there is a wax spot visible but no recognizable image. (For the letter regarding this matter from January 10, 1993, I thank Dr. Gerhard Hammer in Tübingen.)

7. It does appear on the print which was published on the occasion of the Leipziger Disputation published by Wolfgang Stöckel, "Ein Sermon geprediget tzu Leipssgk/ uffm Schloss am tag Petri vn pau/li im xviiij Jar, etc," together with one of the first public pictures of Luther. Cf. Knaake (note 6), p. 55. An illustration of this title page is found in: *Martin Luther. Sein Leben in Bildern und Texten,* ed. Gerhard Bott, Gerhard Ebeling, and Bernd Möller (Frankfurt: Insel, 1983), p. 121. The cross in the middle is difficult to recognize. It must be supposed on the basis of the completed letter seal that it [the cross] also belongs to the seal here.

8. On the title page, for example: "An die Ratsherrn aller Städte deutschen Lands" Wittenberg 1524. Illust. in *Martin Luther* [note 8] 195 or "Der Psalter deutsch," Wittenberg, 1524. Illust. in: Hans Volz, *Martin Luthers deutsche Bibel. Entstehung und Geschichte der Lutherbibel* (Hamburg: Wittig, 1978), p. 134 as a conclusion, for example (next to the picture of a lamb that carries the cross) in the first printing from Luther's translation of the Pentateuch 1524. Illust. in *Martin Luther* (note 8), 212. Here also is the following text: "this sign may be a witness/that such books go through my hands/for the wrong prints and books/this is done by many. Printed in Wittenberg." A summary of this problem is by Hans Volz, "Das Lutherwappen als 'Schutzmarke,'" *Libri International Library Review* 4 (1954): 216-25.

So far there is only speculation about the origin of the seal, which cannot be confidently attributed to either a heraldic[9] or an emblematic[10] tradition. It is most likely that Luther himself created his seal as a bourgeois "Seal of Vocation."[11] That had become customary, as one can see with his father, Hans Luder. When Hans moved from Möhra to Mansfeld, he advertised his new occupation in mining with a coat of arms that depicted two hammers.[12] My hunch is that Luther had reached back beyond the new coat of arms of his father to an old family coat of arms of the Luder family from Möhra, which depicted a crossbow sideways, with two white roses.[13] He had the crossbow erased and retained only one rose.

He could make further use of this element of the old shield, because the northeast window of the choir of the Erfurter Augustinian Church — the place where he lived as a monk — showed a flower motif, dominated by white roses with a red center.[14] In this way, as I interpret the matter, he was able to keep a continuity with his familial origins over and above the biographical break with his father that was caused by his entrance into the Order of the Augustinians.

In the center of the rose, which originated in family tradition but was also appropriate to Luther's own life context, he drew a heart. The heart was the main attribute of the saint of the Order, Augustine.[15] This meant that the innermost meaning of monasticism stood in the

9. Cf. Erich Kittel, "Bürger und Bauren," in *Siegel*, vol. 10 of *Library for Art and Antiquities* (Braunschweig: Klinkhardt and Biermann, 1970), pp. 367-82.

10. Cf. "Herz, Rose, Kreuz, Ring," *Emblemata. Handbuch zur Sinnbildkunst des XVI und XVII Jahrhunderts*, ed. Arthur Henkel and Albrecht Schöne (Stuttgart: J. B. Metzler, 1968).

11. Very informative for this question is the existing work by Julius Klanfer, coming out of the semiotic school of Karl Bühler, unfortunately only in manuscript. Julius Klanfer, "Theorie der heraldischen Zeichen," (Ph.D. diss., Vienna, 1933). Klanfer wrote about the possible free choice of shield pictures by non-noble persons, pp. 13-15; about farmers' shields, p. 43; about occupational symbols in shields, p. 105.

12. Knaake, "Stoffsichtung," (note 5), 480; "Luthers Wappen" (note 5), 53.

13. Knaake, "Stoffsichtung," (note 5), 53f. Illustration in Hermann (note 5), 20. On the doubling of the rose cf. Klanfer (note 12), 15.

14. A relationship between Luther's seal and this rose is also shown in the exhibition at the Augustinian cloister organized by Helmar Junghans. However, the references for this summary are not given there.

15. Cf. "Herz" in *Lexikon der christlichen Ikonographie*, Engelbert Kirschbaum et al., eds., vol. 2 (Rome: Herder, 1968), pp. 248-50; and "Augustinus" vol. 5, pp. 283f.

center of the Erfurt cloister life. But in the middle of the heart, Luther drew the cross. This is not an iconographic innovation, but is known from images of the Heart-of-Jesus depiction.[16] However, with this combination, from the foundation of the heart as the center of love, the cross stands as the only support of theology and faith. Thus, in the arrangement of the seal, Luther expresses a theology of the cross, which points to Augustinian monastic piety and the theology of the Order.

The reasons why the Erfurter monk Martin Luther may have taken steps to develop his own seal might lie in his assuming the office of a district vicar of the Order in 1516. In any case, a certain convergence of biography and theology within the seal points in this direction.[17] No matter how this hypothesis is regarded, one thing is certain: the image reaches relatively far back into Luther's origins, and the interpretation from 1530 is probably not the same as that of 1516; but the image itself has remained constant. That is a recipe for a successful elementary theology: one that can adapt to different situations.

What compelled Luther to reinterpret his seal in 1530? The obvious reason, as can be seen in the letter above, is an inquiry made by Lazarus Spengler[18] about the accuracy of the seal's "portrayal." The wording of

16. Cf. the illustration "Verehrung des Herzens Jesu" (1505) by L. Cranach the Elder in the *Lexikon der christlichen Ikonographie,* vol. 2, p. 252.

17. The seal may be, as suggested by Klanfer, a sign of "attributive representation," which expresses the "membership of an individual" with "an order," for example. The "members of an order take the shield of this order into its own 'family shield,' and use it next to the family shield or unite the family shield with it." Klanfer (note 12), 30. In this context, the heart in the center may also be an exaggerated self-presentation.

18. About him see *Realencyklopädie für protestantische Theologie und Kirche,* 3rd edition, pp. 18, 622-25; Hans von Schubert, "Lazarus Spengler und die Reformation in Nürnberg," H. Holborn, ed. (Leipzig, 1934); reprint [until 1524] (New York/London, 1971); Harold Grimm, *Lazarus Spengler: A Lay Leader of the Reformation* (Columbus: Ohio State University Press, 1978); Berndt Hamm, "Stadt und Kirche unter dem Wort Gottes: Das reformatorische Einheitsmodell des Nürnberger Rattschreibers Lazarus Spengler," in *Literatur und Laienbildung im späten Mittelalter und in der Reformationszeit,* Publication of the Germanistische Symposien, vol. 5, ed. Ludger Grenzmann and Karl Stackmann (Stuttgart: Metzler, 1984), pp. 710-29; see also the biographical sketch and the illustration in "Martin Luther und die Reformation in Deutschland," Exhibition for the 500th birthday of Martin Luther at the German National Museum in Nürnberg in conjunction with the Verein für Reformationsgeschichte, catalog, Gerhard Bott, ed. (Frankfurt: Insel, 1983), p. 329.

the letter leaves open to debate whether Luther approved the portrayal or whether he was concerned to provide a correct version of it.[19]

Another scenario is also possible. Spengler's inquiry can be seen in the context of a signet ring, which the electoral prince, Johann Friedrich (the son of the prince, Johann of Saxony), had made for Luther as a thank-you gift for his translation of the Book of Daniel,[20] which Luther had dedicated to the prince. The prince presented the ring to Luther when he came to the Coburg Castle on the 14th of September, on his trip back from the Imperial Diet in Augsburg.[21] The prince would have had to commission the ring in Nuremberg, which would have coincided with a submission by Spengler and Luther of a model of how the ring should be cut. This scenario does not explain, however, why Luther talked about the colors of his seal (and why he talked about a portrayal) in the letter. Perhaps there were simply two independent events.

But much more important than these external circumstances is Luther's inner condition when he wrote this letter on July 8, 1530. On the 15th of June, and with the arrival of the Emperor, the Imperial Diet in Augsburg finally got underway. It was to decide the further fate of

19. Actually there were probably different variations and different colored versions of the seal in circulation, which was basically used only as an embossing seal. An early example is the colored illustration in an Erfurter schoolbook from 1521 of the Rector Crotus, in which Luther is set (next to Erasmus, Reuchlin, and Mutian) among the row of dominant teachers of the University of Erfurt. Cf. Franz Wilhelm Kampschulte, *Die Universität Erfurt in ihrem Verhältnisse zu dem Humanismus und der Reformation aus den Quellen dargestellt,* vol. 2 (Trier: Lintz, 1858/1860). Reprint in one volume (Aalen, 1970), p. 258. Illust. Nr. 36 in Reiner Groß, ed., *Martin Luther 1483-1546. Dokumente seines Lebens,* (Weimar: Böhlau, 1983), p. 63. However, in Wittenberg itself, variations on printings were used. For example, the seal has an additional type of shield in the outer circle. This can be seen on the title page of "Der Deudsch Psalter" (Wittenberg, 1531), where it is next to the seal of Melanchthon, which has a crucified snake. On the 1541 edition of the Bible (Biblia: das ist "die gantze Heilige Schrift") the shield has a blossoming wreath around the rose. Cf. Volz (note 9), pp. 136, 182.

20. Cf. the illustrations, among which is the illustration of the dedication letter by Volz (note 9), 144f.

21. On July 25, 1530, from Augsburg, Jonas announced to Luther the intentions of Johann Friedrich for Luther. WA Br 5:393. On September 15 Luther reported to Melanchthon the giving-over of the ring. WA Br 5:623. A ring of this type (the original?) is found in a blue vault in Dresden. Illust. in Helmar Junghans, ed., *Leben und Werk Martin Luthers Festgabe zu seinem 500. Geburtstag,* vol. 2 (Göttingen: Vandenhoeck und Ruprecht, 1983), p. 1012. (There is also an illustration of the canopy, formed as the Luther rose, which is over the Katharine portal of the Wittenberg Luther house.)

the Reformation. Luther, who was banned from the Diet, had to remain in the Coburg Castle, which was the nearest place to Augsburg in the electorate of Saxony.[22] Thus, letters were the only connection to the Saxony's Electoral delegation in Augsburg — and the only possibility of influence that Luther had. Under such circumstances, every letter pressed with Luther's seal had special significance.

It was not only for reasons of distance that Luther felt himself to be far away from Augsburg. He felt virtually shut out from what was happening there. In the middle of May he received a draft of what would later be called the Augsburg Confession and had made a few scant comments. News about the important preliminary negotiations with the Diet failed to appear until the middle of June, about which he complained bitterly. Then the situation in Augsburg came to a complete climax: on June 25th the Confession was read out loud, and Luther then finally heard a (restrained) word from Melanchthon about it. This gave rise to a lively correspondence from Luther's side; on the 29th and 30th of June, he sent letters to six different receivers in Augsburg. Luther's reserve as compared to Melanchthon's negotiation strategy in Augsburg is well known, and appears everywhere in his letters.[23]

Spengler's inquiry about the accuracy of the image of the seal probably seems rather unimportant today. But if one can imagine oneself in the position of Luther, the letter writer who could not even bolster his own theological formulation at Augsburg, one can imagine how much weight Luther must have placed on his short letter to the Nuremberger confidante,[24] who in any case also viewed Melanchthon's action at Augsburg with some criticism, as is well known.[25]

---

22. Those details are in Hans von Schubert, "Luther auf der Koburg" in *Luther-Jahrbuch* 12 (Leipzig 1930): 109-61. An overview about Luther's time at Coburg is given in table form in Otto Matthes, *Zehn Briefe aus den Jahren 1523-1590*, owned by Johann Valentin Andreäs (a report of Veit Dietrich from July 8, 1530 about Luther's work as an author in Coburg in the year 1530) in *Blätter für württemberigsche Kirchengeschichte*, vol. 60/61 (1960/61), pp. 19-176 on 104-12.

23. Cf. Bernhard Lohse: "Philip Melanchthon in seinen Beziehungen zu Luther," in Hans Junghans, ed., (note 22) vol. 1, pp. 403-18, esp. 407-9.

24. What emerged at the same time, which Luther dedicated to Spengler, was the "Predigt, dass man Kinder zur Schule halten Solle," WA 30.II:508-88, dedication, 517-20; LW 46:213-58, dedication, 213-19.

25. Cf. the Nürnberger expert report, in which Luther's participation in the reworking of the Augsburg decision is challenged. "Der von Nürnberg Bedenken über die

In sum, it seems that the situation at the Diet of Augsburg, where a confession arose without Luther's participation, compelled him, in July 1530, to interpret the seal that he himself had chosen earlier. This seal showed Luther's characteristic position as a Christian and a theologian, and has come to be understood as an elementary Christian confession.

The Interpretation of the Seal

I come now to the interpretation of the seal itself. Purely as an image, the seal is of noteworthy perfection. It contains the basic forms of geometry: a circle and an intersection of straight lines, the cross. It contains the elementary forms of life: the rose as an image of the plant world, the heart as a sign of animal life. It carries the elementary colors of red, blue, and yellow — and the limit of all color, black and white. These iconographic components alone invite meditation. Their imagery calls forth a certain completeness of content.

It is our method to follow Luther's letter and his own interpretation of his image. This way, we attempt to enter into a discussion with Luther's own understanding by taking him at his word and accepting the sign he proposes.[26] In the end, we will see whether we have an accurate theological interpretation.

1. Our starting point is the middle of the seal.[27] "The first should be a black cross in a heart, which retains its natural color." The center is

---

sogennante unbeschliesslich und unvorgreifliche Antwort der Protestanten . . ." *Dr. Martin Luthers Sämtliche Schriften,* ed. Johann Georg Walch, 2nd edition, vol. 16 (Gross-Oesingen: Verlag des lutherischen Buchhaus Harms, 1880-1910), pp. 1462-69, here p. 1468. Reprint in Concordia Publishing House: St. Louis. See also the letter of Spengler to Veit Dietrich from September 25, 1530 by Moritz Maximilian Mayer, *Spengleriana,* (Nürnberg, 1830), pp. 75-78 as well as Theodor Pressel, "Spengler und der Augsburger Reichstag," in *Lazarus Spengler. Nach gleichzeitigen Quellen* (Elberfeld: Friederichs, 1862), pp. 69-77.

26. The few additional references are taken predominantly from the writings and letters, which had emerged between Spring and Fall 1530 in Coburg.

27. According to the above-mentioned historical hypothesis, the cross in the middle of the seal makes the point. It is noteworthy that the interpretations of 1530 took their beginnings exactly there.

doubled — a cross and a heart, for the middle point cannot contain only one thing. It has begun with an original duality, and this duality must be maintained until the end. Let the alternatives be made clear. If the heart were left alone to bear a cross on its own, it would be a symbol of the burden and effort of life, the presentiment of the final defeat. If the heart were to be left to itself, its cross would be merely a symbol of the transitory nature of all finitude. If the cross were to be left by itself, it would be a sign for the end of a life that hangs on it and miserably dies alone. If the heart were under the cross, it would show a crucified life, burdensome hope, broken promises.

But now, both cross and heart are standing together. The cross is the epitome of the story of Jesus Christ, and the heart under this cross is a sum of human life. Both, being so different in their origins, have become inseparable in their togetherness. If we set this duality at the beginning and in the center, we conclude that Christ's cross approaches human life, and that human life dwells under the cross. Thus, it must be said that the external appearance of the cross is the precondition for a true inward contemplation of the heart, and the inwardness of the heart is the meaning and goal for the external appearance of the cross. When it comes to this unification of heart and cross, there is righteousness and justice: righteousness in that the heart does not need anything else for its fulfillment, and justice when this lack of need is rightly recognized.

However, this union perfects itself in none other than faith in the crucified. Why? The covering of the heart by the crucified is to be understood as a kind of covering over an external object (more precisely — over the only external object) that from its side (the only side) establishes the contemplation within. Among all the relationships that can be taken up by the human heart, it is through the relationship of the heart to the crucified alone that the heart could not be lost on another (in which case it is better for the heart to stay by itself). When the heart relates to the crucified, it wins itself back in a way that it could not do by itself. In this sense, it is to be understood that "faith in the Crucified One saves us. 'For one who believes from the heart will be justified' (Rom. 10:10)."

Regarding the union of the heart and the cross a special reminder is now necessary — as Luther says, "so that I myself would be reminded." One must be reminded, because the threat of abstraction is always close by. The first abstraction is a mere historical understanding of the cross of Jesus Christ, within the horizons of his life that ends, either heroically or disastrously. The second abstraction is when the human heart only gains self-understanding by its own power, apart from the cross of suffering.

The "forming-into-one" of the original differences of the cross and the heart, symbolizing the conformity of humans to Christ in faith,[28] is the original reminder at the center of theology. This is a far-reaching reminder that carries within itself unspoken assumptions about God and the human heart, namely that God is "for us" but the human heart endeavors to remain "in itself."[29] The uniformity of Christ and the human in faith, which expresses itself in the original duality in the center of Luther's seal, leaves theology as an alternative to the opposition between a salvation history of objectivism and a believing subjectivism. Only the one who sees oneself in this alternative has done theology properly, according to Luther.

2. The cross is depicted in black within a naturally colored, red heart. The cross is complete in its contemplative nature, but only in a way that allows it to define this nature from itself. "Although it is indeed a black cross, which mortifies and which should also cause pain, it leaves the heart in its natural color. It does not corrupt nature, that is, it does not kill but keeps one alive."

Now of course this is a deep paradox. But it is exactly this paradox that must be understood if the heart and cross shall remain together, interdependent on one another. I want to carry out my reflections on this fact in two steps.

First, the cross mortifies; but without the cross, the heart is undefined. If the heart does not want to lie unconsciously under heteronomy, then it will feel obligated to define itself and will do this

---

28. The cross is sent to us because God "wants to conform us . . . to his Son Christ" (Sermon on April 16, 1530) WA 32:36,22f.; LW 51:206.

29. "Cognitio dei et hominis est sapientia divina et proprie theologica, et ita cognitio dei et hominis, ut referatur tandem ad deum iustificantem et hominem peccatorem, ut proprie sit subiectum Theologiae homo reus et perditus et deus iustificans vel salvator" (Interpretation from Psalm 51, 1532.43) WA 40/II:327,11-328,2; LW 12:330-31. Cf. "Cognitio Dei et Hominis" in Gerhard Ebeling, ed. *Lutherstudien*, vol. 1. (Tübingen: Mohr, 1971), pp. 221-72, esp. 255-72.

by choosing itself for its own selfish purposes. Further, the heart turns God into an idol when it piously exposes itself. Because it fears the sheer directness of self-determination, the heart chooses God, making its relationship to God into a mere self-serving dependency. The supposedly undefined, neutral heart is, in truth, predefined to be groundless and transitory. This is the heart that lifts itself, pious or godless, above God.

The character of self-choosing belongs to the nature of the heart. However, in this self-choosing, the one who has defined the human heart for this freedom of choice shifts out of focus. So although the human is a creature of God, it is not inscribed on the heart that it can only choose God alone. It is exactly this direct self-definition of the heart that is killed by the cross. Such a *mortificatio* is necessary if the abstract self-mightiness of the heart is to be deprived of power and defined anew. It is no wonder that such a change, such required renunciation, hurts.

The cross mortifies by marking the undefined heart. We can now partly understand the meaning of this. However, we enter ever deeper into the paradox, which is the second step of my reflections. For what does it mean that the cross mortifies but does not kill? *Mortificare*, translated, means nothing else than to bring to death, to kill. Where is the difference then?[30] As we witness in ourselves: there is no difference. To kill is to kill, and to die is to die, no matter which word we use for it. A distinction in the words does not produce a difference of meaning. When the self-defined human dies, it is real. Only through the cross of Jesus Christ is there a difference. How can this be thought through?

---

30. Cf. a parallel from Luther's interpretation of Psalm 118:18 (the Lord has chastened me fully, but has not given me over to death): "He has boasted that he will not die, but live. Thereupon the flesh, world, men, and princes speak up and would not weaken and discourage him: 'Is it not death if you are burned, beheaded, drowned, strangled, condemned, and exiled? I would think that you could tell whether this can be called life. Where is your God? Let Him help you! Of course, Elias will come and take you down (Matt. 27:49)!' To this he replies unshaken, and he comforts himself thus: 'On the contrary, this dying is nothing. It is only a fatherly rod, not wrath. It is only a foxtail, nothing serious. God is only chastising me as a dear father chastises his dear child. It may hurt a little, and it is not sugar; it is a rod. However, it does not kill, but rather helps me live.' This is surely a good interpretation and an effective confutation, to make a benevolent rod out of the word 'death.' Only the Holy Spirit and the right hand of God can teach this art." (*Das Schöne Confitemini* 1530) WA 31/I:158,17-30; LW 14:89.

The cross of Jesus Christ, the epitome of death, becomes the dividing line between death and life in that the crucified Jesus is resurrected. For however the resurrection is to be thought, it is not merely the sheer negation of the crucifixion, which would affect Jesus only as an individual and would amount to either the living again of a dead person or only as a cipher of a future completion. The resurrection of Jesus is, instead, the infinite deepening of his death, the true mortification, even though it did indeed establish for Jesus himself a new life in permanent nearness to God.

Jesus' death is the death of the godless: as Paul correctly cites the law, "cursed is everyone who hangs on wood" (Gal. 3:13; Deut. 21:23). The resurrection shows that Jesus' death is not the punishment for *his* godlessness, but rather it is much more for our own godlessness as indecisive, self-mighty choosers. This insight into the true sense of the death of Jesus is gained precisely when it coincides with a view of the real condition of our hearts:[31] when the actual proximity of one's own life to the death of Jesus is recognized. But if Jesus' death is truly that of the forsaken, which we all are, then our only option is his death. With it, the transitory character of our existence has come to an end, along with our self-established, godless religion.[32]

When we recognize in Jesus' death the death of the godless, we are put into a position where we can no longer choose; where we can only forsake ourselves. However, with this recognition we stand at the place where we are no longer in bondage to anything external. The death of the godless, like the end of an imprisonment, is the completion of negative freedom. It is precisely this negativity that is the beginning of a positive freedom, for if we have died with Jesus then will we also live

31. This idea of a representation that aims for conformity was expressed in an early sermon, "Igitur opus Dei alienum sunt passione Christi et in Christo, crucifixio veteris hominis et mortificatio Adae, Opus autem Dei proprium resurrectio Christi et iustificatio in spiritu, vivicatio novi hominis, Ut Rom 4, 'Christus mortuus est propter peccata nostra et resurrexit propter iustificationem nostram.' Ista itaque conformitas imaginis filii Dei includit utrumque illud opus." (Sermon on December 21, 1516 on Psalm 18 [19], 2) WA 1:112,37-113,3; LW 51:17-23.

32. That includes that one's own cross is to be carried in suffering in order to let the conformity to Christ be completed: "Though our suffering and cross should never be so exalted that we think we can be saved by it or earn the least merit through it, nevertheless we should suffer after Christ that we may be conformed to him." (Sermon from April 16, 1530) WA 32:29,3-6; LW 51:198.

with him (Rom. 6:4). However, we can only live by partaking in Jesus' life, and that means participating in his self-definition with God. This self-definition, as it comes to light in the resurrection, is presented in such a way that it does not choose directly and abstractly. Rather, it comes from God and has its source in the community of the Spirit.

The cross in the heart is, in other words, the true abyss. It is the boundary line between life and death, the necessary death and the real life of every human.[33] It mortifies, but does not kill. It mortifies because Jesus' death is the end of human self-determination by its own power; but the cross does not kill because Jesus' life is the beginning of human self-definition through God. To live with the sign of the cross means to live truly before God.

But this is by no means obvious! The cross is a real abyss and there is no bridge that stretches out across it. Only God's righteousness sustains us over the abyss, with his faithfulness watching over us. Only faith can cling to it,[34] so that the true life before God and the righteousness of faith are absolutely identical. To rely upon God means nothing else than to know that by a glance at Christ one is being carried over this abyss of the cross.[35] "'The just shall live by faith, but by faith in the crucified.'"

3. I have forestalled explaining the white rose in order to interpret fully the cross in the heart, for the center of our seal possesses a dynamic, ex-

---

33. "Here you can see how the right hand of God mightily lifts the heart and comforts it in the midst of death, so that it can say, 'Though I die, I die not. Though I suffer, I suffer not. Though I fall, I am not down. Though I am disgraced, I am not dishonored.' This is the consolation. Furthermore, the psalmist says of the help: 'I shall live.' Isn't this an amazing help? The dying live; the suffering rejoice; the fallen rise; the disgraced are honored." (*Das Schöne Confitemini* 1530) WA 31/I:152,22-30; LW 14:86.

34. "Therefore the Scripture gives to faith the title that it changes the heart and makes the human being completely new; no work can change the human, for it is only faith that can and does it." (Sermon on September 15, 1530) WA 32:100,1-3.

35. "How can now sin and righteousness, death and life, remain next to each other? One must consume the other and one must bite the other off. So now the person is dead, and cannot die. And the flesh is dead and must stay alive for the sake of divinity. This insight and viewpoint makes you into a Christian and when you believe it and hold it for certain then you have the righteousness and the life which he has, for he does such a thing not for his own sake but rather for your sake and well-being." (Sermon on April 17, 1530) WA 32:43,15-23. This also is the heart of Luther's famous interpretation of the first commandment in the Large Catechism.

pansive power that pulls the surrounding elements of the image into itself.

"Such a heart is to be set in the midst of a white rose, to symbolize that faith gives joy, comfort and peace; and at the same time is set in a white joyful rose; for this faith does not give peace and joy as the world gives (John 14:27). That's why the rose should be white and not red, for white is the color of the spirits and all angels (cf. Matt. 28:3; John 20:12)."

The rose is an ancient symbol for Christ.[36] *This* rose is the Christ rose, not only by appearance, but also by definition. It is bright white — like the light of the resurrection, which shines through the proclamations at the open grave. Its whiteness appears as the complete opposite to the blackness of the cross. In the rose, in Christ, this antinomy is embodied.

Characteristic of our seal and of Luther's interpretation is that the contents of this picture are directly applied to faith. According to the Easter sermon of 1530 on the resurrection story, "it does not help much to know a story and to be able to tell a story if one does not know how it is useful to me and you."[37] On the contrary: "this resurrection of Christ has now become yours through the Word, the Gospel carries it for you, that it should be your own. So you can now fasten your heart onto no other monstrance."[38] The heart stands in the rose as it proceeds from the cross, but does not change its color because of the cross. It does not disappear out of the active ways of life. In its vitality, the heart is bathed in light — the resurrection light that at the same time holds the sharp shadow of the cross as a memory. Thus the rose is not red, for it is not just a portrayal of natural, ordinary life. Instead, it is white, symbolizing its paradoxical re-definition through the black cross — its continuation towards a new life.

In my opinion, the resurrection of Jesus does not have significance in and of itself. Instead, it finds its complete meaning in the life of the believer, whom it places into the story of Jesus Christ. This story is characterized by the opposition between death and life, for

36. *Lexikon für Theologie und Kirche,* Michael Buchberger, ed., 2nd edition, vol. 9 (Freiburg im Breisgau: Herder, 1986), p. 44; overtones of the meaning of "paradise" can be heard here too.

37. Sermon on April 17, 1530. WA 32:39,22-24.

38. WA 32:44,6-9.

"whoever can now develop this victory within one's heart is already blessed."[39]

The white rose also shows the believers' participation in Jesus' new, true life before and with God. But this participation only earns its name by remaining near to human life, being felt and experienced. The truth of faith then, is its participation in Christ's life, and its joy, comfort, and peace as it is given in the human sphere.

I want to take Luther at his word again. What produces the feeling of joy? It is knowing myself to be in correspondence to another who corresponds to me. Joy is indeed the inner resonance of positive feeling that comes out of this feeling of faith. The sources of joy become clear when we think back on the description of the choosing heart. If I am destined (or I could say damned) to choose, then joy sets in at that moment only when something I chose or did brings together my intention and my imagination. As soon as I can no longer secure the result of my intentions and imagination, or as soon as something ruins the result, my joy goes with it. Such joy would be that which the world "gives."

The joy of faith is of another kind. For in faith I am not dependent on the products and completion of my choices. Rather, I know myself through God who defined me and liberated me to choose. In being chosen by God, I am brought into correspondence with myself. My nature is not corrupted, but preserved and supported. The joy of believing comes from the unity I feel within myself through God. Therefore I am free from the compulsion to unify myself through choosing. I can do nothing for this joy. I can only allow it. It would be gone if I were to try to acquire it and remove it from its source, which does not lie within me.

Because faith is such joy, it is also comfort. What is to be understood by comfort? In the course of life, it often happens that the inward correspondence, which produces our joy, is contradicted by outer failures. Although the believing human knows as an internal fact that it is in correspondence with itself through God, nevertheless the external fact is that life often does not run according to my plans and pleasure. The inner joy of faith and the outer joy of success are not congruent. Thus it stands to be tested which one is decisive: whether under the failure of my will and acts, the joy of faith wears off or whether the

39. WA 32:45,2.

joy of faith holds up as comfort through the pain of defeat, misconduct, and failure. Faith is comfort, says Luther. Thanks to God's loyalty, Luther reckons that the joy of faith is always maintained, even if it appears as a comforting image in the midst of sadness.

Could it be then, that a permanent opposition between inner joy and outer failures defines the life of the Christian? No, because faith is finally peace. In peace, the moment of faith that correlates inner and outer things is accentuated. Faith aims at such a correlation, so that I am integrated with myself and with the world, thank God. This happens to me as well as all humans. How can such a claim be made in the light of our thoughts here? The decision is based on the one who faith acknowledges as more capable: God. On the one hand, it is God who brought us godless ones into correspondence with himself and with ourselves: it is God who resurrected Jesus from the dead. On the other hand, we must want to choose our own lives as the starting point. But as choosers, we always miss ourselves, even with the most pious intentions. Thus the decision is clear: whoever believes can only trust God to offset the contrast between the fulfillment of faith and the failure of works. If we did not draw this conclusion, it would negate Christ's presence in the Spirit.

4. With that, I have necessarily advanced, without notice, to the next element of our seal. "Such a rose should stand in a sky-blue field, since such joy in spirit and faith is a beginning of the future heavenly joy, which begins already but is grasped in hope, not yet revealed." There is a difference between faith and life, a difference between the joy and the circumstances that make comfort necessary. The white of the rose does not dissolve the color of red (nor is it the indifferent light that is not yet broken into spectral colors), just as faith does not blot out life. However, the white rose makes the color bright indeed. It surrounds transparently itself with the heavenly blue.

Blue can be understood as an image of testing, as an index of temporal endurance. That the heaven wraps itself around in the form of a circle may stand for the fact that faith, joy, comfort, and peace are promised, and they are the future for all life on earth.

Whoever believes knows the difference between faith and life and accepts this difference in hope. Hope in this sense has a double meaning: it is the presence of the future, and the present that is not yet past.

A presence of the future is when the faith in true life is before God and through God. Then nothing else can be expected, nothing higher, nothing more certain throughout all the temporality of life, through all the changes of time. When an individual has faith based on the union of form with Jesus, then that which is called "resurrection" for Jesus is for us still to be expected — the present that is not yet past.

There is now continuity between the presence of the future and the "still here" of the present: the Spirit. "In Spirit" Jesus was resurrected. The community of the Father with the Son in Spirit has triumphed and proven itself against the severing power of death, to which the Son exposed himself. "By the Spirit" the righteousness and fidelity of God is united with the trust of humans and is formed into faith. The community of God — Father, Son, and Spirit — with humanity flows out from the community that God made with Godself. The *vinculum trinitatis* [bond of the Trinity] is also the *vinculum dei et hominis sive fidei* [the bond of God and human or faith].[40]

5. I have now come to the final element of our seal. "And around such a field is a golden ring, symbolizing that such blessedness in Heaven lasts forever and has no end. Such blessedness is exquisite, beyond all joy and goods, just as gold is the most valuable, most precious and best metal."

40. "At this point we should learn the rule that whenever the saints deal with God in the Psalter and Holy Scripture concerning comfort and help in their need, eternal life and the resurrection of the dead are involved. All such texts belong to the doctrine of the resurrection and eternal life, in fact, to the whole Third Article of the Creed, with the doctrines of the Holy Spirit and the Holy Church, the forgiveness of sins, the resurrection and everlasting life. And it all flows out of the First Commandment, where God says: 'I am your God' (Exod. 20:2). This the Third Article of the Creed emphasizes insistently. While Christians deplore the fact that they suffer and die in this life, they comfort themselves with another life than this, namely that of God Himself who is above and beyond this life. It is not possible that they should totally die and not live again in eternity. For one thing, the God on whom they rely and in whom they find their consolation cannot die, and thus they must live in Him. Besides, as Christ says, He is a God of the living, not of the dead and of those who are no more (Matt. 22:32). Therefore Christians must live forever; otherwise He would not be their God, nor could they depend on Him unless they live. For this little group, therefore, death remains no more than a sleep." (*Das Schöne Confitemini*, 1530) WA 31/I:154,27-155,27; LW 14:87. Regarding the Third Article as the summary of the theology of Luther, cf. Eilert Herms, *Luthers Auslegung des Dritten Artikels*, (Tübingen: Mohr, 1987).

The golden ring surrounds everything, even the heavenly blue. For hope does not remain utopian: it has a definite place to which it points. The perfection of the circle, which encompasses everything, signals a definitive conclusion. However, one does not get further, for the circular track of the ring always returns one back to the starting point. One need not go further, for gold stands for the quintessence of worth, over which nothing more worthy is thinkable. One can stay here, because gold is durable and everlasting.

Faith is fulfilled with the golden ring. Here righteousness and salvation are united with each another. It is the epitome of the highest good. Here peace and good exist together: "should be" and "may have" no longer stand in contradiction to one another.

Why is it thus with faith? Only because God is originally perfect in Godself. But the eternity of the ring does not exclude temporality, for time goes back into infinity. However, this endurance is not the wheel of the "always-the-same" that wipes out differences. What remains is that which has the highest worth and gives value to all that it contains.

The perfection of faith is a reflection of the perfection of God. Indeed, God's perfection is his presence to us in the form of the Son through the power of the Spirit in faith. The trinitarian doctrine has, through and through, a soteriological sense.[41]

The Seal and the Course of Theology

"This . . . *compendium theologiae* I have wanted to show you in good friendship." Now, at the end of this letter, in "good company," Luther's *compendium theologiae* is completed. For theology has reached its goal when the community of thoughts becomes friendship in Christ. A compendium contains everything, but in an abbreviated, elementary form. Over all it shows, especially in its compactness, the way to theology.

If we glance back at the course upon which Luther's seal has led us,

41. This is already developed in detail in the "Confession" from 1528: "that are the three Persons/and one God/who gave all of himself completely and fully with all that he is and has" (from *Confession Concerning Christ's Supper*) WA 26:505,38ff.; LW 37:366. Cf. "Die Trinitätslehre als Summe des Evangeliums," in *Einsicht und Glaube,* Jörg Baur, ed. (Göttingen: Vandenhoeck & Ruprecht, 1978), pp. 112-21.

then it can be seen that Luther boldly laid out his compendium as a strict congruence of human existential history and the history of God. From beginning to end it is true: God is for us and we are in God on the basis of being in the likeness of Christ. This congruence grows out of the burgeoning of existence, which seems to be undefined, but in truth concludes itself through the cross of Jesus Christ.[42] From the center out (as the seal was consequently read from inside to out), the logical presuppositions and implications of this event are decoded. Further, from the center out, the existential view of life is manifested in the completeness of congruence between the perfection of faith and the perfection of God. As Ulrich Barth has emphasized, "The necessity of existential learning finally results, not from the *intention to* learn, but rather out of the certainty of that which *is* learned. The intended object of faith is nothing other than the One wanting to be for us and wanting to be learned — Christ himself."[43]

Although Luther's way is exemplary for evangelical Christianity, it is not without its problems. This can be shown in the definitive, modern dogmatic conceptions of Schleiermacher and Barth, but also in a philosophical theology oriented by Hegel.

Luther composed his *compendium theologiae* in the symbolism of his seal. It could be said that the seal is the likeness of Christ himself, which was imprinted on Luther's heart (Song of Sol. 8:6).[44] Luther signified and defined himself through his seal. It is no wonder that he can also call this seal a family coat of arms. The faith, the participation in God's perfection, protects differently and better than any other shielding weapon (Eph. 6:16).

Martin Luther knew himself to be sealed and shielded, imprinted through the congruence of God and humanity established by Christ.

42. "[I]n Christo crucifixo est vera Theologia et cognitio Dei," already describes the *probatio* to Thesis 20 of the *Heidelberg Disputation* of 1518. See this movement in WA 1:362,18ff.; LW 31:52-53.

43. Ulrich Barth, "Luthers Verständnis der Subjektivität des Glaubens" in *Neue Zeitschrift für Systematische Theologie* 34 (1992): 269-91, here 287.

44. "But this is the correct main piece, ground and bottom, that I may learn to look at this Christ with nothing but my heart" (Sermon on April 17, 1530) WA 32:42,35f. "Nam in corde meo iste unus regnat articulus, scilicet Fides Christi, et quo, per quem et in quem omnes meae diu noctuque fluunt et refluunt theologicae cogitationes" (*Preface to the Galatians Commentary* 1535) WA 40/I:33,7-9; LW 27:145-49.

Because of its contents, however, Luther's seal is also open for all other individuals, since the story it tells is not merely Luther's private history.[45] This seal has served Lutheranism well; the whole story of its usage is not yet written.[46]

Luther's seal is an image that calls for an interpretation, so that the subject it describes can be understood. It is a compendium: an introduction to discovery but not the discovery itself. It is this characteristic feature of Luther's seal that challenges us to a richer, self-responsible unfolding. Thus: an elementary theology.

45. In *Das Schöne Confitemini* he says, related to Psalm 118: "But lest anyone, knowing that this psalm belongs to the whole world, raise his eyebrow at my claim that this psalm is mine, may he be assured that no one is being robbed. After all, Christ is mine, and yet belongs to all believers." WA 31/I:66,26-29; LW 14:46.

46. Older, less organized material is found in Urban Gottlieb Haussdorff, *Lebens-Beschreibung eines christlichen Politici, nemlich Lazari Spenglers* . . . (Nürnberg: Schmidt, 1741), pp. 164-71. Besides interpretive, poetic, and meditational texts of differing quality, one would encounter the very formal use of the seal as a sign of identification. For an example of an older interpretation of the seal, see Andreas Kreuch: *Sigillum Lutheri. Eine christliche und einfältige Predigt* . . . (Mühlhausen: self-published, 1579). An example of a newer, more meditative handling of the text is Christian Kröning, "Gedanken zur Betrachtung der Lutherrose" in *Lutherische Kirche in der Welt, Jahrbuch des Martin-Luther-Bundes*, vol. 32 (Neuendettelsau: Martin-Luther-Verlag, 1985), pp. 16-23.

Luther on Creation

JOHANNES SCHWANKE

Luther's doctrine of creation arises out of his study of Scripture. This gives particular weight to his exegetical works, especially his interpretations of Genesis. As an Old Testament scholar, Luther had a particular liking for Genesis,[1] and the sheer number of his expositions of this text bears this out.[2] Among these, the lectures on Genesis are certainly the most prominent;[3] for various reasons they are particularly suited to our present inquiry.[4] They are the longest and, at the same time, the last lectures of Luther's life. Luther delivered them over ten years, from 1535 to 1545, and at their conclusion on November 17, 1545, he had only three months left to live. Luther's whole theology is uniquely comprehended in these lectures. They are indeed the mature testimony of the late Luther and one could even say that they represent his

---

1. WA 44:234,2; LW 6:313; (on Gen. 37:1). Also WA 42:37,1-3; LW 1:39 (on Gen. 1:20).

2. In 1519-1521 Luther gave a first lecture on the book of Genesis (WA 9:329-415). Two sermon series followed: the first 1523-1524 (February 22, 1523–September 18, 1524; WA 14:97-488), the second 1527 (sermons not dated; WA 24:24-710).

3. WA 42-44; LW 1-8.

4. Luther's lectures on Genesis do not deal with the doctrine of creation in an abstract or theoretical way, i.e., as theses for a disputation. Instead, they describe creation in a narrated way, as a creation taking place in time. In addition, the personal character of the lectures is obvious: quite frequently Luther adds personal remarks on his own life and God's acts of creation in it.

Translated by John Betz. This article first appeared in *Lutheran Quarterly* 16 (2002): 1-20, under the same title.

Summa.[5] Although valued for centuries after Luther's death,[6] the Genesis lectures are a source that has more recently been overlooked due to reservations towards them, which were initiated in the critical studies by Erich Seeberg and Peter Meinhold in the 1930s.[7] Among more recent scholars, such as Hans-Ulrich Delius and Ulrich Asendorf, these doubts are regarded as overreactions.[8] Thus the lectures have in recent years once again attracted the attention of scholars.[9]

Human Individuality

"I believe that God has created me together with all that exists."[10] This famous statement, the core of Luther's doctrine of creation, means that the human being owes its individuality solely to God, and may know that this individuality is ordained and accepted by God. God's creation is not a collective, abstract occurrence but something pro-

---

5. Ulrich Asendorf, "Die ökumenische Bedeutung von Luthers Genesis-Vorlesung (1535-1545)" in Oswald Bayer et al., eds., *Caritas Dei, Beiträge zum Verständnis Luthers und der gegenwärtigen Ökumene* (Helsinki: Schriften der Luther-Agricola-Gesellschaft, 1997), pp. 18-40, esp. p. 19. [hereafter cited as Asendorf in Bayer].

6. Peter Meinhold, *Die Genesisvorlesung Luthers und ihre Herausgeber,* vol. 8 in *Forschungen zur Kirchen- und Geistesgeschichte,* Erich Seeberg et al., eds. (Stuttgart: W. Kohlhammer, 1936), pp. 22ff.; cf. WA TR 3:689,8ff. (Nr. 3888); LW 54:288.

7. Erich Seeberg, *Studien zu Luthers Genesisvorlesung: Zugleich ein Beitrag zur Frage nach dem alten Luther* (Gütersloh: Bertelsmann, 1932); and Peter Meinhold, *Die Genesisvorlesung Luthers und ihre Herausgeber* (see footnote 6). Ferdinand Cohrs analyzes the history of the text edition in *Zur Chronologie und Entstehungsgeschichte von Luthers Genesisvorlesung und seiner Schrift 'Von den Konziliis und Kirchen': Lutherstudien zur 4. Jahrhundertfeier der Reformation* (Weimar: Böhlau, 1917), pp. 159-69. A good overview is given by Martin Brecht, *Die Erhaltung der Kirche 1532-1545,* vol. 3 of *Martin Luther* (Stuttgart: Calwer, 1987), pp. 139-43. English translation, Martin Brecht, *The Preservation of the Church 1532-1545,* vol. 3 of *Martin Luther* (Philadelphia: Fortress Press, 1985 [-1993]), pp. 134-41.

8. Hans-Ulrich Delius, *Die Quellen von Martin Luthers Genesisvorlesung* (München: Kaiser, 1992), p. 12.

9. For example Ulrich Asendorf, *Lectura in Biblia. Luthers Genesisvorlesung (1535-1545)* (Göttingen: Vandenhoeck & Ruprecht, 1998); and Asendorf in Bayer, pp. 18-40.

10. "I believe that God has created me together with all that exists. God has given me and still preserves my body and soul: eyes, ears and all limbs and senses; reason and all mental faculties." BC 354,2-3; BC-T 345; BSLK 510,32–511,8; similarly confessed in Ps. 139:14: "I praise you, for I am fearfully and wonderfully made."

foundly personal: The "I" who speaks, the human being who is endowed with individuality, perceives its individuality to be created by God and praises God, according to this faith, as one's own Creator. David Löfgren thus summarizes the matter: "Luther's theology of creation does not begin with a depiction of the creator, but with the concretely created."[11] Indeed, it begins with the concretely created instance of my own person and world. The relevance of the Creator is grounded in the relevance of this Creator to *me*.

In the exposition of creation in his Genesis lectures, Luther considers the beginning of the cosmos and the genesis of various creatures as ultimately of secondary importance, although he was firmly convinced of the historicity of Adam and Eve.[12] Instead, the starting point and center of his doctrine is the creation of himself as a creature who is a person in his own right. Likewise, his personal environment is the effective sphere of divine creativity.[13] From Luther's perspective, therefore, one must first grasp the personal existence of creation before the global aspect of the created world can come into view.

A true Christian doctrine of creation prevents the submersion of the individual into a generalized context of the whole of creation: as a creature the individual stands alone before God, is personally addressed by God, and must also give a personal answer to this same God. To be sure, the human being is nonetheless bound up in the greater context of creation; the fact that God "has created *me*" cannot be divorced from the "*together with* all that exists." This implies that one must give serious consideration to the animal and plant kingdoms. Moreover, Luther does not conceal the individual's responsibility for the greater household of creation. In fact, he condemns a false pride coming out of this special position towards the rest of creation.[14]

Luther's famous, central formula from the Small Catechism is developed further in his lectures on Genesis, where he brings into clear focus what for him constitutes a biblical doctrine of creation:

11. David Löfgren, *Die Theologie der Schöpfung bei Luther* (Göttingen: Vandenhoeck & Ruprecht, 1960), p. 21.

12. WA 42:71,15-17; LW 1:92 (on Gen. 2:9).

13. WA 42:23,16-18; LW 1:30 (on Gen. 1:6). See also WA 42:25,1; LW 1:33 (on Gen. 1:6).

14. See especially WA 45:15,7-21 (House Postil on the Articles of Faith; February 11, 1537).

If you look at my person, I am something new, because sixty years ago I was nothing. Such is the judgment of the world. But God's judgment is different; for in God's sight I was begotten and multiplied immediately when the world began, because this Word, "and God said: 'Let Us make man,'" created me too. Whatever God wanted to create, that He created then when He spoke. Not everything has come into view at once. Similarly, an arrow or a ball which is shot from a cannon (for it has greater speed) is sent to its target in a single moment, as it were, and nevertheless it is shot through a definite space; so God, through His Word, extends His activity from the beginning of the world to its end. For with God there is nothing that is earlier or later, swifter or slower; but in His eyes all things are present things. For He is simply outside the scope of time.[15]

Here it is clear how Luther has included himself, in an utterly surprising and most personal way, in the process of creation. He sees his whole person and individuality as completely embraced by God's creative activity.[16]

Primordial History as Present History

This text brings out a second aspect of the subject, equally important and bound up with the first: Luther interprets primordial history as a history of the present. For Luther, creation is not something past, but something present. Because Luther sees himself in his individuality as created, addressed, and desired by God, the history of creation can be nothing other than present history. Consequently, God's creative activity is not bound to particular periods of life. In spite of the biographi-

---

15. WA 42:57,34-58,2; LW 1:76 (on Gen 2:2).

16. This self-consciousness of Luther, which is grounded in the knowledge of God's relation to every individual human being, lends a voice to God himself, saying: "All that I do in heaven and on earth I direct to the end that it may serve you. You are my only concern; I can and will not forget you. I attend you with such great care and love." WA 44:644,40-42; LW 8:90 (on Gen. 46:19-27). See also WA 42:455,13; LW 2:271 (on Gen. 12:4): "It is not enough, that God speaks; but it is necessary that He speaks to *you*."

cal remark in the above quotation that fixes his age at sixty years,[17] Luther does not situate his own life merely within these limits.

Luther is reluctant to interpret primordial biblical history as the beginning of things, the *initium*, but rather insists that its meaning be understood in terms of a *principium*.[18] He does not allow himself to be distracted by any isolated, past original history, by any "beginning of things," but instead, in the lectures on Genesis, he sees himself radically placed into the creative event of primordial history. It is not Adam who is ultimately relevant here, but Luther. In an interlacing of times, past, present, and future come together in a single moment: "thus through his Word God traverses the world from beginning to end." Pervading time, God's living creative Word is "without end"[19] and is "not dead,"[20] but "to this day"[21] remains ever "effective,"[22] is *verbum efficax*.

God remains with his creation, is effective in it, continually allows new animals and human beings to be born, and continually grants new beginnings and in this way preserves creation.[23] God's *conservatio*, God's sustaining of creation is, to be sure, a sign of his abiding goodness as the creator: "We Christians know that with God, creating and

17. WA 42:57,34f.; LW 1:76 (on Gen. 2:2). As Luther mentions at various places of the lecture that he is sixty years old, this age must be a general comment; compare with WA 43:481,4f.; LW 5:74 (on Gen. 26:24f.) and WA 43:684,3; LW 5:370 (on Gen. 30:28-30).

18. The Vulgate translates "In the beginning" (Gen. 1:1) with *in principio*, not with *in initio*. While *initium* means a beginning, which, once started, stays in the past and has no further influence, *principium* is a beginning that stays relevant for what it initiated. See WA 42:8,34–9,13; LW 1:10 (on Gen. 1:2).

19. WA 42:57,9-12; LW 1:75 (on Gen. 2:2): "Deum per verbum condidisse omnia. . . . Haec verba usque hodie durant. Ideo videmus multiplicationem sine fine." Cf. also WA 42:57,12-20; LW 1:75 (on Gen. 2:2).

20. WA 42:57,27-30; LW 1:75-76 (on Gen. 2:2): "Quia autem crescunt, multiplicantur, conservantur et reguntur adhuc omnia eodem modo quo a principio mundi, Manifeste sequitur verbum adhuc durare nec esse mortuum."

21. WA 42:17,12f.; LW 1:21 (on Gen. 1:5): "Verbum, per quod condita sunt omnia, et adhuc hodie conservantur."

22. WA 42:40,32f.; LW 1:54 (on Gen. 1:22): "Videmus autem, verbum huius diei adhuc esse efficax." And WA 42:40,39; LW 1:54 (on Gen. 1:22): "Hoc verbum adhuc est efficax et operatur ista."

23. WA 42:57,22-24; LW 1:75 (on Gen. 2:2): "Sed in Adamo et primis bestiolis seu animalibus non desierunt ista. Manet adhuc hodie verbum super genus humanum dictum: 'Crescite et multiplicamini'."

preserving are one and the same."[24] The one cannot be without the other; both are and remain indivisibly bound to one another.[25]

Life as Gift from God through Humanity

Although Luther takes his own person as the point of departure of his doctrine of creation, this personal individuality nevertheless does not stand by itself, nor does it originate from an isolated dialogue with God. Human life — indeed, life as such — is life that depends on God. God's action as Creator can only be perceived through the mediation of creatures. God does not act in the abstract, not *nudum* (without means), as it were, but rather binds his activity to creaturely events.

The beginning of human life is mediated. That is to say, it is bound to procreation through one's parents and to birth itself through one's mother. This beginning is determined equally both by the sovereign action of the Creator, in which a human being is miraculously granted life, and also by an utterly human sexual activity. Both the divine act of creation and the human act of love, joined together, simultaneously mark the beginning of life. Not only procreation but also the ensuing care depends equally on human beings and on God.[26] Just how much human beings owe to this interplay, especially in the first months of life, is evident in the following quotation from Luther, in which he investigates the care of a newborn child. Such care bestows life long before one is able to perceive it, to say nothing of being able to respond to it with thanks.

> For no one of those who are alive today knows where he was during the first two years, when he lived either in the womb, or when, after being brought into the light of day, he sucked his mother's milk. He knows nothing about the days, the nights, the times, and the rulers. Yet he lived at that time, and he was a body joined to a soul — a body

24. WA 43:233,24f.; LW 4:136 (on Gen. 22:13): "Nos Christiani scimus, quod apud Deum idem est creare et conservare."

25. WA 43:200,15f.; LW 4:90 (on Gen. 21:34): "Deus enim condidit mundum, et conservat mundum." Also WA 43:564,25f.; LW 5:197 (on Gen. 28:3-5): "Deum, qui non est creator tantum, sed etiam altor et nutritor" and WA 43:335,39f.; LW 4:279 (on Gen. 24:26-28): "Dei authoris et conservatoris omnium rerum."

26. WA 44:648,21-24; LW 8:94 (on Gen. 46:28).

adapted to all natural functions. Therefore this is most certain proof that God wants to preserve man in a wonderful manner altogether unknown to him.[27]

Luther describes parental care as having its foundation and beginning in God's preserving action. This care[28] remains hidden from the infant, is given without being earned, makes life possible, and allows the child to grow and learn. We were taken care of long before we could take care of ourselves;[29] our existence was desired by others long before we ourselves desired it. Before a human being can say "I," he or she is already addressed by the divine and human "you." Thus, human existence is already indebted in the earliest stages of childhood: born into a given family, into a given environment, a given country, a given culture — in words similar to those of the apostle, what do you have — and what are you — that you did not receive? (based on 1 Cor. 4:7).

Creation as Communication

Human creation is grounded in the harmony of divine and human action: on the one hand, in the encounter of God and humanity, Creator and creature; on the other hand, in the encounter of man and woman, body and soul, flesh and spirit. The encounter and union of two different things in a creative act is constitutive of human life. Human life owes itself to a "fundamental communicative event,"[30] which marks the beginning of human life — indeed, of any life whatsoever — and makes it possible in the first place. The constituent duality is not thereby cancel-

27. WA 44:812,28-34; LW 8:316-17 (on Gen. 49:33). See also WA 43:481,2-5; LW 5:75 (on Gen. 26:24f.).

28. WA 44:259,34-37; LW 6:347 (on Gen. 37:12-14): "Nisi matres parerent, lactarent, mundarent, foverent infantes, totum genus humanum interire necesse esset. Cum autem Deus ipse autor sit horum officiorum, . . . esse optima et gratissima exercitia pietatis erga Deum et homines."

29. WA 43:480,40–481,2; LW 5:75 (on Gen. 26:24f.): "Inspice enim tuam infantiam, et cogita, num memineris te fuisse in utero matris, iacuisse in cunis, suxisse ubera matris, plorasse, comedisse pultem, crevisse etc. Atqui vivimus certe etiam primo anno, quo gestatur foetus in utero matris. Sed quomodo vixerimus, nescimus prorsus."

30. Johannes von Lüpke, "Den Zufall ausschalten. Reproduktionsmedizin verhindert Kommunikation," *Evangelische Kommentare* (2000): 32-34, esp. 32.

led out, however, but remains an integral part of the creative union. Thus, for Luther, the creation and development of human life is not a technical-mechanical production, but is embedded in an organic dialogue in which the Word of the Creator, the answer of the creature, and even the protest of the creatures all have their place. This organic communication is not determined by fixed laws, but remains in its dialogical character something living, sensual, and even resistant. The interplay of the divine and the human in a creative communication — which is for this reason also a creative action — can be formulated more precisely in Hamannian terms as a "speech to the creature through the creature."[31]

As the Creator, God's effective Word, which calls the creature into being, both says what it creates and creates what it says.[32] For Luther, God hereby has his own language, his own divine grammar.[33] God is the "author"[34] of the world, whereby all his words are creatures, for "what else is the entire creation than the Word of God uttered by God, or extended to the outside?"[35] As Luther explains:

> Here attention must also be called to this, that the words "Let there be light" are the words of God, not of Moses; this means that they are realities. For God calls into existence the things which do not exist (Rom. 4:17). He does not speak grammatical words; He speaks true and existent realities. Accordingly, that which among us has the sound of a word is a reality with God. Thus sun, moon, earth, Peter, Paul, I, you etc. — we are all words of God, in fact only one single syllable or letter by comparison with the entire creation. We, too, speak, but only according to the rules of language; that is, we assign names to objects which have already been created. But the divine rule of language is different, namely: when He says: "Sun, shine," the sun is there at once and shines. Thus the words of God are realities, not

---

31. Cf. Oswald Bayer, "Schöpfung als 'Rede an die Kreatur durch die Kreatur'" in Oswald Bayer, *Schöpfung als Anrede: Zu einer Hermeneutik der Schöpfung.* 2nd ed. (Tübingen: J. C. B. Mohr [Paul Siebeck], 1990), pp. 9-32.

32. Ezek. 12:25-28; Ps. 33:9.

33. WA 42:17,21-23; LW 1:22 (on Gen. 1:5): "Sed Grammatica divina est alia, nempe ut, cum dicit: Sol splende, statim adsit sol et splendeat. Sic verba Dei res sunt, non nuda vocabula." Also WA 42:37,7; LW 1:49 (on Gen. 1:20).

34. WA 42:20,(20-28) 21; LW 1:25 (on Gen. 1:6).

35. WA 42:17,25f.; LW 1:22 (on Gen. 1:5): "Nam quid est aliud tota creatura quam verbum Dei a Deo prolatum."

bare words. . . . For what else is the entire creation than the Word of God uttered by God, or extended to the outside?[36]

Luther sums it up as follows: "Therefore, any bird whatever and any fish whatever are nothing but nouns in the divine rule of language."[37] It is not the case here that birds and fish stand only for themselves as individual species, but through the opposition of the two environments of the air and the water, in Luther's exposition of Genesis 1, they encompass all living things. Luther's knowledge of God's comprehensive creative activity — precisely in the interconnecting of various ages of the world — is sustained by the following insight: "For when God once said (Gen. 1:28): 'Be fruitful,' that Word is effective to this day and preserves nature in a miraculous way."[38] In spite of the fact that it appears altogether ordinary, this present creation is for Luther nothing short of a miracle: "For the growth of the fruits of the field and the preservation of various kinds, this is as great as the multiplication of the loaves in the wilderness."[39] Despite his marveling over the sovereign Word of the Creator, Luther is not thereby fanatical or overly enthusiastic. He neither risks devaluing the cooperation of the human being in creation, nor disqualifying it as something negative, as a strictly mechanical necessity. Luther understands and recognizes that divine creativity is bound to an earthly referent: God does not wish to create without the human being, without the creature.

Like his creative activity, God's speech is mediated.[40] God addresses one through one's parents, through one's fellow human beings, and through one's environment. For Luther life, which from the start is dependent on God, is grounded in a life-giving and life-sustaining address, which is heard in a creaturely way: indeed, God speaks "through the creature."[41] Luther continually emphasizes the fact that God

36. WA 42:17,15-23; LW 1:21-22 (on Gen. 1:3-5).

37. WA 42:37,6f.; LW 1:49 (on Gen. 1:20): "Quaelibet igitur avis, piscis quilibet sunt nihil nisi nomina divinae Grammaticae."

38. WA 43:138,38f.; LW 4:4 (on Gen. 21:1-3): "Quod enim Deus semel dixit: 'Crescite' id verbum adhuc hodie est efficax, et miraculose conservat naturam."

39. WA 43:139,8-10; LW 4:5 (Gen. 21:1-3).

40. WA 43:183,2f.; LW 4:66 (on Gen. 21:18), translated: "... since through your mouth he [God] speaks with me and through my mouth He speaks with you."

41. WA 42:626,15-19; LW 3:109 (on Gen. 17:3-6), translated: "But you must adhere to and follow this sure and infallible rule: God in His divine wisdom arranges to manifest

wishes to work only through human cooperation,[42] even with the risk that human beings should refuse to cooperate.[43]

> God could gather a church without the Word, manage the state without a government, produce children without parents . . . ; but He commands us and wants us to preach and to pray, and everyone to do his duty in his station.[44]

God's words of institution creatively address the human being and, conversely, establish the possibility of a creative address of the human being to the creature. Human deeds are sanctified by God's address and bound up with God's own divine action.

We know this life-giving and life-promising address of God in no other way but through the care of our own parents. Luther's high regard for marriage as a "nursery"[45] as well as a "fountain"[46] of all the estates is founded precisely in this life-giving and life-preserving commu-

---

Himself to human beings by some definite and visible form which can be seen with the eyes and touched with the hands, in short, is within the scope of the five senses. So near to us does the Divine majesty place Itself."

42. WA 44:648,32-39; LW 8:94 (on Gen. 46:28): "Sic filios potuisset facere absque Adam. Sicut Adam initio nihil prorsus egit, cum formaretur ex limo terrae, neque Heua, cum ex costa Adae conderetur. Sed postea dixit: 'Crescite et multiplicamini'. Quasi diceret: Nunc vobis cooperantibus creabo liberos. Sic in aliis actionibus omnibus communis vitae. Ich soll den paum nicht mit der nasen von einander hauen, sonder soll ein axt, oder segen nehmen. Arbor non est caedenda stipula aut culmo, sed securi, Deus dedit propterea rationem homini, dedit sensus et vires. His utere tanquam mediis et donis Dei." Cf. also WA 43:71,11-13; LW 3:274 (on Gen. 19:14): "nec vult amplius homines ex gleba fingere, sicut Adamum, sed coniunctione maris et foemine utitur, quibus benedicit." and WA 43:68,20-24; LW 3:270 (on Gen. 19:14). On Luther's doctrine on divine and human cooperation see Martin Seils, *Der Gedanke vom Zusammenwirken Gottes und des Menschen in Luthers Theologie,* vol. 50 in *Beiträge zur Förderung christlicher Theologie,* Paul Althaus et al., eds., (Gütersloh: Gütersloher Verlagshaus G. Mohn, 1962).

43. WA 42:346,15-18; 32-35; LW 2:119 (on Gen. 8:21).

44. WA 43:391,3-6; LW 4:354 (on Gen. 25:22) and WA 43:81,21-31; LW 3:288 (on Gen. 19:18-20). Cf. also Max Weber, *Die protestantische Ethik II. Kritiken und Antikritiken,* Johannes Winckelmann, ed. (München/Hamburg: Siebenstern Taschenbuch Verlag, 1965), p. 68.

45. WA 42:178,31-33; LW 1:240 (on Gen. 4:1): "ex quo omnes nascimur, quod seminarium est non solum politiae, sed etiam Ecclesiae et regni Christi usque ad finem mundi."

46. WA 42:579,9f.; LW 3:43 (on Gen. 16:1f.): "ex hoc fonte manare politias et Oeconomias, quas ruere et perire necesse esset, si nulla legitima et certa connubia essent."

nication between man and woman, parents and child, God and human. Nonetheless, Luther's view of marriage as the second estate,[47] following the fundamental estate of the church, underwent change throughout his life. The asceticism of the monastery[48] had brought him earlier to fear marriage as a "damned estate."[49] Not least of all because of his marriage to Katharina von Bora, Luther then became convinced that the estate of marriage was one that was sacred and exceedingly blessed by God, indeed, that he himself was not worthy of it.[50]

Marriage, which is itself established through communication — namely, through God's words of institution — is itself, for Luther, the locus of life-giving communication, in this case, between man and woman. Therefore, a break in communication is here particularly painful.[51] For the human being, who is called to fellowship, cannot exist in isolation: "We have not been created for a solitary life, to be separated from the common society of men."[52] The solitary life leads the human being into desperation;[53] one needs another over against oneself. The human needs conversation.[54]

---

47. Luther can also speak of marriage as the oldest estate, being "der eltist stand unter allen der ganzten welt," "ja, alle andere[n Stände] komen aus dem her." WA 49:797,33-798,1; LW 51:358 (Sermon on Heb. 13:4, August 4, 1545).

48. Cf. for instance WA 43:255,9-11; LW 4:165 (on Gen. 22:16-18): "Quare sustinui ego maximos labores in monasterio? cur corpus meum ieiuniis, vigiliis et frigore adflixi?" and WA 43:615,25-41; LW 5:271 (on Gen. 29:1-3).

49. WA 43:453; LW 5:35-6 (on Gen. 26:8): "Atque ipse ego cum essem adhuc monachus, idem sentiebam, coniugium esse damnatum genus vitae."

50. WA 43:455,1f.; LW 5:38 (on Gen. 26:8): "Uxor servit mihi indignissimo in omnibus praedicamentis substantiae, quantitatis, qualitatis. Sed in praedicamento relationis sum dignus.

51. WA 43:451,26-28; LW 5:33 (on Gen. 26:8).

52. WA 44:573,15f.; LW 7:366 (on Gen. 44:17): "Non enim conditi sumus ad vitam solitariam, ut a communi societate hominum segregemur."

53. WA 42:561,5-7; LW 3:17 (on Gen. 15:5): "Hoc enim sublimium tentationum proprium est, ut occupent animos, cum sunt soli. Ideo in scriptura sancta celebratur oratio nocturna et solitaria, cuius magistra est tentatio."

54. WA 43:18,4-6; LW 3:200 (on Gen. 18:9): "Pia enim colloquia refocillant animos, excitant fidem, accendunt caritatem, ac multis modis erudiunt. Valeant igitur insulsi et muti monachi, qui in silentio cultum et sanctitatem putant positam." Cf. also WA 43:497,12-14; LW 5:99 (on Gen. 13:2): "Et notum est triviale dictum: Homo solitarius aut bestia, aut Deus: Addenda autem est minor, Deus esse non potest, et sequetur optima consequentia, quod solitarium hominem necesse ist esse bestiam."

In summary, divine and human speech are so indivisibly woven together that they cannot be distinguished:

> For God rules us in such a way that He does not want us to be idle. He gives us food and clothing, but in such a way that we should plow, sow, reap, and cook. In addition, He gives offspring, which are born and grow because of the blessing of God and must nevertheless be cherished, cared for, brought up, and instructed by the parents. But when we have done what is in us, then we should entrust the rest to God and cast our care on the Lord; for He will take care of us.[55]

The creation of the human being is neither a purely divine, nor a purely human event. Both sides here are together at work — inextricably bound to one another — in that both promise life.

Given Living Space in the World

God's word of creation and words of institution open up a world for human beings to inhabit, place it and its living spaces at our disposal, and sanctify life in its various estates. This promise-giving and life-empowering speech of God takes place *sola gratia,* "without any merit and worthiness on my part."[56] With this formula from his Small Catechism, Luther links God's grace in the doctrine of creation with the doctrine of justification.

Luther depicts the creation of the world as the building of a house, in which God is both the architect and master builder, who constructs it by means of the creative Word, furnishes it as a suitable living space, and finally places it at the disposal of human landlords. In his lectures on Genesis, Luther paints a picture of creation in most vivid terms. The world, the "elegant domicile"[57] of humanity, is exquisitely furnished. The roof of the house of the "world" is heaven, the foundation is the earth, the walls are the oceans. This "shell" is then painted, adorned,

55. WA 44:648,21-24; LW 8:94 (on Gen. 46:28).

56. The Small Catechism, First Article, BC 354; BC-T 345; BSLK 511,5; similarly: "Gott kunde auff viele weyse reich werden, wenn ers thun wolte. . . . Er thuts aber nicht, sondern giebt alles umbsonst." WA TR 5:132,12f., 17f. (Nr. 5422).

57. "domicilium . . . elegans"; WA 42:29,28; LW 1:39 (on Gen. 1:11).

and filled by God: The kitchen and the cellar are equipped with plants, which human beings can eat for nutrition.[58] Once the "great and glorious house"[59] is finally ready to be moved into, human beings are permitted and even ordered to enjoy [fruit!][60] its goods. For Luther, moreover, it is a specific sign of God's goodness as Creator that God cares first for the house and the dwelling of human beings before furnishing God's own dwelling — namely heaven.[61] This providential care by which God protects human beings and gives them what they need during their earthly existence is entirely directed toward human beings and remains — in an entirely unspectacular way — continually bound to creaturely mediation.

> For so God has given us reason and all creatures and all our temporal blessings to serve our uses. The man who wants to travel will require provisions for his journey from which he may secure food and lodging for himself. But he would act very foolishly if he thought that he had no need of money or food and that everything would be offered him on all sides by the providence of God. God has created all things that are necessary for this life not that you should expect them from Him directly, but that you should enjoy those things that are at hand and in the order which He himself has prescribed. By no means therefore should the use and the ministry of creatures be despised since, indeed, God has created them to serve us.[62]

Luther's use of the image of the building of a house can certainly lead to misinterpretations. The image of God as the master builder and architect of the world should not be misconstrued to mean that, after

58. WA 42:29,31; LW 1:39 (on Gen. 1:11). Cf. also WA 42:355,21f., and 26-30, 33; LW 2:133 (on Gen. 9:2): "These words, therefore, establish the butcher shop; attach hares, chicken and geese to the spit; and fill the table with all sorts of foods. . . . God sets himself up as a butcher [Deus igitur hoc in loco se constituit quasi Lanium]."

59. WA 42:29,31; LW 1:39 (on Gen. 1:11): "diviciis tam amplae domus."

60. WA 42:29,30f.; LW 1:39 (on Gen. 1:11): "in quam a Deo deducitur et iubetur frui omnibus."

61. WA 42:26,41–27,7; LW 1:35-36 (on Gen. 1:10).

62. WA 44:17,32-41; LW 6:24-25 (on Gen. 31:19). Also WA 44:78,3f.; LW 6:105 (on Gen. 32:6-8): "sed utaris necessariis ad hanc vitam sustentandam"; and WA 44:78,8-10; LW 6:105 (on Gen. 32:6-8): "ideo mane in functione tua et intra limites verbi: et utere mediis et consiliis, quae Deus ordinavit."

the construction and furnishing of his work, God leaves it to its own devices. Rather, the opposite is the case: as the master builder God equally desires to dwell within the house he has furnished.[63] God remains with the creation, wraps himself entirely into it, and is grasped in a creaturely way.[64] For Luther, God remains the "father of the house"[65] of the world. Likewise, the gift of the world as a house should not be misconstrued to mean that the habitation of the world is a permanent one; it is rather an inn, a temporary lodging.[66] Luther consistently emphasizes that the true home of human beings is heaven and that the world, as something prepared by God for human beings, does not possess any enduring character.

In spite of the multiple images of God as a skilled master builder, for Luther, the creation of the world is no mechanical process,[67] but something profoundly organic; birth and growth, procreation and life are the decisive terms here — not production, but bestowal.[68]

The Space of the Estates

Beyond this living space a further area of life opens up. Church, household, and politics are likewise stations in life that are granted to hu-

63. WA 46:558,20-32; LW 22:26 (on John 1:3 and John 2 from 1537).

64. WA 42:10,4-7; LW 1:11 (on Gen. 1:1f.): "velle comprehendere nudam divinitatem, seu nudam essentiam divinam . . . impossibile est, ideo involvit se Deus in opera et certas species, sicut hodie se involvit in Baptismum, Absolutionem etc. Ab his si discedas, tunc abis extra mensuram, locum et in merissimum nihil." God does not leave the world, but stays by his creation and takes care for it. WA 42:27,9-13; LW 1:35-36 (on Gen. 1:10): "Nunc etiam aream instruit et producit terram aptam habitationi et ministerio hominum. Hoc opus sibi placere bis dicit propter nos, qui sic ei sumus curae, ut etiam confirmet nos futurum, ut huius operis, quod tam sollicite aedificavit, etiam posthac magnam sit habiturus curam et affuturus ac porhibiturus sit hostem et mortem certissimam, nempe aquam."

65. WA 42:443,30f.; LW 2:255 (on Gen. 12:2): "quas hunc patremfamilias gessisse constat, qui est Deus aeternus, conditor et Servator omnium."

66. WA 42:441,40-442,4; LW 2:253 (on Gen. 12:1). Cf. WA 43:278,37-279,2; LW 4:198 (on Gen. 23:3f.).

67. WA 40/3:509,18-510,22; LW 13:91-92 (Enarratio Psalmi XC; 1534/35; on Ps. 90:2).

68. Johannes von Lüpke, "Schöpfer/Schöpfung VII" and Oswald Bayer, "Schöpfer/Schöpfung VIII," *Theologische Realenzyklopädie*, vol. 30, (Berlin/New York: Walter de Gruyter, 1999), pp. 307,1-5; 326-48.

man beings as promised living and work places; they are granted through God's words of institution and, hence, through his Word as creator. As Luther writes:

> Age, sex, and callings differ greatly in this life. One teaches the church; another serves the government; still another instructs the youth; a mother busies herself with the care and upbringing of children; and the husband is concerned with providing an honest living. In the opinion of the world these are not very grand and impressive works. But if you look at the Word, that heavenly adornment and divine glory, why should you not act proudly over against Satan, and why should you not give thanks to God for such great gifts? For these are not bare works; they are adorned with the Word of God, since they have been enjoined on you by God.[69]

For Luther, the words of institution hereby become the decisive criterion: as the performative Word of the Creator it sanctifies the stations and it places the human being in the world.[70] Luther's discovery of the world as a given, promised domain[71] extricates him from a monastic denial of life and corresponding flight from the world. As a reformer living entirely out of joy in creation, he discovers worldliness as a theological category. Everything that the human being is and possesses is "God's gift,"[72] which should be "used"[73] by human beings; Lu-

---

69. WA 42:516,33-39; LW 2:356 (on Gen. 13:14f.).

70. "Deinde incedamus in simplici vocatione: Maritus alat familiam, ancilla pareat Dominae suae, materfamilias lavet, ornet, doceat liberos. Haec opera, quia in vocatione et in fide filii DEI fiunt, fulgent in conspectu Dei, angelorum et totius ecclesiae Dei. Sunt enim vestitia caelesti luce, verbo Dei: Etsi in conspectu ecclesiae Pontificis contemnuntur, quod vulgaria et usitata sint." WA 42:517,12-18; LW 2:356-57 (on Gen. 13:14f.).

71. God's blessing in the three estates is especially mentioned in WA 43:523,16–524,31; LW 5:135-39 (on Gen. 27:28f.).

72. "Siquidem omnia, quae habemus, tantum Dei munere et dono habemus." WA 42:544,27f.; LW 2:392-93 (on Gen. 14:20). See also: "Sicut autem Deus natura optimus non potest omittere, quin nos variis donis ornet et cumulet, sicut sunt incolume et integrum corpus, opes, sapientia, industria, cognitio scripturae etc." WA 42:265,39-41; LW 2:5 (on Gen. 6:1).

73. "non cogitemus mali aliquid esse in gubernatione, seu usu rerum: Si quid vitii est, in corde est, id curemus, ut rectum ist, et omnia habebunt recte." WA 42:497,7-9; LW 2:329 (on Gen. 13:2).

ther even sees money in a positive light as a gift of God, and refuses to follow an indiscriminate Franciscan ideal of poverty.[74]

In addition to being entirely opposed to the monastic flight from the world and its denial of the estates, Luther directs his polemic against a third category: the monastic hatred of the body.

Not only the habitation of the human being, but even the human being himself or herself is furnished by God. Luther views human beings as well equipped by God and emphasizes not only the bodily organs like eyes, hands, and feet[75] as gifts of God, but bodiliness as such.[76] The human being receives his or her own body,[77] just as he or she receives spiritual gifts.[78]

Life in these promised domains requires time. Thus, God promises human beings time, a lifetime, and with this gift is also given room to follow the course of their lives as a measure against human impatience. This path of human beings with themselves, with other people, and with God is no momentary one, but constitutes a single path with a given amount of time, with all its joys and experiences, all its suffering and mistaken paths. To be sure, the endangerment of this given space by an untimely death, by the withholding of a full life, cannot be concealed.

In the granting of all these domains of life (the world, the estates, the body, and time) God says to the human being: "You may live in the world!" Along with this opening up of the world and the empowerment to live in it, human beings are equally exhorted with the second command: "You may give shape to the world!"

---

74. WA 42:496,17f.; LW 2:328 (on Gen. 13:2). WA 42:495,24f.; LW 2:327 (on Gen. 13:2).

75. "Oculi, pedes, manus sunt Dei dona"; WA 42:497,1; LW 2:328-29 (on Gen. 13:2).

76. WA 43:331,17-19; LW 4:273 (on Gen. 24:19f.): "qui sunt dona Dei, non tantum quae spiritu, sed etiam quae foris et erga homines honeste fiunt, Deus enim etiam corporum Deus est. Ideo corporalia dona suppeditat, et vult nos iis cum gaudio frui." Cf. WA 44:422,12f.; LW 7:166 (on Gen. 41:39): "Id nimirum egregium et insigne donum est oculi videntis et auris audientis."

77. "Hi enim intelligunt, et agnoscunt creatorem et creaturam eius, norunt, unde ipsi orti, et unde omnia accipiant."; WA 43:299,23-25; LW 4:228 (on Gen. 24:1-4).

78. "Agnoscere, quod sis eruditus, sapiens, dives, non malum est: Ingratitudo enim esset dona haec contemnere."; WA 42:588,31f.; LW 3:56 (on Gen. 16:6).

The Shaping of the Given World

The formation of the world that is given to human beings takes place first of all in that what is promised to human beings can also be claimed by human beings. Human beings should not harden themselves to the promise of God and withdraw themselves from it. Instead these promised domains of life are given us in order to be filled out and shaped. To deny that human beings are called to give shape to the world is to deny life itself. Luther sees human beings as duty bound to make use of the gifts and domains that have been placed at their disposal. As he puts it:

> For in this way I, too, have been absolved through the Word and have partaken of the Sacrament of the Altar. Surely, then, I am not going to say: "I will not work. I will sit in idleness. If I must live, I will live, etc." This would be tempting God. Indeed, you must use the things given and granted to you by God in His kindness. You must rule, work, and strive not to tempt God.[79]

For Luther, the government and rule of human beings is grounded in the fact that God does not keep the "divine grammar" for himself: The ability to communicate, to engage with others, to have and establish fellowship, and thereby to create something new, is also given to human beings. As a God who empties himself completely into his creature and shares himself without reservation, God gives human beings a share in the divine attributes, makes them able to speak.[80] Along with this capacity for language, human beings are also given the gift of verbal power: Adam's governance and rule is manifested in the naming of the animals.[81] With this gift of God's participation and the resulting participation of the human being, a marvelous cooperation of divine and human energies takes place in the strictest sense: God gives himself into human hands, into human mouths, gives human beings the divine creative attributes and therewith a share in God's own work.

79. WA 43:605,32-36; LW 5:256 (on Gen. 28:20-22).
80. The gift of language is for Luther God's most precious gift: "Inter omnia opera seu dona praestantissimum est loqui. Hoc enim solo opere homo differt ab omnibus animalibus." WA TR 1:565,22-24 (Nr. 1148). Cf. also WA TR 4:546,11-13 (Nr. 4855).
81. WA 42:90,14-20; LW 1:119.

Luther distinguishes himself sharply from monks who have left the world and in so doing failed to perceive their commission to give shape to the world. They spurn the *mandatum Dei* and the tasks given with their stations in life precisely because they do not heed God's words of institution and therewith the God who entrusted human beings with this task, however miserable and lowly it may seem.

Hence when a maid milks the cows or a hired man hoes the field — provided that they are believers, namely, that they conclude that this kind of life is pleasing to God and was instituted by God — they serve God more than all the monks and nuns.[82]

For Luther, the free gift of the world through God's promise, "You may have dominion!," does not remain something indeterminate:

This should be stressed in opposition to the gloomy hypocrites, who consider it piety and saintliness to abstain from gold, silver, food, clothing, or the like. Such abstinence does not please God. Indeed, He has appointed us lords and rulers of all things, over sheep and oxen and the entire earth (Ps. 8:7-8; Gen. 1:29-30). He assigns to us not only the possession of and the dominion over things but also their use. He wants us to preserve our bodies, not to kill them. Therefore, He has given us food, drink, clothing, the sun, and the moon.[83]

On the other hand, the reversal of this mandate to rule over creation is sin:

[I] know that God does not give out his gifts so that we can rule and have power over others or so that we should spurn their opinion and judgment: rather so that we should serve those who are in such a case as to need our counsel and help.[84]

Our fellow creatures are not commodities for consumption; instead, to rule means: "Rule, so that everything blooms." At the same

82. WA 43:106,2-6; LW 3:321 (on Gen. 20:2).
83. WA 43:333,28-34; LW 4:276 (on Gen. 24:22).
84. WA 42:432,13-15; LW 2:239 (on Gen. 11:27f.).

time, Luther does not conceal the fact that such rule is endangered and can even be lost through sin.[85]

At first glance, the increasing possibilities of influence, for instance associated with biological and genetic research, certainly enlarge the sphere of human rule; at the same time, they stand in danger of linguistically impoverishing creative speech. For this reason, the sovereignty of the human being cannot be miserly and egocentric, rather it must remain communicative.[86] Otherwise the rule of human beings, and the language whereby creatures are addressed, ceases to become creative and instead becomes deadly — as *incurvatus in seipsum.*

The Monologue of Narcissus

The dual structure of communication, which Luther views as indispensable to the creation and formation of human life, is increasingly susceptible to circumvention so that it no longer seems elementary or necessary. Modern genetic technology of reproduction challenges the elementary structure of communication in the theology of creation. Soliloquy and monologue increasingly gain ground over creative communication, for instance, in the technology of cloning. In his monologue Narcissus denies himself a partner: the creative communication, which is devoted to one's partner, breaks off, or, as the case may be, gives way to the desire to meet with nothing other than one's own image.

If the value of a human being as the likeness of God is no longer grounded in the creative address of God, and if this is no longer unconditionally true for every human being, promising him or her, as a mat-

85. WA 42:50,32-34; LW 1:67 (on Gen. 1:26): "cum iuberentur Adam et Heua dominari eis. Ergo nomen et vocabulum dominii retinemus ceu nudum titulum, Ipsa autem res fere tota amissa est." Cf.: "Etsi igitur dominium fere in totum amissum est, tamen ingens beneficium est extare adhuc eius reliquias aliquas."; WA 42:100,1f.; LW 1:133 (on Gen. 2:22).

86. "Selbstabschluß ist Götzendienst. Wer sich dem Schöpfer, der durch die Mitgeschöpfe redet, verschließt, sich der mitgeteilten Freude und Bitte versagt, besitzindividualistisch lebt, macht sich und seinen Besitz zum Selbstzweck und Fetisch. Wer nicht Gott und dem Nächsten dient, sondern allein sich selbst, wird zusammen mit seinem Besitz starr und tot." Bayer, *Schöpfung als Anrede,* p. 68.

ter of principle, an entitlement to life, then other criteria gain ascendancy. Subjective preference leads to a selective communication, which is particularly noticeable at the beginning and end of life. God's unconditional promise of life, as well as the domain bound up with it, stand in danger of no longer being perceived as a promised gift. Instead it becomes a possession to be defended, refused, and appropriated according to a pragmatic outlook. The transmission of received life and the domains of life that result from it no longer follow unconditionally, as they were first received, but conditionally.

A Christian doctrine of creation, by contrast, cannot condone the view that human sympathies and personal preferences should qualify the promise of creation. If the divine address and exhortation to life apply to humanity, as Luther says, "independent of my merit and worth," then one cannot apply self-serving criteria of personal history or merit particularly in the cases of the physically handicapped or those with Alzheimer's disease. The unassailable worth of each individual applies unconditionally to all human persons. This worth is unmerited, and therefore cannot be lost. It is promised and God's promise cannot be rescinded; it is, as it were, an indelible character.

Communication in the Face of Contradiction

God's creative word grants humanity freedom and value; it respects the contradiction and otherness of humanity. It hears the answer of humanity, which is no echo, and allows time for its answer. God addresses humanity creatively, but does not dictate to humanity; God is a poet, not a dictator. If one differentiates between creation and mechanistic reproduction, one of the distinguishing characteristics is the indeterminacy of the former. The vivacity at the outset of human life consists precisely in the fact that this process has the capacity to avoid a totalitarian control and demonstrates the independence of the newly arisen personality, which eludes the manipulative ideals of its parents' wishful thinking. This resistance and genetic contradiction on the part of the creature is the first instance of an entire life of evasion, as it were — a history of individual paths, desires, and ideas. These are to be respected.

In contrast to autocratic objectives, God grants human beings freedom in creation. This value and freedom of the human being are manifested precisely where the human being is addressed creatively through the creature, equally by God and one's fellow human beings. This freedom is manifested where one receives the room to live, which is promised; when one fills this space and shapes it; and where, in this unconditional freedom and value that is given, human beings now grant on their own behalf the same value and freedom to creation.

Luther on the Resurrection

GERHARD SAUTER

"If for this life only we have hoped in Christ, we are of all men most to be pitied."[1] Thus Luther translates 1 Corinthians 15:19, where Paul goes on to summarize precisely the reasons for Christian hope in the resurrection. In Luther's series of sermons on 1 Corinthians 15 from August 11, 1532 to April 27, 1533, this sentence constitutes faith's ground of confidence.[2] Here the Reformer develops his theological understanding of the resurrection in a more comprehensive and multifaceted way than anywhere else. Therefore, in this essay I seek to concentrate on Luther's line of thought in these homilies, and to follow it as closely as possible.

"If for this life only we have hoped in Christ, we are of all people most to be pitied." This statement obliges Luther the preacher to engage the congregation in the complexity of preaching. Arguments and counterarguments characterize every evangelical sermon, not only a sermon on

---

1. "Hoffen wir allein in diesem Leben auff Christum, So sind wir die elendsten vnter allen Menschen." WA DB 7:131; LW 28:59-213.

2. WA 36:478-696. The texts cited are Luther's as recorded by Rörer.

This article first appeared in *Lutheran Quarterly* 15 (2001): 195-216, under the title "Luther on the Resurrection: The Proclamation of the Risen One as the Promise of Our Everlasting Life with God." Translated by Austra Reinis from "Die Verkündigung des Auferstandenen als Zusage des Lebens bei Gott" in *Relationen-Studien zum Übergang vom Spätmittelalter zur Reformation: Festschrift zu Ehren von Prof. Dr. Karl-Heinz zur Mühlen.* Edited by Athina Lexutt and Wolfgang Matz (Münster: Lit Verlag, 2000), pp. 383-98, dedicated to Bishop William H. Lazareth, Princeton.

the resurrection. The proclamation of the resurrection of the dead as the promise of life with God is the heart of every sermon; it is not one theme among others, which may be brought forth when the need arises. The evangelical sermon is not meant to teach a more successful way of life, or better management of one's life, or mastery of responsibility for others. These things reasonable people can find of their own accord; for such things no preaching is needed.[3] Preaching is needed because it leads us out of the "vale of tears" into the future life.[4] If this does not happen, then preaching is wasted time and a useless or even damaging enterprise.

If one preaches and people come to hear what is proclaimed to them, then surely in this situation a tremendous number of assumptions come into play. The connection between preaching and such assumptions must be explained. Luther encourages the congregation to take responsibility for the challenges posed to it through preaching, sacraments, and the creed. First Corinthians 15:19 provides the impetus for this claim, saying in its own logic, "*if* this were the case, *then* that would follow." Such logic need not reduce anyone to silence by its formality; rather, it leads to reflection and deliberation. What basis does such an if-then statement have? Have we simply invented it in order to lead to an absurd conclusion? How can we find its foundation — a foundation that might surprise us to the extent that much else on which we build might turn out to be without foundation?

The Arguments in Theological Sequence

Luther demands considerable mental effort on the part of his congregation by exposing it to the challenges of evangelical preaching. In an afternoon sermon he does not hesitate, for example, to expect his

3. "non erecta praedicatio propter praesentem vitam, vivit, ut haushaltest und land und leut regirst, hoc noverunt gentiles etc. et ration docuit et necessitas." WA 36:534,6-8; LW 28:101; "Hoc sit vobis Christianis praedicatum. Drauff seid baptizati, vocati et Euangelium etc. Non ut reich werden, quia Iuristae land regieren, fursten zu." WA 36:544,10-12; LW 28:100.

4. "Sed si baptizatus, ut incipiam aliam vitam, et ista praedicatio ist nicht gericht ad praesentem vitam, sed quodmodo ex isto jamertal in futuram." WA 36:534,17-19; LW 28:100; "Sed hoc discite, ut cor vestrum zu richten auff ein ander leben und wesen." WA 36:544,12-13; LW 28:108.

sleepy audience to follow the use of the terminology of formal logic.[5] Is Luther confusing a worship service with a seminar in philosophy? Would it not be more appropriate to speak of the resurrection of the dead as a mystery of faith, and to seek different bases for this conviction, bases that have nothing to do with reason, especially since Luther has just declared reason incompatible with evangelical preaching?

Nothing of the sort. The close interweaving of sermon and expectation of the future life needs to be explained within its theological context. Otherwise we run the risk of arriving at erroneous conclusions, which threaten life precisely because they appear to be serving life in such an eminent way. All too easily we become entangled in conclusions that make us lose our footing in faith and hope.

Luther's first significant step in his discourse is to appreciate the connection between preaching and the hope of the resurrection. He finds this in verse 14: "And if Christ is not risen, then our proclamation is in vain and your faith, too, is in vain." It is to understand that if Christ is not risen then evangelical preachers are not messengers sent by God. In such case, it has not been God who has authorized us to proclaim the resurrection. Indeed, then God is not truly God, and we have ourselves been deceived and have deceived others.[6] This is the theological sequence which Luther develops. Its premise is that God is true because God cannot negate God's self.[7] The living God cannot abandon us to death, or God would be contradicting God's self.

---

5. "Proving what has been denied by what has been denied" and "begging the question" *(petitio principii)*: WA 36:524,10ff.; LW 28:94. Cruciger's text speaks additionally of "weak dialectics," WA 36:525,16; LW 28:95; an argument "from the particular to the universal," WA 36:525,5-6; LW 28:95; a device that disproves by arguing to an impossible or false conclusion, WA 36:526,3; 533,21; LW 28:94-95.

6. "Ista omnia sequuntur: Si fides unrecht, et verbum, si verbum unrecht, praedicator non recte gesand. Si etiam deus falsch, qui misit, et non recht." WA 36:526,6-8; LW 28:96; "Ideo hengt als an einander: Gott, sein wort, Christus, Apostolorum praedicatio, fides. Ideo so Gott lebt, nicht liegen kann, so gewis der Apostolorum praedicatio recht et fides, so gewis resurrectio mortuorum. Sic concludit Paulus." WA 36:528,4-7; LW 28:97.

7. "Si vero credis Christum etc. zwingt die [dich] die consequentz, quia deus se non potest negare, est verax. Ideo verbum eius et Apostolorum praedicatio et fides ecclesiae, quae dran hengt." WA 36:533,2-4; LW 28:99; Hans Joachim Iwand, *Luthers Theologie, Nachgelassene Werke*, vol. 5, ed. Johann Haar (München: Kaiser, 1974), p. 203, "Die Auferstehung ist so gewiß wie Gott Gott ist."

I would like to call this line of argument a typical example of eschatological rationality.[8] It does not offer a chain of proofs that we may choose to accept should we come to appreciate its brilliance. Neither does Luther proceed on the basis of tradition, resting his case on the recognized authority of witnesses. Nor does he — as became common after the Enlightenment — search for reasons supporting the plausibility of the resurrection; that is to say, he does not seek to prove the credibility of Jesus' resurrection on the basis of the empty tomb. He also does not attempt to ground the resurrection of the dead in Jewish tradition, asserting that the Easter event certifies it. Instead Luther speaks to "us" who are challenged to examine ourselves with respect to the load capacity and the range of faith and hope. Luther wishes to argue along with Paul, to assess the strength of the argument by clarifying its context and deducing from it the correct conclusions.

Only the preaching of the resurrection can awaken the hope of the future life. This is not a rationalization by Luther simply because he happens to be speaking from the pulpit. What is true of faith — that it comes from preaching (Rom. 10:17) — is equally true of hope. Preaching is the indispensable ground of hope because hope comes from God and cannot be invented by human beings. Preaching declares to us what we could never tell ourselves. How else are we able to speak of resurrection, of which we cannot discover even a trace within ourselves?

Luther can only *speak* of the resurrection — with every effort to be clear in his argumentation! — in that he speaks as a preacher, to whom has been entrusted the task of proclaiming the promise of the future life with God. In preaching the resurrection of the dead as the Word of the God who does not lie but remains faithful, Luther differs from the late Middle Ages, indeed even from earlier theological traditions. Luther does share many of the "eschatological" ideas of his time — in these he was no innovator. Yet, what is distinctive about Luther is that he "focuses" these ideas "theologically in the certainty, that all who die in the faith, have their 'place' in God's Word and promise in Jesus Christ."[9]

---

8. Cf. Gerhard Sauter, "Eschatological Rationality," in *Eschatological Rationality: Theological Issues in Focus* (Grand Rapids: Baker, 1996), pp. 171-200.

9. Karl-Heinz zur Mühlen, "Luther II. Theologie," in *Theologische Realenzyklopädie* (Berlin/New York: Walter de Gruyter, 1976 ff.), 21:560. Hereafter cited as TRE.

Without attempting to systematize the ideas and thoughts about the resurrection, which interacted in theology and popular piety prior to Luther, one can say that two perspectives dominated. The first proceeded from the distinction between body and soul, understanding death as the separation of the two.[10] The dead were often referred to as "souls," which at the resurrection had to be reunited with their bodies, lest they remain incomplete.[11] Even when theologians objected to such a separation, it continued to appear generally convincing to popular piety, not least because it seemed to make plausible the continuation of the person beyond death. This supported the other perspective: The human soul was regarded as capable of acting and suffering even after death. Souls could even travel, and this could be described by means of visions.[12] Above all they could be progressively cleansed and perfected. Even though heaven remained closed to them, God's mercy was not going to be denied to them forever and they could even receive help from the church. Thus, in purgatory the progress of human beings towards perfection continued — the combination of "Way" and "Ascent" that characterized medieval theological anthropology.

From the time of Benedict XII (1336) the dogma that after death the soul either experiences the beatific vision or is doomed to eternal damnation assumed decisive importance. The twofold outcome of the judgment decided the fate of the soul. Though all human beings in fact had to answer for their deeds and misdeeds before Christ at the last judgment, nevertheless, each individual soul at the moment of death either ascended immediately to the beatific vision, stood in purgatorial need of purification, or descended directly to hell.[13] Ideas about the gradual purification of souls — namely, the doctrine of purgatory, masses for the dead, and the practices of indulgences — developed on this basis.

Luther's Reformation insights regarding theological anthropology and eschatology forced him to discard all practices, along with their

---

10. Reinhard Staats, "Auferstehung I/4. Auferstehung der Toten — Alte Kirche," in TRE, 4:477.

11. Arnold Angenendt, *Geschichte der Religiosität im Mittelalter* (Darmstadt: Primus, 1997), pp. 722-24.

12. Angenendt, *Geschichte,* pp. 695-705.

13. Heinrich Denzinger, ed., *The Sources of Catholic Dogma,* trans. Roy J. Deferrari (St. Louis: Herder, 1957), pp. 1000-1002. Hereafter cited as DH.

theological rationalities, related to the medieval understanding of the resurrection. If we cannot depend on anything but God's promises and faithfulness, then our identity is bound up and preserved in these promises. What we do or leave undone is held in the hands of God. That which is promised to us in the message of justification concerning our journey on earth applies in full and without end to dying in the faith, as well as to that which can be done for dying persons.

In the Middle Ages and even earlier, Christian education and pastoral care alternated between threat and consolation. This type of instruction was supported and intensified by means of Christian art. Christian iconography of the "Last Things" later went so far as to imagine death, purgatory, the last judgment, hell and heaven as states of the soul that could be depicted by means of various facial expressions.[14] Luther instead took support from biblical texts — and not only when he was preaching — because accounting for hope (1 Pet. 3:15) involves simultaneously proclaiming the judging and saving work of God. He thinks and speaks as a biblical theologian who derives theological insight from the tension existing within biblical texts. He expounds these tensions only to the extent that is required for the clarity of the account that he gives. For this reason he is not bothered by the fact that Paul can speak of life with Christ immediately after death[15] and the future resurrection in the face of the last judgment side by side. Luther does not systematically iron out such differences and avoids any rationalization leading to scurrilous speculation, as for example concerning the return of reanimated, quasi-bodily souls into the grave, in order from there again to proceed to the resurrection. In any case, Luther holds considerations concerning the interim state between death and the resurrection to be missing the point, because they entail concepts of empirical time, which never reaches God's time. That which happens to us and in which we cannot participate cannot be measured in terms of human time; it remains hidden from our sight. For this reason Luther speaks about "the sleep of death" rather than of an "in-

14. See, for example, four copperplate engravings by Raphael Sadaler I (1560/61-1632) in Peter Jezler, ed., *Himmel, Hölle, Fegefeuer: das Jenseits im Mittelalter; eine Ausstellung des Schweizerischen Landesmuseums*, 2nd ed. (Zürich: Neue Zürcher Zeitung, 1994), pp. 320f.

15. This note is sounded for example in Luther's preface to Urbanus Rhegius' "Prophetiae veteris testamenti de Christo" (1542), WA 53:400,14-19.

terim state." This interpretation, which he takes amongst others from Paul's words concerning the dead as those who have "fallen asleep in Christ" (1 Cor. 15:18; 1 Thess. 4:14), we have yet to consider, suffice it to say here that it corresponds to the early Christian eschatological metaphor of waking at the dawn of the new world (see Rom. 13:11-12; Eph. 5:14).

Hope in the Midst of the Misery of Affliction and Tribulation ("Anfechtung")

First Corinthians 15:19 also provides the second move in Luther's discourse. This key statement does not stand alone. If it did, then one might wonder whether it was truly conclusive. If Christ were hope for this life alone, it would not so much be a formula for despair as an exhortation to spend ourselves in the interest of making the most of this life.

"[Then] we are of all people most to be pitied": Luther regards this primarily as a fact — not a hypothetical prospect. In doing so he leads us onto a track, which in turn can lead onto an extremely slippery path: the misery of Christian existence. Christians, he says, are demonstrably worse off than other people; they are subjected to suffering and persecution from which others are spared.[16] (Luther argues the fact sociologically, depicting peasants, knights, and burghers to be happy, godless people without sorrow — as though there weren't Christians among them as well!) From this point of view the future life easily becomes the compensation for all that which people have missed in this life.

However, Luther immediately qualifies his point: "Evil persons," he admits, are also being oppressed, robbed, and killed. But what if people involuntarily take difficulties upon themselves for the sake of the future life — and here the hypothesis cuts painfully, it hits the nerve of life — they are merely deceiving themselves? What if there truly isn't anything after death? In Luther's opinion this is only the

16. "So sind keine menschen nicht geplagter, elender quam Christiani i.e. si scirem hoc verum, so lies ich Taufe und gleuben, predigstuhl das hertzleid." WA 36:537,4-6; LW 28:103.

excuse of those who deceive themselves. But who can vouch for the contrary? This question reaches so deeply that one cannot simply reply: The resurrected Christ, indeed God himself, vouches for it! As much as this is true, how can this become our answer, an answer out of which the character of our hope today is formed? In what sense may Christians hold the eschatological hope of the resurrection as one that does not stand on the same level with all other possible hopes, subject as they are to the risk of disappointment? Disappointed hopes, of course, have the power to spur us to new daring, provided that we do not give up the hope that keeps us alive. If, however, we were to be disappointed in the hope of eternal life, then this would necessarily hit us to the core. If we were to be deceived in this hope, then we would be lost. Not only because then it would be irrevocably too late to change one's mind and to lead a different life. Rather, our entire life, during which we would have placed our hope in Christ, would have lost its grounding for good. We would be miserable if the *futura vita* turned out to be a grandiose lie. We would be more miserable than other people, who had no such hope of truth, and who therefore did not have to see themselves deceived when all came to an end with death.

Luther does say in passing that all those who do not expect anything after death, who simply take life and death as they come, must one day become aware of their self-deception. But he refuses to weigh one calculation against the other, in the fashion of Blaise Pascal's mathematical "wager" of eternity against nothingness.[17] Rather, Luther focuses on *Anfechtung*, though not on an *Anfechtung* that originates in the fear of death or dying. He drives his congregation with utter radicalness into the question of the most profound reason for despair in life. The misery of Christians only becomes clear when they begin however vaguely to sense what "misery" means: desperate forlornness in the life-and-death struggle. It is not sufficient to answer that Christians — or many Christians — have taken upon themselves some difficulties in the hope of a better life. Misery is experienced in *Anfechtung* under the anger of God.

17. Blaise Pascal, *Pensées,* ed. Leon Brunschvicg (Paris: Edition de Ch.-M. des Granges, 1961), Fragment 233; English translation: *Pascal's Pensees,* trans. A. J. Krailsheimer, Fragment 418, "Infinity — nothing" (233), p. 149-53.

"Misery" is thus not simply a mood, it is the condition of the absence of God (as in the thirteenth-century hymn by Berthold of Regensburg: "Now we pray the Holy Spirit . . . that he would protect us at the end, when we leave this misery"). Misery is *Anfechtung* in the "vale of tears," and the "vale of tears" is the misery[18] into which we have fallen, deservedly or not. It is estrangement as such, it is not a world full of misery in which we notice only valleys and shadows, or even a world in which human beings feel sorry for themselves and complain, a world of whiners. In the "vale of tears" *Anfechtung* assaults us, and this is not a psychological state of depression.

Anfechtung cuts us off from our trust in God. It is the suffocation of hope, as it were, a contraction of the vessels of which the causes are not only spiritual. *Anfechtung* is the foretaste of the peril of death. In *Anfechtung* human beings fall between God and the devil, and the terrible thing about it is that they no longer know who is crushing them, because it seems as though they have gotten themselves into these dire straits, in that they become aware that they cannot stand before the judgment of God. Tormenting thoughts of eternal damnation do not let them go because they know they must be destroyed in the face of God, in spite of their good works, even in spite of their practice of the faith.[19] *Anfechtung* is not a private matter, but the assault of the devil on our own judgments. That the devil attempts to convince Christians of their damnation in order to drive them away from God — how can Christians know this, as long as they remain entangled in their own judgments? For this reason Christians need a much stronger assurance than that which the prospect of a simple continuation of life after death would offer. Christians need nothing less than hope in Christ: the hope that can now rely on the Resurrected One. For this reason — as Luther can say elsewhere — in every thanksgiving for salva-

---

18. *Deutsches Wörterbuch von Jakob und Wilhelm Grimm,* vol. 4: 2 (Leipzig: S. Hirzel, 1877), pp. 2260ff., "Jammerthal." See also Martin Luther, *Studienausgabe,* vol. 6, *Frühneuhochdeutsches Glossar zur Luthersprache,* ed. H.-U. Delius (Leipzig: Ev. Verlagsanstalt, 1999), p. 97, "jamerig": "elend, trauervoll."

19. "Ideo Christianus ein elender mensch, qui in hoc kampff sthet, quod semper blode, erschrocken hertz, cogitationes de morte incidunt in cor de hoc iudicio, da bricht ym der kalt schweis. Ideo tregt er quotidie am hals. Ego quidem vivo, cogitat, sed cogitationes veniunt: tu peccasti. Si etiam ein wol geubter man in fide, habet mher etc." WA 36:539,2-6; LW 28:104.

tion from *Anfechtung* we confess faith in eternal life and the resurrection.[20]

Were Christ not the Resurrected One, but instead a great teacher of a better life, then we would have been deceived not only in our expectations, but in Christ himself. Through this, Luther indirectly indicates that what is important is not the *hope of the resurrection* but the *Christ-Hope*. Our hope is focused on Christ. Those who hope in Christ are not more clear-sighted than those who despair, but they can hope that Christ has gone ahead of them. Had Christ not risen from the dead — he who promises us life, he who says that he himself is the truth and the life — then he would have been exposed as a liar, and not simply a person who had built his life and death on an illusion.

But Jesus Christ has experienced "not only the way to life through death, but also the life out of death,"[21] as Luther in 1530 had explained in his exegesis of Psalm 16:7 ("I bless the Lord who gives me counsel; in the night also my heart instructs me"). In that Christ learns obedience in his suffering (Heb. 5:8), because he submits to God's action and follows God's will, he becomes a "doctor," a "learned one" and "teacher" of a very different kind; learned in the Word of God.[22] His experience consists of this and not of anything else. This is the unique experience in which he precedes us and which we cannot anticipate. Yet he does let us participate in the experience by granting us hope in himself. Be-

20. See the Commentary on Psalm 118, *Das Schöne Confitemini* (1530): "Und hie sollen wir die regel lernen, das, wo jm Psalter und jnn der schrifft die heiligen also mit Gott handeln vom trost und hülffe jnn jhren nöten, das daselbst gewislich vom ewigen leben und afferstehung der todten gehandelt wird, Und das solche text allzu mal gehören auff den artickel von der aufferstehung und ewigem leben, Ja auff das gantze dritte stück des glaubens, als vom heiligen geist, von der heiligen Christenheit, von vergebung der sünde, von der aufferstehung, vom ewigen leben. Und fleusst alles aus dem ersten gebot, da Gott spricht: 'Ich bin dein Gott etc.'" WA 31/I,154,27-34; "The Beautiful Confitemini," LW 14:87.

21. ". . . nicht nur den Weg zum Leben durch den Tod, sondern auch das Leben aus dem Tod. . . ." Sebastian Degkwitz, *Wort Gottes und Erfahrung: Luthers Erfahrungsbegriff und seine Rezeption im 20. Jahrhundert*, Beiträge zur Theologischen Urteilsbildung 6 (Frankfurt am Main/Berlin/Bern/New York/Paris/Wien: Lang, 1998), p. 161.

22. "Haec est experientia passionis. Duo igitur allegat: consilium divinum et experientiam carnis propriam. Deus docuit me et ipse expertus sum in mea passione. . . . Das ist denn ein rechter Doctor, qui primo a Deo docetur, deinde experitur. Experientia autem est, wenn Gott mit dem rat hilfft, das einer denckt: ich wills ausharren." WA 31/I:317,4-9.

cause Christ "depends on God in his Word, he hopes contrary to the experience of death, that God will save him in his own, inconceivable way — not from death, but through death."[23]

Given the nature of this hope, it cannot be fulfilled in this life only; indeed, it cannot even thoroughly take effect here. Had Christ not risen from the dead, this hope would not even be required. Because it is hope in Christ alone, it would be vain and the monstrosity of all wretchedness if Christ had not truly risen. The key argument in 1 Corinthians 15:19 takes for granted the character of hope as participation in Christ, in his experience of death and resurrection. The experience of Christ is shared with us solely in the form of faith and hope — and both are (as Luther noted in his gloss to Rom. 10:15) not yet experiences for us "until the coming of the future life."[24] "Faith and hope reach not for another life, but rather for the overcoming of this life marked by death, through that life which has been awakened from death and created anew."[25]

Thus we are not talking about an evaluation of "this" life from the virtual perspective of another life, or even from the perspective of the knowledge of our death. We are not reflecting on the hope of a life to come based on the worth or lack of worth of this life. This logic will determine the interpretation of 1 Corinthians 15:19 three hundred years later with the "enlightened" objection raised, for example, by the Swiss writer Gottfried Keller[26] in his "Gruner Heinrich" (1854-55, 1879-80), the literary version of Ludwig Feuerbach's critique of religion. Is life not worth much more if it is limited, if it ends with death? Does not a

---

23. "sich auf Gott in seinem Wort verläßt, hofft er wider die Erfahrung des Todes, Gott werde ihn auf seine, unvorstellbare Weise retten — nicht vor dem Tod, sondern durch ihn hindurch." Sebastian Degkwitz, *Wort Gottes und Erfahrung,* p. 195.

24. "Sunt enim non exhibita ad sensum bona et pax, Sed nunciata verbo ac sic fide tantum percipienda i.e. sine experientia, donec vita futura veniat." WA 56:425,3-5; LW 25:416.

25. "Glaube und Hoffnung strecken sich nicht nach einem anderen Leben aus, sondern nach der Überwindung dieses vom Tode gezeichneten Lebens durch das aus dem Tod erweckte, neugeschaffene Leben." Sebastian Degkwitz, *Wort Gottes und Erfahrung,* p. 195.

26. On this topic see Wolfgang Schrage, *Der erste Brief an die Korinther,* Evangelisch-Katholischer Kommentar zum Neuen Testament, vol. 7/:4 (Zürich: Benziger and Neukirchen-Vluyn: Neukirchener, 2000), pp. 134f; see also Gottfried Keller, "Der Grüne Heinrich," in *Sämtliche Werke in zwei Bänden,* vol. 1 (München: Droemersche Verlagsanstalt, 1953), pp. 29-605.

hope that reaches beyond death lead to a lower evaluation of "this" life? Can this life be considered a way station to which we no longer need to devote all our efforts?

These are psychological considerations concerning an attitude towards life as limited by death. Another such consideration is the notion of a human — all too human — hope beyond death. As heterogeneous as these attitudes may be — the attitude is basically the same. Luther does not concern himself with such things, or at most peripherally. He is not moved by the consideration of the limitedness of human life or by the question of the "other world." Neither does Paul write, "Would we have to leave this life at that, then we would be miserable."

Luther, in typical fashion, does not go into the syntactic connection of the word "alone." "Are the Christians, in the case of no resurrection, only *the hopeful ones* in this life or are they then the hopeful ones *only in this life?*"[27] The key for Luther lies in "hope in Christ." Such hope does not end with this life. The hope in Christ reaches beyond our death. To hope means to cling to Christ. We cling to the Resurrected One, even when we have died, and especially when we are resurrected. Jesus Christ is God's living promise for our life with God. It is hope that joins us to this Christ. If truly we have hoped in Christ, then this cannot be valid only for this life.

Hope in Christ is therefore not a hope beyond death in the sense of an intentionality that might vault beyond every space-time limit of human life. The hope of the resurrection remains joined to Christ, thus it pulls us out of the grave — to the side of the Resurrected One. And for this reason this hope does not end with our death, nor can it be dispensed with after the resurrection. It cannot be replaced with or overtaken by "having been attained" in some way. Resurrection is not bound to any time-continuum. Resurrection is not an end to hope, otherwise it would be a hope in the resurrection. Confidence in the resurrection remains joined to Christ, and thus remains hope in Christ, even though in a transformed and transfigured way.

First Corinthians 15:19 leads all readers — not only the "ideal reader" of Paul, who might have been a disguised heretic! — to ask: "On what hope have I based my life? What is the source of this hope? How far does this hope reach?"

27. Schrage, *Der erste Brief an die Korinther,* p. 132.

What May We Hope? Whom May We Expect?
Jesus Christ as the Head of His Own!

The third step in our discourse: Our resurrection depends on Christ's conquest of death. "But in fact Christ has been raised from the dead, the first fruits of those who have fallen asleep" (1 Cor. 15:20). Jesus Christ is the first of many, of an immeasurable number: One could understand this as meaning that Christ has "made the beginning" in that he has been the first to demonstrate the possibility of the resurrection of the dead and by doing so has, as it were, opened the door through which we may follow him, or that he clears the way so that we can enter a further reality behind him, namely the hereafter. Jesus Christ, however, is not a pioneer; he is not one who has been the first to explore an unknown and hitherto untrodden territory into which now others may follow him. Many do follow him; they cling to each other[28] — but only those who also cling to Christ[29] will live.

That Jesus Christ is the "first fruits" links the announcement of the "general" resurrection of the dead with the promise of the Resurrected One to his own: the promise that they will once be where he already is. The mere prospect of a resurrection of all the dead cannot truly awaken hope; on the contrary, it may even engender anxiety and fear. All depends — and this too, the medieval pictures of the last judgment have visually depicted — on where people are drawn in their resurrection. People cling to each other, in life as in death. But the one whom Christ has drawn to himself — in baptism into his death — for that one he, the first fruits of the resurrected, is also the "Head" to whom all who belong to him cling as its members. This is an indissoluble connection, which proves to be sustaining in the hope that intimately binds Christ with his own. The body of Christ as a picture for the church reveals an entirely different type of union from the common fate of all people, which could simply be sealed once more through the resurrection.

The resurrection with Christ may be compared with childbirth, in which the head emerges first, and pulls all the other members out with it. When in childbirth the head has emerged — and that is the most difficult and painful part, jeopardized by many potential complications —

---

28. WA 36:542,12; LW 28:106.
29. WA 36:546,1; LW 28:108.

then the rest happens in seconds; the body follows.[30] Because Christ has risen, our resurrection is already half-accomplished,[31] because it happened for our sake. United with him, Christians already have their head outside the realm of death. And for this reason they no longer find themselves entirely where they know themselves to be in misery. They have already emerged from the world of the grave, more than halfway, as Luther repeats.[32] The passage from death into life cannot be compared with a gradual transition, with a progressive process of purification, maturation, and perfection, as is suggested by the doctrine of purgatory.

Any concept of a passage from life into an existence after death, difficult as that passage may be, is inadequate in the face of the message of the victory of Christ over death. Only through this victory does it become clear where Christ descended when he came to us human beings. His descent into the realm of the dead, of which the Creed speaks ("descended into hell"), exposes him to the power of death and breaks this power once and for all, it is therefore anything but a mere passage.

Luther initially understood this descent, which is contrasted with the ascent to heaven as God's realm of action, as a descent into hell, with which Christ consummates his work of salvation, according to the traditional medieval perception.[33] Later — and perhaps not coincidentally in the course of the exegesis of Old Testament texts — he describes *infernus* as "everything that there is where we descend after this life, whether the grave or anything else."[34] It would be a misunderstanding, however, to understand this in terms of a location. In the explanation of the creedal statement "he descended into hell" in the Large Catechism (1529) it is concisely stated that the confession serves

30. "ut mulieres dicunt: infantem natum capite, hats nicht not." WA 36:548,1-2; LW 28:108-9.

31. "Ideo nostra resurrectio mortuorum ist freilich mher den helfft geschehen, quia caput nostrum da." WA 36:548,5-6; LW 28:110-11.

32. "sind mher denn die helfft lebendig." Here it would be idle to quibble over whether the glass is half-full or half-empty. WA 36:547,9; LW 28:109.

33. Werner Thiede, "Luthers individuelle Eschatologie," *Luther-Jahrbuch* 49 (1982): 43.

34. "alles, was es ist, da wir hinfaren post vitam sive sepulchrum sive aliud quiddam" WA 31/I: 318,17-18 (concerning Ps. 16:11); cf. the "Lectures on Ecclesiastes" (1526), WA 20:162,31-33: "Infernus . . . significat foveam, sepulchrum, proprie vero me iudice . . . illum abditum recessum, in quo dormiunt mortui extra hanc vitam" (concerning Eccl. 9:10).

to "clarify [transfigure] and express" the work of salvation as do the other elements of the story of Jesus Christ.[35] Christ subjects himself to the power of death. He has joined those who sleep; even more, he has descended into the realm of death, which is not limited to the dead, but stretches out its clutches towards us, the living. This death is a hostile power, which is manifested in raging sin. Jesus Christ struggled with this power for the sake of all who were forced to succumb to it. Without his victory over death they have not merely fallen asleep, but are irretrievably lost.

However, not only they, but we too, who still consider ourselves a ways from death, would still be under its power without Christ. The descent of the crucified one into the realm of the dead shows us, that we, too, live in the realm of death, that we coexist with the dead — and they with us. If the life of Christ projects into our world, then it intervenes in the world of death, which constantly threatens to grasp us and to which we submit in that we cling to our life. In the realm of death human beings have submitted to death. It is the place where the dead are locked up without any hope at all. The realm of death is our place, the place in which our time collapses and where the net of hope that we have woven is torn. So that we fall into the abyss and in falling still see what our condition is. Thus all categories of time and space are transcended and we are struck with an inconceivable fear. Death is concealed underneath the appearance of life. In going there, Christ has taken upon himself the hopelessness of those who have no hope. Jesus Christ has overcome death in that he has entered the realm of death, where no one is able to revolt, where no one is able to rise up, and where perhaps no one even wishes to do so!

The community of the living and the dead with Christ, their hope, reaches further and is considerably stronger than the "solidarity of the living with the dead,"[36] which is expressed in medieval piety by the efforts of the living on behalf of the dead in the form of prayers, offerings, and so forth.[37] According to this view, the living were considered capable of accomplishing something on behalf of the dead. In the sign

35. "verkleren und ausdrücken." WA 30/I,186,33; BSLK 652,33; BC-T 414; BC 434.
36. Angenendt, *Geschichte*, p. 711.
37. "Solidargemeinschaft von Lebenden und Toten," in Angenendt, *Geschichte*, pp. 708-11. Compare with Luther's criticism for example in "An den christlichen Adel deutscher Nation" (1520), WA 6:444,22-445,6; LW 44:180-81.

of the victory of Christ over death, however, we are the ones *to whom* something is done, as are those who have already died.

The resurrection of Christ is the victory over death. "Death has been swallowed up in victory. Where, O death, is your victory? Where, O death, is your sting?" (1 Cor. 15:55). Luther reads this in Paul, who had found the destruction of death by God in Isaiah 25:8 and Hosea 13:14. But here in particular we must listen carefully. The resurrection of Christ has become the death of death.[38] Christ has "swallowed up and devoured death."[39] However, "'swallowed up,' not yet finished but well begun."[40] The victory is and remains the victory of Christ. In us death is not yet swallowed up. Nevertheless the victory of Christ is made ours through baptism and the gospel,[41] without, however, awakening any sort of feelings of superiority in us. We must fight with death, and this in and of itself would be a hopeless struggle, hopeless at least in that we must die and in that we have no control over death. There everyone is and remains alone, and cannot find a substitute, as Luther expressed it incomparably in the beginning of his Invocavit sermon on March 9, 1522.[42] Yet Christians are not left to themselves, and certainly they are not surrendered to that which they can see in themselves. They are not allowed to look back over the debits and credits of their lives, assuming they are even still capable to take stock in such a way. Having been baptized, they do at least have a foretaste of what it means to have died. It means that something has definitely come to an end: their life lived only for itself, turned in upon itself. Once this curvature has been broken, then the believer is free to gaze on Christ, the crucified and resurrected one, the victor. He is our judge and our savior. Here hope in the resurrection links with the message of justification. The one who has died with Christ participates in his victory. He is not spared from

---

38. See Gerhard Ebeling, "Des Todes Tod. Luthers Theologie der Konfrontation mit dem Tode," *Zeitschrift für Theologie und Kirche* 84 (1987): 162-87.

39. "den tod verschlungen und gefressen." Thus the explanation of "descended into hell" in the Large Catechism, WA 30/I:187,6; BSLK, 652,31; BC-T, 414; BC, 435.

40. "'*Verschlungen*' nondum factum, sed ghet im schwang." WA 36:685,1; LW 28:206.

41. "Victoria est resurrectio Christi. Nondum in nobis, sed tamen sieg ist da, quae nostra per baptismum, Euangelium." WA 36:685,2-3; LW 28:206.

42. "Wir seindt allsampt zu dem tod gefodert und wirt keyner für den andern sterben, Sonder ein yglicher in eygner person für sich mit dem todt kempffen." WA 10/III:1,7-10; LW 51:70.

death, but he has already been delivered from the realm of death. For this reason he can struggle with death in a different way, and no longer has to deal with it alone.

Thus the metaphor of "struggle and victory" shapes language about the resurrection, particularly in view of the fact that the resurrected Christ reigns over the life and death of Christians. "Struggle and victory" is an entirely different metaphor than "dying and becoming." The metaphor "struggle and victory" causes questions concerning a continuation of life after death or the signature of immortality to appear pale. Struggle and victory characterize the way of Jesus, which was not a passing through the gates of death, nor a crossing over the boundaries of death, and not even the overcoming of the power of death by means of a power appertaining to Jesus alone. He entered into the realm of death. In entering into death, he took up the struggle for life and death as such, not merely his own struggle for life and death.

Christians, through faith, participate in the victory of Christ and are thus given hope in the Resurrected One. His victory grasps them; it is not simply transferred to them. Therefore it is not possible to derive human resurrection from the resurrection of Christ. The modern spiritualism of Ernst Troeltsch — who had hewn in his gravestone the inscription: "Why do you look for the living among the dead?" — would have been theologically inconceivable for Luther. With this question the Resurrected One calls his own out of the realm of the dead, in which they — apparently consciously — exist (Luke 24:5). The promising question of the risen Christ is not to be recast into a slogan for one's own fate, for then it turns into a puzzle of religious self-certainty which ought to endure, but upon closer inspection is the manifestation of abandonment: "on a hope where there was nothing to hope for" (Rom. 4:18). Decisive for the character of this hope is the perception of Christ: who are we expecting him to come as — the Resurrected as the Coming One, the Coming One as the Resurrected?

Let us insert a question: What does "resurrection" mean — "rising again" or "being awakened"? The term "resurrection" leads one to think of "rising again" after falling, meaning that one stands up again, that one has not become infirm, in contrast to "being resurrected." For Christ this is one and the same thing, but not for us. God has torn him from death, and Christ has conquered death. This can only be expressed more precisely and unequivocally with the help of the subtle distinctions of the doctrine of the Trinity. Luther himself did not discuss this, but does refer to it indirectly by his strong emphasis on the victory of Christ.

Here the metaphor of "the sleep of death" receives its theological locus.[43] The ones who sleep are withdrawn from space and time; they do not know what is happening to them and with them. Christ awakens them, because he alone has the power to end the world's sleep of death. The metaphor is meant above all to make clear the fact that what is important in the resurrection is the miracle of the awakening — as well as that we do not sink unexpectedly into a coma. That which happens to us then cannot be measured in terms of time any longer. For this reason there is no "interim" for the dead — this period of time, which has arisen out of concepts such as purgatory or the sleep of the soul (Calvin).[44]

What the resurrection will look like hardly interests Luther, though. The experience of *Anfechtung* has long driven out any spiritualism. Luther's detailed (and occasionally redundant) exegesis of the passage 1 Corinthians 15:35-49 — the miracle of the new creation — can be summarized as follows: You cannot have an adequate conception of how wonderful it will be — actually, you can't imagine it at all![45] And: Look around you, look at your gardens,[46] they are an eloquent witness to that which God can create, they are signs of hope for you, who are so quick to lose hope.

The resurrection of the body? At least since Augustine this phrase of the Creed has engendered great perplexity.[47] In Augustine's understanding, which is steeped in neo-Platonism, the resurrection begins in the here and now. The revived souls participate in eternal life. The theme of the resurrection of the body is retained, but it is a secondary

43. See Werner Thiede, "Luthers individuelle Eschatologie," pp. 28-33.

44. John Calvin, *Psychopannychia*, in *Opera quae supersunt omnia*, vol. 5 (Braunschweig: C.A. Schwetschke, 1834-1900), p. 33.

45. Cf. WA TR 3:276,26-27 (Nr. 3339; June-September 1533): "Als wenig die kinder wissen in mutterleib von ihrer anfart, so wenig wissen wir vom ewigen leben."

46. Sermon on 1 Cor. 15:35 on May 3, 1545, WA 49:72,9-10: "Quilibet homo in horto legit librum de resurrectione et testem et pignus resurrectionis."

47. Concerning that which follows see Reinhard Staats, "Auferstehung I/4. Auferstehung der Toten — Alte Kirche," in TRE, 4: 477.

theme, which does not uphold Christian hope. Later considerations concerning the state of the soul after death arise out of this coexistence, also as contrasted with the resurrection of the dead and the last judgment.

There is hardly a trace of this left in Luther. Luther rejected the teaching concerning the immortality of the soul as dogmatized in the bull *Apostolici regiminis* of the Fifth Lateran Council (December 19, 1513).[48] Nevertheless he thought that body and soul were separated at death and were reunited later.[49] In any case, human beings would be resurrected to wholeness: "the whole man shall live."[50] Resurrection is transfiguration, a new shaping of the whole person. On the phrase "resurrection of the flesh" Luther could thus comment in the Large Catechism that "it is awkward language"[51] because it makes one think of the butcher shop. For this reason Luther preferred "resurrection of the body." Whether this can be paraphrased as "completion of creation,"[52] seems questionable to me; occasionally Luther suggests that the new creation is incomparable to anything that we know based on nature and history.[53] Even though he was aware that the new creation comprises more than newly created human beings, he did not engage in any speculation about it.

We may lift our heads, because the breakthrough to the new life has already taken place: in our baptism into the death of Christ. Of that which to us appears to be an abiding in the vale of tears we cannot have a proper estimation. Under a different appearance this vale of tears is that which no longer has any power over us under Christ, and this will in time be made clear to us, as though coalesced in a time lapse.

48. DH, pp. 1440-41.

49. Ole Modalsli, "Luther über die letzten Dinge," in: *Leben und Werk Martin Luthers von 1526 bis 1546. Festgabe zu seinem 500. Geburtstag,* ed. Helmar Junghans, vol. 1 (Berlin: Ev. Verlagsanstalt, 1983), p. 335.

50. "der gantze mensch soll leben." WA TR 5:219,13-14 (Nr. 5534); LW 54:447; cited by Ole Modalsli, p. 335.

51. "nicht wol deudsch geredt." WA 30/I:191,13; BSLK 659,59; BC-T 418,60; BC 439,60.

52. Ole Modalsli, p. 344; Friedrich Beißer, *Hoffnung und Vollendung,* Handbuch Systematischer Theologie 15 (Gütersloh: Gütersloher Verlagshaus G. Mohn, 1993), pp. 73-76.

53. "das Gott werde uns thun, wie er verheissen hat, das er uns wolle aufferwecken und verkleren viel heller und schöner, denn itzt keine Creatur auff erden ist." WA 36:638,32-34; LW 28:175.

What dare we hope? We may hope that God will be faithful to those who are created anew in Christ. The fact that many will be lying deep under the earth and long will have decayed (Luther cannot paint it drastically enough)[54] — this need not dismay God. He is the God who creates life out of death, in that he swallows up death — as surely as God is God.[55] The God who awakened Jesus Christ from the dead is the God of the living, not of the dead. Yet this does not mean an exclusion of the dead. It is rather a promise of life with the creating and living God to the living and to the dead.

In an eleventh-century Strasbourg manuscript entitled *Mement mori* (Remember that you must die!) God is at the end requested:

Tu muozist uns gebin ten sin
Tie churzun wila so wir hie sin
Daz wir die sela bewarin
Wanda wir dur not hinnan sulen varn

You must give us a right understanding
For the short time that we are here
That we may preserve our souls
When out of distress we depart from here.[56]

For Martin Luther the time of human existence is not a period of preparation for eternal life, nor is it simply a period of testing, however much he has emphasized — and had to emphasize to be faithful to Scripture — that the decision concerning life with God is made now and not sometime in the future. In our lifetime the promise of life with God reaches us. For this very reason "this lifetime" is the space in which hope can grow, because it is held in the confidence in "life as such," for Jesus Christ, the Crucified, Resurrected, and Coming One embraces life. What has been experienced, suffered, done or left undone, in communion with him will perish nevermore.

54. For example in the sermon on 1 Cor. 15:51-55 on May 10, 1545, WA 49:728-29, esp. line 1: "in unehr, verweset, stinckt, verfaulet ut kein ass auff Erden etc."

55. "Unser herr Gott fragt nichts darnach, sed dicit: Tod, ich wil dich fressen, dein tod sein, quod vorasti, wil ich vivificare vel non ero deus." WA 36:531,13-14; LW 28:99.

56. *Tod und Unsterblichkeit: Texte aus Philosophie, Theologie und Dichtung vom Mittelalter bis zur Gegenwart*, vol. 1, *Von der Mystik des Mittelalters bis zur Aufklärung*, ed. Erich und Annemarie Ruprecht (Stuttgart: Urachhaus, 1992), pp. 18-19.

Luther and God's World

Luther on Vocation

KARLFRIED FROEHLICH

From Luther, Lutherans have a doctrine on vocation. Remember the point about any job, every occupation being equal and precious in God's sight, no matter how unglamorous or menial it may be? The assembly-line welder's job or the custodian's work is just as valuable and important as the pastor's counseling session or the U.S. president's daily schedule. From Luther's *Babylonian Captivity:*

> Therefore I advise no one to enter any religious order or the priesthood, indeed, I advise everyone against it — unless he is forearmed with this knowledge and understands that the works of monks and priests, however holy and arduous they may be, do not differ one whit in the sight of God from the works of the rustic laborer in the field or the woman going about her household tasks, but that all works are measured before God by faith alone.[1]

Vocation — is this really a doctrine? The Trinity, predestination, and the real presence of the entire Christ in the Lord's Supper are doctrines, but "vocation"? That is what the standard book on Luther's thought in this matter calls it: *Luthers Lära om Kalelsen.* It was written by the great Swedish theologian Gustav Wingren in 1942 and has been

1. LW 36:78; WA 6:541.

This article first appeared in *Lutheran Quarterly* 13 (1991): 195-207, under the same title.

translated into many languages. The English translator of Wingren's book rendered the Swedish title without referring to doctrine: *The Christian's Calling: Luther on Vocation.*[2] As George Lindbeck reminds us, however, "doctrine" is a linguistic phenomenon, a web of language that functions dynamically to express and develop the faith and self-understanding of the community in which it is operative by setting the parameters of acceptable speech for its members. So, perhaps Wingren's *Lära* (doctrine) may have a point. As Wingren says himself, he set out to describe "vocation" in the context of Luther's total theology; everything hangs together there. And this, of course, does have to do with a web of doctrine. This essay presents Luther's teaching on vocation in four steps: To begin with, we will examine the word and its meaning; we will then, more briefly, look at its importance for the self-understanding of every Christian, the self-understanding of the pastor and minister, and finally the self-understanding of a seminary.

Vocatio

"Vocation" is a Latin word, *vocatio,* derived from the verb, *vocare,* to call. The English equivalent would be the noun "call" or more precisely, "calling." If you look at a dictionary for equivalents, you find terms such as "occupation, profession, trade, work," perhaps even "job." What the meaning is seems therefore clear and unambiguous. Without being misunderstood, one could ask on a personnel questionnaire for a person's family name and a person's occupation or trade. Could you ask for a person's name and "calling"? It would not sound right. If you think of it, it sounds religious. The English word "calling," despite its clear secular meaning, has a definitely religious flavor! If I am describing my work or occupation as a "calling," then someone must have "called" me. But who? An inner voice? Perhaps God?

It is instructive to compare this odd situation with German, Luther's language. "Vocation" in German is *Beruf* — today a totally neutral word. There is no sense of religious overtones when it appears on a questionnaire: *Name, Vorname, Beruf.* It is the technical term for one's

2. Gustaf Wingren, *The Christian's Calling: Luther on Vocation* (Edinburgh: Oliver and Boyd, 1958).

regular work or occupation, nothing more. Strangely enough, that this is so has to do especially with Martin Luther. Linguists agree that it was Luther who created this meaning of the term through his bold theological move of equalizing the value of all work before God: works have nothing to do with salvation. They belong to our human existence in this world, a world where neighbors need our works, not in the world beyond. Luther prepared the way for the total secularization of the term, which is simply a fact today.

When he used the word with this new meaning, Luther thought he was translating a biblical term: *klesis* (Greek), from *kaleo,* to call. It occurs eleven times in the New Testament, almost exclusively in Paul and the Pastoral Epistles. "Consider your *klesis,* brothers and sisters; not many of you were wise by human standards" (1 Cor. 1:26); or: "the gifts and the *klesis* of God are irrevocable" (Rom. 11:29). The meaning is quite clear: "*Klesis,*" "calling," refers to the call from God that has made a person a child of God, a Christian. Paul connects it with God's election and the spiritual gifts, the *charismata; klesis* has to do with conversion and the transition from a false to the true, saving religion. The most interesting case is 1 Corinthians 7:20. In this chapter, Paul gives advice on questions of Christian living that were posed to him by the Corinthians. He does so in an eschatological framework, that is, under the expectation that Christ will return soon: "Let everyone remain in the *klesis* in which he or she was called." Paul gives this advice with an eye on several concrete issues: should one seek, or try to undo, circumcision now? Should a slave seek freedom now? Should a person marry now? Unfortunately, the sentence is ambiguous. One could read: "Let everyone remain in the calling (of God) *by* which he/she was called"; or "Let everyone remain in the calling (meaning the external condition) *in* which he/she was called." Luther translated *klesis* here, and only here, as *Beruf;* he read it in the second sense, understanding it as an external condition, and this is quite clear from his rendering of a parallel that he found in Sirach 11:20-21. He translates: "Remain in God's Word and stay in your *Beruf.* . . . Trust in God and stay in your *Beruf,*" where the Greek has *ergon* (work) and *ponos* (toil). Luther may have pressed Paul too far, making 1 Corinthians 7:20 a witness to *klesis* as *Beruf,* that is, as an external condition. But his term was a polemical one, coined with a contemporary edge to protest against the concept of higher and lower callings in the Roman church, the presupposition of all forms of monasticism. Luther's "doctrine" of vocation, if it was one, belonged in the context of his rejection of monasticism.

To help us situate Luther's teaching on vocation within the context of his critique of monasticism, a little history is in order. "Vocation" (*vocatio*) was the Latin equivalent for Paul's *klesis*, God's calling of people to become Christians. After Constantine, by the end of the fourth century, everyone was (or was supposed to be) a Christian by imperial decree and was baptized as an infant. How do you become a Christian when you and everyone else around you already is one — never mind that most people's Christianity did not go very deep when it was just the civil religion of the realm? It is no wonder that the fourth century saw not only the conversion of the Roman Empire but also the first flowering of monasticism, the movement of people who wanted to be serious Christians at a time of lowered standards. Their argument was clear: Christ challenged his disciples to be "perfect." He gave general commands for every Christian such as "love God and neighbor," but he also gave special "counsels" to those who wanted more: The counsel of absolute poverty ("Go sell what you own" Matt. 19:21); the counsel of total renunciation of marriage ("there are eunuchs who have made themselves eunuchs for the sake of the kingdom of heaven" Matt. 19:12); the counsel of obedience — obedience to the Sermon on the Mount, which Christians understood as the marching orders of the true *militia Christi*. Now, this was the foundation of monasticism. Poverty, chastity, and obedience became the basic vows of monks and nuns upon entering the monastery. Monks and nuns followed a higher calling. They opted for a Christian way apart from and above the crowd.

Under these circumstances, basic terms that applied to all Christians originally underwent a decisive narrowing of their meaning. After the fourth century, "to convert" meant to leave the world and embrace the monastic "vocation"; the term "vocation" itself now referred exclusively to the divine call to the monastic "profession," and "profession" was now the word for the solemn act of taking the monastic vows. Most tellingly, "religion" no longer meant the totality of the Christian faith or other faiths but served simply as the technical term for monasticism. Hard to believe? When I was visiting St. John's Abbey at Collegeville, Minnesota, a couple of years ago, the abbot reported that they had "a slight rise of vocations recently"; he meant candidates for the community. And when you don't want to say that an acquaintance is a "monk" or "nun," what *do* you say? You say: "He or she is a religious." Monasticism *is* religion.

This is what Luther reacted against. He rejected the idea of a better, holier, more God-pleasing way of salvation than that which applied to all. He rejected the double standard of commands and counsels. He himself had opted for the harder, "higher" way, but in pushing its promise to the limit, had learned not only that it did not deliver on the promise, but that it was a wrong idea. His insight into justification by faith alone taught him that there are not two levels of salvation or two classes of Christians.

The final clarification of his thought on monastic vocations came with his treatise, *On Monastic Vows,* of October 1521. Luther wrote it during his time out at the Wartburg Castle when word reached him that colleagues at Wittenberg were getting married and confreres were leaving his monastery. The pastoral intention of instructing and strengthening the consciences of people like this appears in the title already. At issue was not the monastic lifestyle. Luther himself did not leave the monastery — quite literally. He continued to live in the Augustinian Friary on the east side of Wittenberg to the end of his life; his prince gave him the building as a gift after he got married. The Christian, he explained, justified and sinner at the same time, was perfectly free to choose a life in community, even a life of poverty and celibacy. The problem was the vows. Luther states the problem this way:

> No one can deny that the command to offer vows was instituted by divine authority. Scripture says, "Make your vows and keep them" [Psalm 76:11], so there is no point in disputing whether a vow may be offered. What we are trying to show is how to distinguish one vow from another and recognize which vows are godly, good, and pleasing to God. Only these must be considered as vows. They are named and demanded in Scripture. Further, we are trying to show how we may distinguish which vows are ungodly, evil, and displeasing to God, vows which would not otherwise be regarded as vows.[3]

Thus, the problem was not even "vows" as such — if vows are made before God, they must be kept. But they must be true vows, vows according to the will of God. Monastic vows, his own included, were not. They

3. LW 44:252; WA 8:577.

contradicted everything we know about God's will: the universality of God's promise of salvation, salvation by faith alone, Christian freedom, reason (monastic vows demanded what no young person could reasonably promise), and finally the ten commandments, especially the fourth: "Honor your father and mother." Luther dedicated the treatise to his father Hans Luther, who had strongly opposed young Martin's decision to become a monk; in the dedication letter he asked his father's forgiveness for his, the son's, willful violation of the commandment.

It was in the sermons of this period that Luther spelled out his new notion of *Beruf*. One's *Beruf* was not something special, but something down-to-earth, something exercised right in the world of everyday work and toil. It was the word for the Christian's calling, wherever exercised, as an act of faith active in the love of God and neighbor. In a Christmas sermon, he reflected on the shepherds:

> Christian liberty is not tied to any specific work. On the contrary, all works are the same to a Christian, no matter what they are. These shepherds do not run away into the desert, they do not don monk's garb, they do not shave their heads, neither do they change their clothing, schedule, food, drink, nor any external work. They return to their place in the fields to serve God there.[4]

He made the same point in his interpretation of Jesus' curt answer to Peter's question about the beloved disciple after the resurrection (John 21:21f.). Peter had asked: "Lord, what about him?", and Jesus answered: "If it is my will that he remain until I come, what is that to you?" Luther paraphrased:

> Do you think, Peter, that I want the same from you as I want from him? No, it is not this way. You keep to your own task and wait for what I tell you. He will find out about his task as well. I desire many different servants, and they will not all have the same work to do.[5]

4. LW 52:37; WA 10/1/1:137.
5. WA 10 I/1:307,9-12.

The Vocation of Every Christian

It is easy to see how strongly this exegesis is influenced by Luther's conviction about the priesthood of all believers, or of all the baptized, as the Evangelical Lutheran Church in America prefers to say these days. With this, we are in the middle of point two already: the importance of vocation for the self-understanding of every Christian. Luther regarded the priesthood of all the baptized as a thoroughly biblical doctrine, taught in the New Testament as well as in the Old: "Like living stones, let yourselves be built into a spiritual house, to be a holy priesthood, to offer spiritual sacrifices acceptable to God through Jesus Christ," as the baptismal homily in 1 Peter 2:5 puts it. With his new definition of "vocation," Luther calls us back behind a two-tiered Christianity of monastics and non-monastics, perfect and less perfect, spiritual and secular Christians, and back to the early Christian *klesis,* the understanding that all have a calling from God, regardless of their station and condition in society. The distinction of a higher, spiritual sphere from a secular was the first wall of Romanism that had to be torn down according to his *Appeal to the Ruling Class of German Nationality,* one of the three great Reformation tracts of 1520. Grounding his argument in Paul's first letter to the Corinthians, Luther writes:

> It is pure invention that pope, bishop, priests, and monks are called the spiritual estate while princes, lords, artisans, and farmers are called the temporal estate. This is indeed a piece of deceit and hypocrisy. Yet no one need be intimidated by it, and for this reason: all Christians are truly of the spiritual estate, and there is no difference among them except that of office. Paul says in 1 Corinthians 12[:12-13] that we are all one body, yet every member has its own work by which it serves the others. This is because we are all Christians alike; for baptism, gospel, and faith alone make us spiritual and a Christian people.[6]

But note well: In tearing down this wall, Luther did not eliminate priests or do away with the priesthood. Instead he eliminated the laity! All are holy, all are spiritual and have a special call from God to faith

---

6. LW 44:127; WA 6:407.

and witness, the call to do whatever they do in church and society as priests of the Most High:

> Therefore, just as those who are now called "spiritual," that is, priests, bishops, or popes, are neither different from other Christians nor superior to them, except that they are charged with the administration of the word of God and the sacraments, which is their work and office, so it is with the temporal authorities. They bear the sword and rod in their hand to punish the wicked and protect the good. A cobbler, a smith, a peasant — each has the work and office of his trade, and yet they are all alike consecrated priests and bishops. Further, everyone must benefit and serve every other by means of his own work or office so that in this way many kinds of work may be done for the bodily and spiritual welfare of the community, just as all the members of the body serve one another [1 Cor. 12:14-26].[7]

However, Luther fought on two fronts. Many people took his message of Christian freedom under God's call to radical consequences in political and societal life, to which he reacted with fear and apprehension. He called them *Schwärmer,* Enthusiasts, and developed against them his doctrine of the *Zwei Reiche,* the two kingdoms or realms, one of the most embattled pieces of the Lutheran heritage. Yes, there is one God, Lord and Ruler of all, but in this world, where saints are still sinners, the divine rule is not experienced in one way only. For humans, God's wrath is as real as God's mercy. God rules differently as creator and redeemer; he governs people in two ways — his "proper" way of giving freely, and his "strange" way of demanding sternly: gospel and law, distinct but never separated. Apply this tension to our self-understanding of being called by God regardless of our station or occupation, and the importance of "vocation" becomes clear: The "two kingdoms or realms" cut right through every Christian's heart and experience. As sinners, we experience our secular occupations negatively as a self-inflicted discipline (Luther calls it "mortification"), a burden that must be endured. As justified children of God, we experience them as transformed into divine vocations in the service of neighbor. And this existential dialectic is a reality, not a choice.

7. LW 44:130; WA 6:409.

The Vocation of the Pastor

This brings us to our third point, the importance of "vocation" for the pastor and minister. Pastors would not blink at the questionnaire asking for their "name, given name, and calling." Yes, they have a calling in the true sense of the English word. Theirs is not just an "occupation, trade, or profession." They are not in it for worldly gain: not for money (have you looked at salary scales recently?); not for status (the clergy sign behind your windshield will hardly spare you that parking ticket); and certainly not for power (has your clergy association's protest had much effect?). Rather, they know that *God* has called them in one way or another. Many pastors and probably many who are seeking ordination have a vivid sense of a personal call to this ministry, which you tend to compare to the biblical call of prophets and disciples. God told you: This is what I want you to do, and you are doing it. I think this personal conviction is a precious gift, not only to yourself, but to the church, and must not be taken lightly.

Luther understood the pastoral ministry as the ministry of Word and sacrament, God's *external* means of grace. As such, they are not at our personal disposal. From this angle, he had a natural distrust of claims that a person had God's immediate call to this vocation. He always exhorted future pastors to test their calling. This may still be a good idea in our time. Luther would suggest starting where he started: with the troubled conscience. Do you know this phenomenon? Have you ever asked the question whether you really should inflict yourself with all your foibles and wrinkles on an unsuspecting congregation? If this is a serious question for you, there is only one solution apart from sustained prayer: stop applying just your own discernment process. Ask others. Seek out the discernment of your brothers and sisters in the smaller and larger context of your church.

This side of the test is stressed by the Augsburg Confession. Article 5 does not speak of pastors being personally called by God to preach the Word and administer the sacraments. Without any reference to persons, it speaks of God having "instituted the office of Ministry, that is, provided the Gospel and the sacraments." And when Article 14 finally does come around to mentioning the persons in this ministry, it insists only that "nobody should preach publicly in the church or administer the sacraments unless he or she is regularly called." "Called" here does

not mean "called by God" but by human authority, and "regularly"
means that certain set procedures of communal discernment apply.
For the Augsburg Confession as for Luther, the "vocation" of pastors
like any *Beruf* is first of all work in this world for others, and in this case
on behalf of others who also are called to be priests in their various occupations and, because they cannot hold two *Berufe,* must call a suitable person to do this central work of God for and among them, so
that it may be done for all people everywhere. What Luther says of every
Christian applies quite poignantly to the pastor:

> We have a double vocation, a spiritual and an external. The spiritual
> vocation is that we have all been called through the Gospel to bap-
> tism and the Christian faith. . . . this calling is common and similar
> for all. . . . The other contains a differentiation: It is earthly, though
> also divine.[8]

The Vocation of a Seminary

There is not much time left to address the fourth point at any length:
The importance of vocation for the self-understanding of the seminary. Seminaries are a peculiarly American phenomenon. Under the
circumstances of life in the colonies and the early years of the United
States, seminaries were founded by churches for the purpose of training the much-needed pastors and ministers for pastoral vocations in
the new congregations. In this sense, seminaries are clearly "vocational
schools." We do not like this label. In today's hierarchy of educational
institutions, vocational schools do not rank high. They are the places
where one learns the practical skills necessary to ply a trade or engage
in a specific occupation, and learning in such institutions is largely by
doing. A student once reported a remark that a simple soul in his
hometown made to him only half-jokingly. It illustrates this kind of
perception with regard to seminaries: "Oh, you are attending seminary!
Isn't that the place where you compose and memorize the five hundred
sermons you will have to preach?"

Seminaries are surely more than that. Many seminaries like to

8. WA 34/II:300,306.

think of themselves as "professional" schools. During the late 1960s there was much discussion in the American Association of Theological Schools of a proposed "Curriculum for the Seventies." Those were the heydays of the "Pastoral Theology Movement," and the curriculum was designed to transform theological education into professional education like medicine and law, complete with hands-on training and a D.Min. as the first professional degree. After all, ministry is a "helping profession," is it not? The initiative failed, fortunately. It built on the sheer hope of change in practice at the expense of solid heritage in theology. I think it is time that seminaries, especially in the Lutheran orbit, reaffirm their identity as vocational schools in the proper sense. There will have to be training in practical skills for the *Beruf* of a pastor. Much of this is already in place as a result of the experiments in the 1970s. But since, in Luther's understanding, vocation involves *God's* call in every work we do, this training must involve an "academic" component, the concern for *"God-speech,"* theology, the study and the science of God. In the Middle Ages, theology was launched as an intellectual discipline in and with the "academy," the world of new schools and universities in the twelfth and thirteenth centuries. Its booster rocket was the Bible as the foundational document of the Christian faith and the questions this motley collection of writings was bound to raise in curious, and even not so curious, minds. Enthusiasm for a theo-logy nourished by the Bible as an integral part of all vocational training of pastors and ministers never diminished after those beginnings, from the efforts of Dominican and Franciscan teachers instructing Friar Preachers in their study halls to the apprenticeships of pastoral candidates in the parsonages of colonial New England, and the makeshift training schools of pastors in the Confessing Church in Nazi Germany. Where ministry is ministry of the *Word,* its biblical basis requires theological learning. Seminaries must be centers of such learning.

This necessary emphasis on theology and learning, including the study of biblical languages, the details of history, and the material of the doctrinal heritage is an important asset for another task of seminaries as vocational schools: helping future pastors and ministers to test their vocation. By seriously tackling these routines, students will find out whether they are really up to the kinds of demands that will be imposed on them by the calling they have perceived. If they realize that these exercises are not for them, there is nothing wrong with leaving seminary. In his critique of monasticism, Luther fought for the freedom to leave, not the freedom to enter the monastery. The concept of vocation as an expression of the priesthood of all the baptized allows anyone to serve God's call with his or her specific charism elsewhere in a full-time ministry of the church or even in a different kind of occupation.

Finally, seminaries in the Lutheran orbit have an inherent obligation to invite *all* members of the universal priesthood into their preoccupation with *theo-logy,* which is part of any Christian's work considered as vocation. Different from Luther's time, one of the greatest problems of the pastoral vocation today is the immense overload of expectation. The pastor of a congregation is supposed to be an expert in too many things; the job description requires too many different activities, and the list is still growing. Our church has tried to deal with this problem by redefining ministry more broadly and getting the tasks shared more widely. We have now multiple-rostered ministries that can indeed relieve the burden placed on what should be the one ministry of Word and sacrament. For the seminaries this cannot mean that they multiply professional tracks *ad infinitum* and only dissipate their energies. Clustering may be one of the ways to cope. But seminaries will have to strengthen even more their theological involvement because under these circumstances *theo-logy* will have to be offered to so many more participants in church work as members of the shared priesthood of the baptized. Without this indispensable "academic" element in which every Christian has a right and duty to be vocationally trained, a Christian's work would cease to be "vocation," "calling," and revert to what the dictionary calls an "occupation," a "trade," a "job" — nothing more.

Like other Lutheran churches, the Evangelical Lutheran Church in America has wrestled and continues to wrestle with these issues. The 1993 Churchwide Assembly adopted a substantial document on ministry, "Together for Ministry," which had been several years in the making. Its most conspicuous feature was the establishment of a diaconal ministry that is now in place. But this was only part of the content of a rich harvest of serious discussion. It seems regrettable to me to observe how fast the fruits of such intense and valid labors are forgotten. "Together for Ministry" did not give a central place to the topic of vocation. It focused on mission and service. There is, however, a section in which "vocation" plays a role. It occurs in the section on the pastoral call and ordination where the wider context is sketched out:

> God calls all Christians to a life of vocation. To have a vocation means to live out one's call. For Christians that call is answered in the structures of daily life — family, work, state, service to neighbor, care of creation — as the setting in which to live out their identity in the Gospel.[9]

These are clear and good words. They do not formulate a doctrine of vocation, but they reformulate in contemporary language a venerable tradition of Lutheran thinking about vocation, beginning with Luther.

---

9. Evangelical Lutheran Church in America, Division for Ministry, *Together for Ministry: Final Report and Recommendations of the Task Force on the Study of Ministry 1988-1993* (Chicago: Evangelical Lutheran Church in America, 1993), p. 16, para. III.

Luther on Poverty

CARTER LINDBERG

The topic "Luther on poverty" is not quite the proverbial exam question on the history of the universe with a few examples, but certainly is far too comprehensive and complex for a brief essay. Nevertheless, with a tweak on the venerable maxim "to sin boldly,"[1] I shall try to traverse the lush and intertwined terrains of Luther studies[2] and poverty studies.[3] I say intertwined because studies of the Reformation's influence

---

1. Authors, teachers, pundits, and other assorted folks like to (mis)use this much overworked phrase as a segue and attention-getter. Hence, being myself party to such, we ought to recall the whole phrase and its proclamation of justification by grace alone. In a letter of 1 August 1521 to Melanchthon written from the Wartburg, Luther discusses the unsettling theological issues being advanced in Wittenberg by Karlstadt, issues that would in the next months lead to the "Wittenberg Disturbances" of 1521-1522. "If you are a preacher of grace, then preach a true and not fictitious grace; if grace is true, you must bear a true and not fictitious sin. God does not save people who are only fictitious sinners. Be a sinner and sin boldly, but believe and rejoice in Christ even more boldly, for he is victorious over sin, death, and the world." WA Br 2:370-72; LW 48:281-82. See also LW 48: 12-13; WA Br 1:35,24ff. (8 April 1516).

2. The author of Ecclesiastes undoubtedly had Luther studies in mind when he wrote: "Of making of many books there is no end, and much study is a weariness of the flesh" (12:12). A good introduction to Luther's theology is Bernhard Lohse, *Luthers Theologie in ihrer historischen Entwicklung und in ihrem systematischen Zusammenhang* (Göttingen: Vandenhoeck & Ruprecht, 1995).

3. Poverty studies have mushroomed in recent decades. For overviews see the bibli-

---

This article first appeared in *Lutheran Quarterly* 15 (2001): 85-101, under the same title.

upon the early modern shift from charity to social welfare have been subject to both confessional theological inflation and deflation, and social-historical debunking. At the turn of the last century, the Lutheran scholar Gerhard Uhlhorn posited that Luther's theology facilitated early modern social welfare, whereas the Catholic scholars Georg Ratzinger and Franz Ehrle claimed the Reformation was ethically degenerate and that credit for the modern development of social welfare belongs to ancient and medieval Catholic theology and canon law. With a pox on both confessional houses, contemporary social historians argue that theological motivation was negligible, at best a cosmetic cover for economic and demographic factors.[4] These conflicts, while

---

ographies in Emily Albu Hanawalt and Carter Lindberg, eds., *Through the Eye of a Needle: Judeo-Christian Roots of Social Welfare* (Kirksville, Mo.: Thomas Jefferson University Press, 1994), pp. 215-45; and my *Beyond Charity: Reformation Initiatives for the Poor* (Minneapolis: Fortress, 1993), pp. 207-29. Recent pertinent studies include Bronislaw Geremek, *Poverty: A History* (Oxford: Blackwell, 1994); Ole Peter Grell and Andrew Cunningham, eds., *Health Care and Poor Relief in Protestant Europe 1500-1700* (London/New York: Routledge, 1997); Robert Jütte, *Poverty and Deviance in Early Modern Europe* (Cambridge: Cambridge University Press, 1994); Andreas Pawlas, *Die lutherische Berufs- und Wirtschaftsethik* (Neukirchen-Vluyn: Neukirchener, 1999); and Hans-Jürgen Prien, *Luthers Wirtschaftsethik* (Göttingen: Vandenhoeck & Ruprecht, 1992). The classic comprehensive study, although dated, remains the work stimulated by the nineteenth-century rise of the Lutheran diaconate and the Inner Mission: Gerhard Uhlhorn, *Die christliche Liebestätigkeit*, 3 vols. (2nd ed., Stuttgart: Gundert, 1895; reprint Neukirchen, 1959), pp. 1882ff. A study closely related to our topic is Ricardo Rieth, *"Habsucht" bei Martin Luther: Ökonomisches und theologisches Denken, Tradition und soziale Wirklichkeit im Zeitalter der Reformation* (Weimar: Böhlau, 1996); see also "Luther on Greed" in this volume.

4. For a review of the literature and arguments see my *Beyond Charity*, 9-13; "'There Should Be No Beggars Among Christians': Karlstadt, Luther, and the Origins of Protestant Poor Relief," *Church History* 46 (September 1977): 313-34; and Ole Peter Grell, "The Protestant Imperative of Christian Care and Neighborly Love," in Grell and Cunningham, pp. 43-65, especially p. 44: "Undoubtedly, the removal of religion from this scenario can to some extent be seen as a healthy reaction to the confessionally biased historiography which had characterized this field until the 1960s, but that this conclusion was reached by predominantly social historians, influenced by the radical cultural climate of the late 1960s, when the impact of neo-Marxism and economic explanations was strong, can hardly surprise. . . . That Otto Winckelmann's response to Ratzinger and Ehrle . . . has now been forgotten is perhaps understandable, but that the more recent articles by Harold Grimm and Carter Lindberg have been largely ignored is less excusable, even if Grimm and Lindberg are primarily concerned with Luther's influence and theological rationale for encouraging changes in poor relief."

beyond the scope of the present essay, are mentioned as a kind of historiographical caveat emptor for the reader as we look at Luther's understanding of poverty and what to do about it.

Poverty in Theological Perspective

The first point to remember in discussing any "Luther and . . ." topic is that he understood himself as a proclaimer of the good news that salvation is received not achieved. His understanding of justification by grace alone is a sharp break with the scholastic — and universally human — religion of achievement. As Luther affirmed in his theological testament, *The Schmalkald Articles,* our justification before God "must be believed and cannot be obtained or apprehended by any work, law, or merit."[5]

To be sure, Luther was a professional theologian in terms of his training and his academic position. He was thoroughly versed in the scholastic method of disputation and had no qualms about entering the academic arena with anyone. But, and this is a crucial but, his understanding of theology and ethics always had a pastoral focus.[6] Theology was not an intellectual game for the lecture hall, an application of science to the subject, "God." Rather, theology is for proclamation.[7] Not God in his absolute majesty, the "naked God," but God "clothed in His Word and promises" for us *(pro nobis)* is the subject of theology.

> God says: "I do not choose to come to you in My majesty and in the company of Angels but in the guise of a poor beggar asking for bread." You may ask: "How do you know this?" Christ replies: "I have revealed to you in My Word what Form I would assume and to whom you should give. You do not ascend into Heaven, where I am seated at the right hand of My heavenly Father, to give me something; no, I come down to you in humility. I place flesh and blood before your door with the plea: "Give me a drink! . . . I do not need food in

5. BC 301; BC-T 292; BSLK 415. See William R. Russell, trans., *The Schmalkald Articles* (Minneapolis: Fortress Press, 1995), pp. 5-6.

6. In his article on poverty Gerhard Krause asserts that Luther's social ethics in relation to economics reflected his pastoral responsibility for the poor. "Armut," *Theologische Realenzyklopädie* 4 (1979): 99.

7. See Gerhard Forde, *Theology Is for Proclamation* (Minneapolis: Fortress, 1990).

heaven. I have come all the way from Judea. Give me a drink! I have had it announced to all the world that whatever is done to the least of My brethren is done to me" (Matt. 25:40).[8]

Luther, therefore, approached the topic of poverty not as an economist, sociologist, or politician, but as a theologian proclaiming God's promise and judgment.

> Let no one, therefore, ponder the Divine Majesty, what God has done and how mighty He is; or think of man as the master of his property, the way the lawyer does; or of his health the way the physician does. But let him think of man as sinner. The proper subject of theology is man guilty of sin and condemned, and God the Justifier and Savior of man the sinner. Whatever is asked or discussed in theology outside this subject is error and poison.[9]

This meant that his orientation to social issues was not in the mode of the Aristotelian (and modern!) progress from vice to virtue.[10] In short, service to the neighbor does not depend upon its results, upon progress or success, but upon God's promise. Faith active in love is not naïve — remember, "man the sinner" — but liberating. "From Christ the good things have flowed and are flowing into us. . . . From us they flow on to those who have need of them. . . ."[11]

In a moment we shall see how Luther's theology liberated poor relief from its medieval strictures. But first we must note that Luther viewed the flow of goods to the needy through the lens of the dialectic of law and gospel. The significance of this dialectic cannot be overestimated, for the right knowledge of theology depends upon it.[12] Luther

---

8. LW 22:519-20; WA 47:222,21-42.

9. LW 12:311-12; WA 40/2:327,36-328,19. See Oswald Bayer, *Theologie,* Handbuch Systematischer Theologie, 1 (Gütersloh: Gütersloher Verlagshaus, 1994), pp. 35-42, and "Martin Luther" in C. Lindberg, ed., *The Reformation Theologians* (Oxford: Blackwell, forthcoming).

10. The usual discussion of Luther's break with Aristotelian-influenced scholasticism focuses on movement from sin to sanctification. My point here is that this discussion is directly relevant to social ethics. See my "Do Lutherans Shout Justification But Whisper Sanctification?" *Lutheran Quarterly* 13 (Spring 1999): 1-20.

11. LW 31:371; WA 7:69,3,5.

12. WA 7:502,34f.: "Next to knowledge of the whole of Scripture, the knowledge of the whole of theology depends upon the right knowledge of law and gospel."

never separated law and gospel, but always retained their dialectical relationship. Theologically, the law functions to reveal sin and drive the sinner to God. But in the realm of civil society God's law functions to restrain evil and promote the common good. An essential tool for this constructive social activity is reason. We tend to remember in this context Luther's colorful statement that reason is "the devil's whore." What he meant by that phrase is the displacing of revelation by speculation, that is, the striving to ascend to God by reason, to try to fathom God in his majesty.[13] In relation to the building of society, however, "reason is the most important and the highest rank among all things. . . . It is the inventor and mentor of all the arts, medicines, laws, and of whatever wisdom, power, virtue, and glory men possess in this life."[14] For Luther social ethics, good works, are not salvatory, but they do serve the neighbor. Since works are not ultimate but penultimate activities of the sinner saved by the justifying God, they are this-worldly rather than other-worldly, directed to the neighbor rather than to God. Works are a response to God's promise; a response that flows from faith active in love; from worship. Thus Luther's social ethics are aptly described by the phrase "the liturgy after the liturgy." "Now there is no greater service of God [dienst gottis; Gottesdienst = "worship"] than Christian love which helps and serves the needy, as Christ himself will judge and testify at the Last Day, Matthew 25[:31-46]."[15] "The world would be full of worship (Gottesdienst) if everyone served his neighbor, the farmhand in the stable, the boy in school, maid and mistress in the home."[16]

13. The contrast between Luther and medieval theology, both scholastic and mystical, may be diagrammatically conceived. For Luther, God descends to the sinner: "Christ cannot be dragged too deeply into the flesh." For medieval theology and piety, the sinner is to ascend to God: hence the widespread image and metaphor of the ladder to heaven. See Margaret Miles, "Staying Is Nowhere: Ascent," ch. 4 in The Image and Practice of Holiness (London: SCM, 1988); and Christian Heck, L'Échelle Céleste dans l'Art du Moyen Âge: Une Histoire de la Quête du Ciel (Paris: Flammarion, 1997). Luther criticized the Turks, Jews, and papacy for prescribing "heavenward journeys on which the travelers will break their necks." LW 22:334; WA 47:61,10ff.

14. LW 34:137; WA 39/1:175,9-10. See also Bayer, "Martin Luther."

15. LW 45:172; WA 12:13,26-28. The phrase "liturgy after the liturgy" comes from Orthodoxy. See Myra Blyth, "Liturgy after the Liturgy," The Ecumenical Review 44, no. 1 (January 1992): 73-79, and my essay "Luther's Concept of Offering," Dialog 35, no. 4 (Fall 1996): 251-57.

16. WA 36:340,12-16; LW 51:259-87. Cited by Prien, Luthers Wirtschaftsethik, p. 145.

These theological convictions informed Luther's response to the endemic poverty of his medieval context.

Medieval Poverty and the Poor

The medieval understanding of poverty accommodated itself to the changing socio-economic conditions accompanying the shift from feudal relations to the early profit economy.[17] The red thread running through changing views was the view that almsgiving (charity; *caritas*) — bluntly put — could purchase paradise.[18] Major biblical warrants for this conviction came from the apocryphal writings of Tobit (4:9-11; 12:9) and Sirach (Ecclesiasticus). The latter provided the key themes that almsgiving atones for sin (Ecc. 3:30) and that poverty itself may prevent sinning (Ecc. 20:21). The theological focus was thus upon the almsgiver, not the receiver. Alleviation of physical need remained "second to the main priority, namely the salvation of the souls of both donor and receiver."[19]

Even a weak hermeneutics of suspicion may detect a potential ideology of poverty that with the rise of the profit economy could function as a way to maintain people on the physical and economic margins, thereby creating a cheap labor pool. This ideology was further strengthened by the long-standing conviction that poverty is the preferred status for Christians (God's "preferential option for the poor"). After all, "it is easier for a camel to go through the eye of a needle than for someone who is rich to enter the kingdom of God" (Matt. 19:24; Mark 10:25; Luke 18:25). The poor therefore, as necessary "objects" for almsgiving served the soteriological (and economic!) interests of the rich. Thus it seemed to the well-off that you *can* take it with you. Augustine himself suggested a kind of "higher hedonism" when he said

17. For a discussion of these developments in relation to the "rich" vocabulary for poverty and the poor, see Michel Mollat, *The Poor in the Middle Ages*, trans. Arthur Goldhammer (New Haven: Yale University Press, 1986), pp. 1-11; Jütte, *Poverty and Deviance,* pp. 8-21; and Lester K. Little, *Religious Poverty and the Profit Economy in Medieval Europe* (Ithaca, N.Y.: Cornell University Press, 1978).

18. Joel Rosenthal, *The Purchase of Paradise: Gift Giving and the Aristocracy, 1307-1485* (London/Toronto: Routledge/University of Toronto Press, 1972).

19. Grell, "Christian Care," p. 48.

the poor carry our alms to heaven "where we shall not lose them."[20] This orientation was institutionally structured by monasticism in general and by the Franciscan and Dominican mendicant movements in particular. A consequence was church-sanctioned begging by monks and anyone else whether needy[21] or opportunistic.

Luther's Response to Medieval Almsgiving

The widespread poverty, vagrancy, and underemployment of the late medieval period was legitimated by the church's ideology of poverty and exacerbated by the new economic developments. The schema of salvation that presented poverty as the ideal Christian life and anchored it in society through the promises of earthly and heavenly rewards due the almsgiver kept people from recognizing and therefore from changing the social structures causing poverty.

Luther's doctrine of justification cut the nerve of this medieval ideology of poverty. Since salvation is a gift of God apart from human works, both poverty and almsgiving lose saving significance. By despiritualizing poverty, the Reformers could recognize poverty in every form as a personal and social evil to be combated. Justification by grace alone through faith alone effected a paradigm shift in the understanding of poverty and the poor. Poverty is no longer seen as the favored status of the Christian, but rather a social ill to be ameliorated even if it cannot be ultimately cured.

20. *The Fathers of the Catholic Church,* vol. 11 (Washington, D.C.: Catholic University Press, 1963), p. 268. For a fuller explication see my *Beyond Charity,* pp. 22-33, and passim.

21. There is now a wealth of material on the medieval and early modern marginalized and their conditions. See for example: Bronislaw Geremek, *Les fils de Caïn: L'image des pauvres et des vagabonds dans la littérature du xve au xviie siècle* (Paris: Flammarion, 1991); Bernd-Ulrich Hergemöller, ed., *Randgruppen der spätmittelalterlichen Gesellschaft* (Warendorf: Fahlbusch, 1994); Wolfgang von Hippel, *Armut, Unterschichten, Randgruppen in der Frühneuzeit* (München: Oldenbourg, 1995); Robert Jütte, *Abbild und soziale Wirklichkeit des Bettler- und Gaunertums zu Beginn der Neuzeit* (Köln: Böhlau, 1988); F. Irsigler and A. Lassotta, *Bettler und Gaukler, Dirnen und Henker: Randgruppen und Aussenseiter in Köln 1300-1600* (Köln: Greven, 1984); and Bernd Roeck, *Aussenseiter, Randgruppen, Minderheiten: Fremde in Deutschland der frühen Neuzeit* (Göttingen: Vandenhoeck & Ruprecht, 1993).

Poverty, I say, is not to be recommended, chosen, or taught; for there is enough of that by itself, as He says (John 12:8): "The poor you always have with you," just as you will have all other evils. But constant care should be taken that, since these evils are always in evidence, they are always opposed.[22]

The poor are no longer the objects of meritorious charity, but neighbors to be served through justice and equity. "This means that in order to diminish need and injustice, structural changes have to be effected."[23] Under the rubrics of justice and love to the neighbor, i.e., the civil use of the law, Luther and his colleagues quickly moved in alliance with local governments to establish new welfare policies and legislation.

The first major effort was the Wittenberg Church Order of 1522 that established a "common chest" for welfare work. Initially funded by medieval ecclesiastical endowments and later supplemented by taxes, the Wittenberg Order prohibited begging; provided interest-free loans to artisans, who were to repay them whenever possible; provided for poor orphans, the children of poor people, and poor maidens who needed an appropriate dowry for marriage; provided refinancing of high-interest loans at 4 percent annual interest for burdened citizens; and supported the education or vocational training of poor children. The Wittenberg common chest was a new creation of the Reformation that transformed theology into social praxis. Its financial basis soon included sales of grain, public collections, and a primitive banking operation. These resources enabled it to exercise a broad spectrum of social welfare including care of the sick and elderly in hospitals, a medical office for the poor whose doctor, Melchior Fendt, established prophylactic measures in times of hunger and inflation, and support of communal schools and churches. The common chest also served early capitalist economic enterprises such as the rapidly expanding printing trade.[24] To the objection that social welfare was open to

---

22. LW 9:148; WA 14:657,30-32.

23. Prien, *Luthers Wirtschaftsethik*, p. 190. This of course did not replace personal concern for others. Luther, himself — often to Katie's consternation — was quite generous to others. See Eberhard Schendel, "Martin Luther und die Armen," *Lutherischen Kirche in der Welt* 36 (1989): 112-24, here 113-14.

24. For a detailed study of the Wittenberg common chest program, see Stefan Oehmig, "Der Wittenberger Gemeine Kasten in den ersten zweieinhalb Jahrzehnten

abuse, Luther replied, "He who has nothing to live should be aided. If he deceives us, what then? He must be aided again." Other communities quickly picked up these ideas. By 1523 there were common chest provisions for social welfare in the church orders of Leisnig, Augsburg, Nuremberg, Altenburg, Kitzingen, Strasbourg, Breslau, and Regensburg.[25]

These ordinances for poor relief were efforts to implement Luther's conviction that social welfare policies designed to prevent as well as remedy poverty are a Christian social responsibility. Under the motto "there should be no beggars among Christians," the early Reformation movement set about implementing concern for personal dignity and public alleviation of suffering.

It has been said that a key to the character of a society is how it treats its youth and its elderly. The intention of the Leisnig Order reveals what Luther and his colleagues had in mind:

> Poor and neglected orphans within the city and villages of our entire parish shall as occasion arises be provided with training and physical necessities by the directors out of the common chest until such time as they can work and earn their bread. If there be found among such orphans, or the children of impoverished parents, young boys with an aptitude for schooling and a capacity for arts and letters, the directors should support and provide for them. . . . The girls among the neglected orphans, and likewise the daughters of impoverished parents shall be provided by the directors out of the common chest with a suitable dowry for marriage.
>
> Those individuals . . . who are impoverished by force of circumstance and left without assistance by their relatives . . . and those who are unable to work because of illness or old age and are so poor as to suffer real need, shall receive each week on Sunday, and at other times as occasion demands, maintenance and support from our

seines Bestehens (1522/23 bis 1547)," *Jahrbuch für Geschichte des Feudalismus* 12 (1988): 229-69; 13 (1989): 133-79.

25. The "church orders," i.e., the legislation introducing the Reformation, are a rich but largely untapped resource for social as well as liturgical reforms. See E. Sehling, ed., *Die evangelischen Kirchenordnungen des XVI. Jahrhunderts*, 16 vols. (Leipzig/Tübingen, 1902-1913/1955-); and Gerta Scharffenorth, *Den Glauben ins Leben ziehen* . . . (München: Kaiser, 1982), pp. 114-18, 182-83.

common chest. . . . This is to be done out of Christian love, to the honor and praise of God, so that their lives and health may be preserved from further deterioration, enfeeblement, and foreshortening through lack of shelter, clothing, nourishment, and care, and so that no impoverished person in our assembly need ever publicly cry out, lament, or beg for such items of daily necessity.[26]

Grell points out that Luther's Wittenberg colleague, Johannes Bugenhagen, the writer of significant church orders for northern Europe, elaborated on the health care mentioned above. "For Bugenhagen health care provision became as essential a part of the proper Protestant church order as the reform of poor relief had originally been for Luther. The attention these issues received in Bugenhagen's church orders centered around four main points: baptism, midwifery, nursing and hospitals."[27]

While Luther's efforts to develop welfare legislation were well received in the cities and territories that accepted the Reformation, his efforts to encourage civic control of capitalism gained little support. Of course, it is hardly surprising that, when interest rates could soar to 40 percent, bankers turned a deaf ear to his call for a 4 to 5 percent ceiling on interest. Also, Luther's criticism of capitalism included far more than exorbitant interest rates. Social need always stood above personal gain. "[I]n a well-arranged commonwealth the debts of the poor who are in need ought to be cancelled, and they ought to be helped; hence the action of collecting has its place only against the lazy and the ne'er-do-well."[28]

Luther found that it is easier to motivate assistance to individuals than it is to curb the economic practices that create their poverty. Poverty's squalor calls out for redress, whereas the attractive trappings of business muffle criticism. Yet the effects of early capitalism could be felt. In Wittenberg between 1520 and 1538, prices doubled but wages remained the same. Luther called this murder and robbery in disguise.

26. LW 45:189-90; WA 12:25,31-26,7.
27. Grell, "The Protestant Imperative of Christian Care," p. 53. See pp. 53-60 for Grell's description of these four areas.
28. LW 9:243; WA 14:715,31-33.

How skillfully Sir Greed can dress up to look like a pious man if that seems to be what the occasion requires, while he is actually a double scoundrel and a liar.[29]

God opposes usury and greed, yet no one realizes this because it is not simple murder and robbery. Rather usury is a more diverse, insatiable murder and robbery. . . . Thus everyone should see to his worldly and spiritual office as commanded to punish the wicked and protect the pious.[30]

In his 1525 advice to the Town Council of Danzig, Luther stated that government regulation of interest should be according to the principle of equity. For example, a mortgage of 5 percent would be equitable, but it should be reduced if it does not yield this return. At the same time, one should consider persons. The well-to-do could be induced to waive a part of his interest, whereas an old person without means should retain it.

But these views were of minimal influence. Legislation was introduced in Dresden in 1529 that prohibited 15 to 20 percent interest in favor of a 5 percent rate. This in turn influenced the reform of the Zwickau city laws in 1539. Yet it was also noted then how often the Dresden legislation was violated.

That these examples may indicate more failure than success is confirmed by the 1564-1565 controversy in Rudolfstadt. The Lutheran pastor there refused to commune two parishioners who lived by "usury." The theological faculties of Wittenberg, Leipzig, and Jena were requested to give their opinions. They concluded against the pastor, who then had to leave town; and they did not recognize Luther as an authority on this issue.

After this, there was never again a serious effort to acknowledge Luther's position on usury. Luther's followers first ignored and then forgot his position against early capitalism. On the question of money, even Luther's followers thought he was too wild to follow. Yet, clearly, it is difficult to discuss poverty without discussing wealth or the poor without discussing the rich.

29. LW 21:183; WA 32:450,35-37.
30. WA 51:422,15-423,2.

Luther on Money

Medieval monasticism narrowed the spiritual asceticism of the early church to renunciation of the world. As mentioned earlier, poverty was idealized into a kind of spiritual capitalism for poor and rich alike. The poor were on the preferred path of salvation, and the rich earned merit for salvation by almsgiving. The foremost figure in the medieval poverty movement was certainly Francis of Assisi, whose rejection of money served to radicalize discipleship and to alleviate anxiety about the corrupting effect of money and business.

On Francis, Luther commented: "I do not think that Francis was an evil man; but the facts prove that he was naïve or, to state it more truthfully, foolish." His foolishness was in supposing that money was evil in itself, and in displacing the free forgiveness of sins through Christ by a new law of renunciation.

> If silver and gold are things evil in themselves, then those who keep away from them deserve to be praised. But if they are good creatures of God, which we can use for the needs of our neighbor and for the glory of God, is not a person silly, yes, even unthankful to God, if he refrains from them as though they were evil? For they are not evil, even though they have been subjected to vanity and evil. . . . If God has given you wealth, give thanks to God, and see that you make right use of it. . . .[31]

The problem is not money but its use. The greedy misuse the world by striving to acquire it; the monastics, by struggling to renounce it. The end result for both is personal insecurity because trust is placed in self-achievement rather than in God. Meanwhile, the neighbor is neglected.

Luther's response was unequivocal: "Many people, of both low and high estate, yes, all the world, were deceived by this pretense. They were taken in by it, thinking: 'Ah, this is something extraordinary! The dear fathers lead such an ascetic life. . . .' Indeed, if you want to dupe people, you must play the eccentric."[32]

It is of interest that Luther criticized not just monasticism but every effort to seek "extraordinary" works rather than living out the vo-

31. LW 2:327,331; WA 42:495,24-25 and 498,28-32.
32. LW 22:50; WA 46:579,14-20.

cation to which one is called. Luther's point is that we are to do what God commands, not what we fancy God would like. The temptation then and now is the desire to do "important" things rather than the mundane tasks attendant upon our place in the web of relationships that is our calling. Luther's point is that we are not called to self-chosen extraordinary tasks but to service in the world. "Vocation is the work of faith; vocation is worship in the realm of the world."[33] Indeed, daily work is the mask behind which God provides life's necessities.[34]

In his commentary on the Sermon on the Mount, Luther warns that the "monkery" of substituting our works for the commands of God can take all sorts of guises.

> In other words, monkery must remain as long as the world stands, although it may assume other names and new activities. Anyone who takes it upon himself to start something special that goes beyond faith and the common occupations is and remains a monk, though he may not affect the same manner or habit or bearing. Of course, it is easy to beware those who go around with cowl and tonsure; they have been described often enough for everyone to recognize them. But beware of the new monks. . . . [Who] make a pretense of great devotion and sanctity. . . .[35]

The medieval ideology of poverty had been entrenched for centuries, but the acceptance of the idea that money can make money was a relatively recent development with the rise of cities from the twelfth century on. Usury, the taking of interest where there is no production, had long been condemned. Already Pope Leo I in the mid-fifth century had stated that "taking interest is the death of the soul" (*Fenus pecuniae, funus est animae*), and usury had been prohibited by numerous councils from Lateran II (1139) to Lateran V (1515). But by

33. Vilmos Vajta, *Die Theologie des Gottesdienstes bei Luther* (Stockholm: Svenska Kyrkans Diakonistyrelses Bokförlag, 1952), p. 314. In a similar vein, Hans J. Hillerbrand speaks of the "doxology of the ordinary." Idem, "The Road Less Traveled? Reflections in the Enigma of Lutheran Spirituality" in Daniel N. Harmelink, ed., *Let Christ Be Christ: Theology, Ethics & World Religions in the Two Kingdoms* (Huntington Beach, Calif.: Tentatio Press, 1999), p. 142.

34. WA 31/1:437,7; LW 14:115; and LW 40:130; WA 18:112-13.

35. LW 21:259; WA 32:514,12-14.

all accounts, the entrepreneur was well established by Luther's time.[36]

Luther found the calculating entrepreneur extremely distasteful. He was convinced that the capitalist spirit divorced money from use for human needs and necessitated an economy of acquisition.[37] From his brief "Sermon on Usury" (1519) to his "Admonition to the Clergy that they Preach Against Usury" (1540), Luther consistently preached and wrote against the expanding money and credit economy as a great sin.

> After the devil there is no greater human enemy on earth than a miser and usurer, for he desires to be above everyone. Turks, soldiers, and tyrants are also evil men, yet they allow the people to live . . . ; indeed, they must now and then be somewhat merciful. But a usurer and miser-belly desires that the entire world be ruined in order that there be hunger, thirst, misery, and need so that he can have everything and so that everyone must depend upon him and be his slave as if he were God.[38]

In his Large Catechism, Luther wrote: "Daily the poor are defrauded. New burdens and high prices are imposed. Everyone misuses the market in his own willful, conceited, arrogant way, as if it were his right and privilege to sell his goods as dearly as he pleases without a word of criticism."[39]

This "lust for profits," Luther observed, had many clever expressions: selling on time and credit, manipulating the market by withholding or dumping goods, developing cartels and monopolies, falsifying bankruptcies, trading in futures, and just plain misrepresenting goods.[40] Such usury, Luther argued, affects everyone. "The usury which

36. Prien, *Luthers Wirtschaftsethik,* pp. 56-68. See also Jacques Le Goff, *Your Money or Your Life: Economy and Religion in the Middle Ages,* trans. Patricia Ranum (New York: Zone Books, 1988). Le Goff describes the development of the doctrine of Purgatory in relation to the rise of usury.

37. For a discussion of Luther's perceptive analysis of the powerful economic and social processes of his day, see Hermann Lehmann, "Luthers Platz in der Geschichte der politischen Ökonomie" in Günter Vogler, ed., *Martin Luther. Leben — Werk — Wirkung,* 2nd ed. (Berlin: Akademie Verlag, 1986), pp. 279-94.

38. WA 51:396,12.

39. BC 418; BC-T 397; BSLK 621.

40. LW 45:261-73; WA 15:304-5.

occurs in Leipzig, Augsburg, Frankfurt, and other comparable cities is felt in our market and our kitchen. The usurers are eating our food and drinking our drink." Even worse, however, is that by manipulating prices "usury lives off the bodies of the poor."[41] In his own inimitable style, Luther exploded, "The world is one big whorehouse, completely submerged in greed," where the "big thieves hang the little thieves" and the big fish eat the little fish.[42] Thus he exhorted pastors to condemn usury as stealing and murder, and to refuse absolution and the sacrament to usurers unless they repent.[43]

It is important to note that Luther's concern was not merely about an individual's use of money, but also the structural social damage inherent in the idolatry of the "laws" of the market. Ideas of an "impersonal market" and "autonomous laws of economics" were abhorrent to Luther because he saw them as both idolatrous and socially destructive. He saw the entire community endangered by the financial power of a few great economic centers. The rising world economy was already beginning to suck up urban and local economics, and to threaten an as yet unheard of opposition between rich and poor. He saw an economic coercion immune to normal jurisdiction that would destroy the ethos of the community. This is why Luther considered early capitalism to constitute a *status confessionis* for the church,[44] in spite of the fact that many of his contemporaries thought he was tilting at windmills.

Luther believed that not only was the church called publicly and unequivocally to reject these economic developments, but also to develop a constructive social ethic in response to them. This social ethic developed social welfare policies and legislation, and called for public accountability of large business through government regulation. It is common to think of Luther as a Pauline theologian; true enough, but he and his colleague Johann Bugenhagen understood the relevance of Matthew 25:31-46. This text appears not only in Bugenhagen's church orders but also in Luther's exposition of the fifth commandment.

41. WA 51:417,11-17.

42. LW 21:180,221; WA 32:447-48; and WA 51:362; and LW 25:172; WA 56:189-90; and LW 13:60; WA 31/1:206,31f.; and LW 45:270; WA 15:312-13.

43. WA 51:367,10-368,16.

44. See Prien, *Luthers Wirtschaftsethik*, pp. 221-22, and Ulrich Duchrow, *Global Economy: A Confessional Issue for the Churches?* (Geneva: WCC Publications, 1987).

Therefore God rightly calls all persons murderers who do not offer counsel and aid to men in need and in peril of body and life. He will pass a most terrible sentence upon them in the day of judgment, as Christ himself declares. He will say: "I was hungry and thirsty and you gave me no food or drink, I was a stranger, and you did not welcome me, I was naked and you did not clothe me, I was sick and in prison, and you did not visit me." . . . What else is this but to reproach such persons as murderers and bloodhounds? For although you have not actually committed all these crimes, as far as you were concerned you have nevertheless permitted your neighbor to languish and perish in his misfortune.[45]

Conclusion

Luther's efforts to turn the early capitalist world upside down by insisting on government regulation of business and the remission of burdensome debts was countered by the powerful of his day. But it was not only Luther who was powerless. When Emperor Charles V made motions in the direction of stricter business controls, the Fugger banking house reminded him of his outstanding debts to them, and the mining monopolies claimed the right to act as they pleased. Luther was not utopian in these matters. He commented that the world cannot be without usury any more than it can be without sin, but woe to the person by whom it comes.

Nevertheless, throughout his career, Luther fought against what he saw as the two-sided coin of mammonism: ascetic flight from money and the acquisitive drive for it. His foundation for this battle was the great reversal of the gospel that a person's worth is not determined by what he or she does or does not possess, but rather by God's promise in Christ. Thus money is not the lord of life, but the gift of God for serving the neighbor and building up the community.

"There is nothing new under the sun," or as our Gallic friends say, "the more things change, the more they remain the same" are especially pertinent phrases in relation to poverty and the poor. In historical perspective, the statement that "the poor are always with us" is more than

45. BC 412; BC-T 391; BSLK 608-9.

a dominical cliché. The converse, "the rich are always with us," is equally true as is most recently evident in the lavish parties and contributions designed to influence political parties and representatives of government to enhance their privileges. The dark side of these incredible expenditures — in spite of touted reductions in welfare rolls — remains visible with those who have eyes to see. Perhaps at no time since the Great Depression is there such widespread homelessness and child poverty. Editorials and public figures condemn and exhort both "the system" and the "victims." Yet the poor remain with us. Nearly one in four American children live in poverty while the wealthiest 20 percent of Americans control 84 percent of the nation's wealth, and the incomes of the poorest 20 percent continue to shrink.[46]

In the medieval context of almsgiving and personal charity, Luther's understanding of justification was a paradigm shift that facilitated rational and secular approaches to poverty. Because salvation is the foundation rather than the goal of life, because salvation is received, not achieved, neither poverty nor almsgiving is meritorious before God. Poverty is not a peculiar form of blessedness but a social blight to be addressed by social means. While the common chest program cannot be simply repristinated in our day, the principles that informed it remain timely. Faith active in love embraced rational and legal structures for the well-being of the neighbor. Without denigrating personal concern for others, Luther's tracts and their enactment in church orders saw that the common good required government regulation of commerce and financial instruments. A recent example from Luther's homeland is the German government's effort to curtail below-market prices by international chain stores. Without price regulation the big fish eat the little fish, and then the big fish can do what they want. Counterexamples in our own context include deregulation (Firestone tires being a case in point) and privatization. The latter includes not only the effort to shift the responsibility for welfare from government to charity organizations (and their highly paid CEOs), including the churches, but also the moves to shift health care and elder care to private profit-making enterprises. For Luther, the government

46. *The Boston Sunday Globe,* 3 September 2000, sec. E4, report on the Columbia University study released in August 2000.

is to help the poor, the orphans, and the widows to justice, and to further their cause. . . . [T]his virtue includes all the works of righteousness: as when a prince or lord or city has good laws and customs; when everything is regulated in an orderly way; and when order is kept by people in all ranks, occupations, trades, businesses, services, and works, so that it is not said: "The people are without laws." For where there are no laws, the poor, the widows, and the orphans are oppressed. . . . And this is equally true of buying, selling, inheriting, lending, paying, borrowing, and the like. It is only a matter of one getting the better of another, robbing him, stealing from him, and cheating him. This happens most of all to the poor, the widows, and the orphans.[47]

47. LW 13:53; WA 31/1:200,11-16.

Luther on Greed

RICARDO WILLY RIETH

The typical starting point for academic research into Luther's thoughts on economics and ethics is his writings on usury from 1519/20, 1524, and 1540.[1] Certainly it is possible to learn much about the economic ideas of the Reformer through these writings. Yet this procedure limits the perspective in that it reduces considerably the range of documents to be examined. Luther also expressed his opinions on economic subjects in sermons, translations, lectures, letters, and "table talks." In this presentation of his concept of greed, we intend therefore to survey Luther's various writings, with special emphasis on the contrast between greed and faith.[2] Carter Lindberg proceeded the same way in his essay on a closely related topic, "Luther on Poverty," which offers a solid basis to the material presented here.[3]

What does "greed" mean in the writings of the Reformer? Luther

---

1. "Sermon von dem Wucher," WA 6:36-60; "Von Kaufshandlung und Wucher," WA 15:294-322; LW 45:245-310; "An die Pfarrherrn, wider den Wucher zu predigen," WA 51:331-424.

2. This essay represents a brief exposition of a larger work on the same theme: Ricardo Rieth, *"Habsucht" bei Martin Luther: Ökonomisches und theologisches Denken, Tradition und soziale Wirklichkeit im Zeitalter der Reformation* (Weimar: Böhlau, 1996).

3. See Carter Lindberg, "Luther on Poverty," *Lutheran Quarterly* 15 (Spring 2001): 85-101.

This article first appeared in *Lutheran Quarterly* 15 (2001): 336-51, under the same title.

spoke and wrote the words *geitz* in German, and *avaritia* in Latin. Considering the common usage of both words in the sixteenth century, it is possible to recognize two principal meanings: on the one hand, "to retain," "to maintain for him/herself," "to accumulate" (covetousness, avarice, to be avaricious); on the other hand, "wanting to have more" (greed, to be greedy). Both meanings were linked very closely in *geitz* and *avaritia* and their correlatives during the Reformation era. In Luther's case the meaning "wanting to have more" (to be greedy) is more frequent.[4] For this reason, we are using the English term "greed" here.

Not only linguistic differences but also opposing value judgments can impede a full understanding of Luther's usage of greed. Since the eighteenth century, especially under the influence of the classical political economy, greed with connotations of "personal interest," or "selfishness" was seen as a positive element of human behavior. Greed became a virtue of economic management. Although this affirmative view of greed is sometimes present in ancient and medieval thought, it represented an exception. Greed was normally seen as a negative quality or a bad behavior, irrational and unjust, as sin and addiction. Such was the predominant opinion at Luther's time.[5]

Greed in Luther's Biblical Interpretation

Luther developed his theological understanding of greed amid the challenges of his everyday experience, examining them in the light of his biblical interpretation. He studied Old and New Testament passages where specific Hebrew and Greek terms for greed appear. As well, he studied texts that he understood to involve greedy behavior in people or group relations and real situations. He critically and constantly revised the knowledge growing out of this exegesis and applied it to his writings, sermons, translations, and lectures. He found his hermeneutical guidelines for interpreting most of the passages on greed especially in the first, seventh, and ninth commandments in the Sermon on the Mount and in New Testament statements on greed as root of evil (I Tim. 6:10) and idolatry (Eph. 5:3, 5; Col. 3:5).

4. Cf. Rieth, *"Habsucht,"* pp. 74-78.
5. Rieth, *"Habsucht,"* p. 41.

Unbelief (incredulitas) as a Root of Injustice: Psalm 5:10 and 14:4

Interpreting Psalm 5:10 in his second *Lectures on the Psalms* (1519-1521), Luther strongly criticized greedy people and idolaters inside the church. He related the text to other Scripture testimonies, as Luke 20:47; Amos 4:1; and Isaiah 56:10-12. These impious masters do not point to God's way with their teaching, but maintain their self-interest under the appearance of serving God. The best interpretation for Psalm 5, according to Luther, comes from the situation of his own time, namely, the material exploitation of the people, mediated through the preaching of works righteousness by a complicit clergy.[6]

Writing about Psalm 14:4 on the occasion of his first *Lectures on the Psalms* (1513-1516), Luther early on raised the subject of idolatry. "Evildoers" are those who "eat up my people as they eat bread." Here, the greedy are judged as those who want to be admired for their good works and recognized as the salt of humanity. Faith, the true worship of God, however, is incompatible with greed. Greed should thus be understood as idolatry.[7] Some years later, in his second *Lectures on the Psalms,* Luther interpreted this text again. Especially the second part of the verse ("eat up my people as they eat bread") offers a description of greed that has to be related to unbelief and impiety. Based on these words, Luther presented a scathing criticism against the Roman church. With the words "they do not call on the Lord," the psalmist is pointing to unbelief as the origin of injustice caused by greed. The fact that God's name was not being invoked means that there is no trust in him as the maintainer and supporter of humankind and creation. The link to the critique against the Roman church comes when this text speaks in the first line about prophets devouring the people. Clergy in Luther's time were teaching doctrines and practices based on their greed, that is, they were exploiting the people. These people, for their part, living under such a bad influence, were being transformed from victims into authors of injustice.[8] Also in the German Bible Luther wrote marginal notes to verses 1 and 5 of Psalm 14,

---

6. Cf. WA 5:148,39–149,4.
7. WA 5:421,30-35.
8. WA 5:421,10–423,7.

pointing out the theme of unbelief *(Unglaube)* and its consequences for human behavior.[9]

Masking and Unmasking Greed and Idolatry: Ephesians 5:3-5

Luther considered crucial the Pauline connection between idolatry and greed. "The one who is greedy is an idolater" (Eph. 5:5). In a 1525 sermon on Ephesians 5:1-10, he affirmed that this passage forbids to Christians all forms of spoliation against their neighbor and all quarrels over material things. However, if something like this does happen, it should not be left without reprimand and prospects for improvement. In order not to defame the ecclesiastical ministry, the evangelical teaching should be freely maintained in the community.[10] The holiness of Christians has to be demonstrated through their practice. Even with all of their imperfections, they should daily desire a chaste existence without greed. Thereby is God praised and honored and the behavior of unbelievers improved.[11] Who does not confirm his faith through the fruits that it brings is in reality a heathen with a Christian name.[12] Paul's casting of greedy persons as idolaters demonstrates that the apostle was an enemy, above all, of the greedy. A greedy person only keeps money and goods according to his own interest, as if those things were a god. Instead of using it to support churches and schools, he prefers the ruin of both, the spiritual and secular governments. He places his certainty and confidence in money and not in the living God, who is responsible for his subsistence. Thus the circle inaugurated with greed and idolatry closes itself with unbelief.[13]

In the same sermon, Luther interpreted Ephesians 5:6 as the apostle's exhortation to unmask greed's face and the pretense of justice. The fact that people are exploited and the poor suffer constantly does not deter the greedy person since he considers his practice rational and necessary because of economic determinations.[14] Such greed

9. WA DB 10/I:138f.
10. Cf. WA 17/II:207,21-26.
11. WA 17/II:205,19-23.
12. WA 17/II:210,18f. Luther quoted here 1 Tim. 5:8.
13. WA 17/II:211,10-20.
14. WA 17/II:211,22-35.

causes God's wrath. Together with licentiousness it caused the flood. Other biblical texts (for example, Num. 25:18; 1 Cor. 10:8) also demonstrate God's stern intervention in such cases. Whoever does not confirm his faith by action is the equal of a heathen before God, a deserter of Christ and faith. In Luther's own time, God's wrath against greed manifested itself in forms of shortage, plague, war, and bloodshed.[15] Paul is really speaking here about people who do not consider greed to be sin. He is also thinking about people who are supposedly conscious of their sinful condition and recognize faith as indispensable to salvation, but ignore good works as the consequence of a living faith. Their lives are not marked by generosity, the opposite of greed, thus provoking God's wrath.[16]

Living Gospel against Greed and Idolatry: Matthew 6:24

Just hearing and repeating God's Word does not transform someone into a believer. The gospel is alive. It turns itself into acts of love and brings force and comfort to people. To be a Christian presupposes faith active in love. "Mammon" refers in this context to goods that people merely accumulate and do not use for their own subsistence. Someone who limits life's meaning to this aim does not really understand God's Word and kingdom, and lives under the influence of greed. True Christians, however, pray for "our daily bread" (Matt. 6:11) and are satisfied with their possessions. The words "to serve mammon" coincide with "greed, which is idolatry" (Col. 3:5). In Luther's opinion, the Gospels and Paul almost always put greed in particular (and not the other sins, like lust and wrath, which are also against God) in connection with idolatry.[17]

Virtue before the World, Sin before God: Isaiah 5:8

The words "Woe to you who add house to house" can in no way, according to the Reformer, be interpreted allegorically. In agreement with the

15. WA 17/II:212,1-12.
16. WA 17/II:212,13-22.
17. WA 17/I:414,7-12; 415,22-32.

testimony of Ephesians 5:3; Colossians 3:5; and Matthew 6:24, they were aimed against greed and have to be understood literally. Regarding greed, itself an idol against faith, God and the world have absolutely contrary judgments. The world does not punish it and indeed considers it a virtue.

Luther also pointed out in other contexts the importance of the historical sense of an Old Testament passage rather than an allegorical interpretation. In his introduction to Isaiah, first published in 1528, he described the prophet's action and preaching as combat against disobedience of the first commandment and against idolatry. The same orientation was adopted in the general introduction to the prophetic books.[18] To the readers of Isaiah he recommended the prior reading of 2 Kings and 2 Chronicles:

> For if one would understand the prophecies, it is necessary that one know how things were in the land, how matters lay, what was in the mind of the people — what plans they had with respect to their neighbors, friends, and enemies — and especially what attitude they took in their country toward God and toward the prophet, whether they held to his word and worship or to idolatry.[19]

In the same introduction, Luther wrote that Isaiah primarily denounced idolatry and only partly reprimanded other addictions, as greed, pride, and intemperance. Nevertheless, when interpreting specific passages, such as Isaiah 5:8, he saw idolatry and greed as very closely related. In his introduction, Luther wanted to develop the relationship of the prophet's message with the two fundamental themes of faith and sin against the first commandment. This was followed by the critique of greed as idolatry and not merely as a minor form of evil.[20]

Idolatry and Accumulation: Colossians 3:5

The identification of greed as idolatry in Colossians 3:5 moved Luther to highlight both in a very special way within the wide catalogue of sins

18. Cf. WA DB 11/I:6,27–10,7.
19. WA DB 11/I:16,21–26; LW 35:274.
20. Cf. WA DB 11/I:22,29–24,4.

presented in that text. This can be observed in a 1534 sermon on Colossians 3:17. Faith is not only related to what Christians say and hear, but also has to change itself into a form of good works and to improve. With this catalogue of sins the apostle was characterizing a mundane and carnal life, a life in opposition to existence in the Spirit. Further, this list characterizes the devil's kingdom. This sort of life could be expressed both in the spiritual sphere — through false doctrine, unbelief, contempt for the Word — and also in the carnal sphere — through greed.[21] The listed sins belong to the carnal sphere and, because of their crudeness, it is possible to identify and to condemn them solely by human reason.[22]

If Luther were to speak in full detail just on greed, his sermon would be much too long, he says, since it manifests itself in all professional categories and trades. In opposition to greed, a Christian person should live generously. This consists not only in liberality toward the neighbor, but also in being satisfied with all that is received from God and in being anxious rather for the goods of the kingdom of God.[23] One could never sufficiently describe how perfectly greed disguises itself as something beautiful, virtuous, correct, and honest. It seems normal to apologize for mammon's idolatry with the excuse of seeking personal and family subsistence — both necessary and ordered by God — and thus to disguise greed or anxiety for sinful wealth. This deception is so common and broadly shared in society that neither preachers nor authorities can combat it in an efficient way.[24]

Humanity's Devastation: Genesis 29–31

Laban's person and life show in an exemplary way, according to Luther, the repercussions of greed in human existence. Laban's behavior in relation to Jacob especially shows how deep the injustice practiced by a greedy person against his neighbor can be. While Jacob should be characterized as fair and saintly, Laban would represent exactly the oppo-

---

21. Cf. WA 37:368,11-369,29.
22. WA 37:370,31-371,1.
23. WA 37:372,1-8.
24. WA 37:372,14-373,11.

site, because of his greed. Genesis 31:1 should be read in connection with 1 Timothy 6:10. The text presents an authentic description of greed, a sort of combination of all sins. The example of Laban, someone who despised and exploited his own children, reveals the capacity of greed to destroy someone's individual humanity. In the same way, the very close bond between greed and idolatry is extremely important in Laban's case. Even Rachel's theft of Laban's household idols (Gen. 31:19) would have been appreciated by God, who in this way finally punished Laban. As an idolater he sinned against the first tablet of the law; as a greedy person, against the second.[25]

Golden Calf and Spoliation: *1 Corinthians 10:1-13*

According to Luther, Paul wrote these words concerning the Corinthians' idolatry, having in mind the practice of heathen cults. Although Luther's contemporaries could say they did not celebrate those cults, they could not say that they were not idolatrous. Idolatry unfortunately remains a current theme. Based on this text, Luther discussed two forms of idolatry, which he recognized in his own time: the one was the idolatry of false masters, who announce a false faith; the other was the idolatry of greedy people, examined in Luke 16 and Colossians 3:5. Scarcely anyone, among all social classes, would be able to declare freedom from the second form of idolatry. Nobody could claim, on the basis of Paul's delineation of Old Testament sins, to be better than the Jews. Greed was for Luther the "golden calf" (Exod. 32) of his time, which would be adored whenever the neighbor is exploited, even to produce a small profit. God would in no way, however, tolerate this "golden calf" but would punish the idolaters through the Turks or the papacy.[26]

Idolatry and Service to Mammon

Luther stressed that true service to God *(Gottesdienst)* starts only with faith. He understood "service to God" not merely in a narrow sense, as

25. See also WA 9:509,19; 579,13-30; 581,28-31; 583,4-26.
26. WA 49:540,16–542,11; 540,32–542,31.

liturgical activity (worship), but much more as faith's manifestation in all aspects of human life. Both forms of sin frequently appear as antagonistic forces in opposition to faith and to the true service toward God, especially in interpretations of the first commandment, the Sermon on the Mount, and classical Pauline passages on greed and idolatry — Ephesians 5:5; Colossians 3:5; and 1 Timothy 6:10.[27]

Explaining Psalm 136:2 ("give thanks to the God of gods"), Luther asserts that the Lord's recognition as the true God before all gods would prove those gods' nonexistence. In his time, such gods should be identified among greedy people. Luther's reading of Paul led him to this conclusion, because of the apostle's definition of greed as idolatry.[28]

Luther related all other commandments and their respective transgressions to the first commandment. For him sin is always contempt for God. This should be underlined especially in relation to greed as idolatry. The specific concern of the apostle about the sin of greed is clear, because of its preference — in distinction to other sins — for images and idols.[29] Moses, when explaining the first commandment (Deut. 6:1-13), demonstrated how someone disobeys it and the reasons for this disobedience. He mentioned in first place wealth and abundance, that is, according to Luther, mammon and greed. There are other texts in the Scripture also — like Baruch 3:17; 1 Timothy 6:10; and Colossians 3:5 — where greed appears in very close connection with sinning against the first commandment. The human heart lays its confidence on present things and not on the ones that are absent. Wealth's trust in mammon, by governing the heart, excludes faith and love. This is effectively forgetting the Lord. Moses understood the first commandment in the spiritual sense, that is, regarding trust in God over against the heart's idolatry and trust in the creatures.[30]

In explaining Isaiah 2:8 ("Their land is full of idols"), Luther pointed out that the word "idol" should express more than just an image or statue. Every opinion, originating from an impious mentality, that presents itself as coming from God but has no basis in Scripture, should be understood as an idol. Examples of such idols would be

27. Cf., for example, WA 17/II:211,4-20.
28. WA 4:427,27-32.
29. WA 1:519,14-21.
30. WA 14:612,29–613,16; LW 9:70-71.

opinions, such as the mass produces an effect because of the human work done, or fasting is an obligation, or special attire should be worn on the occasion of certain religious ceremonies. Gluttony and greed would be directly linked with the raising of those idols.[31]

Luther's General Understanding concerning Greed

In his own critical way, Luther adopted much from the long tradition of thinking about greed. In his ideas, it is possible to identify opinions and statements based particularly on the thought of Church Fathers. Unlike some of them, especially some scholastic theologians, Luther did not establish a hierarchical structure for a catalogue of vices, where greed occupies a certain position and is put in relationship with other sins. The catalogues of vices found in Luther's writings are generally New Testament quotations.

Greed as Sin

Through an intensive analysis of the biblical texts, Luther promoted a radicalization of the meaning of sin. He was supported in this by early church exegesis and his recently acquired conception of justification. Thus, greed became for him more than merely one matter among other errant human behaviors. Starting from the biblical and patristic understanding, he realized that greed was something directly involved in the relationship between God and humanity.[32]

Luther understood greed as a mentality or human attitude against God and the neighbor. From this point of view, he criticized most of the scholastic tradition, which had classified greed as a radical sin, but did not identify it with the original sin. Luther defined original sin as unbelief. Inspired by 1 John 2:16, Luther identified greed with the concupiscence of the eyes, a force and a power inside the person that compels one to commit evil. Besides breaking with most scholastic views, Luther distanced his critique of greed also from pre-Reformation con-

31. WA 25:100,40–101,9; 31/II:24,24-26.
32. Cf. Rieth, *"Habsucht,"* pp. 122-26.

temporary moralism. The moralism of Luther's time was partly linked to some intellectuals of the humanist movement. Luther made it clear that his aim was not to promote a moralization of public lives based on the norms of Christian thought. Nevertheless, through his censure of greed, he wanted to find answers to fundamental subjects in theology and the church, that were, of course, in indissoluble connection to questions of social and economical reality.[33]

According to Luther, greed is a form of sin that hides injustice and conceals spoliation under a mask of good works and apparent good intentions. It expands itself in uninterrupted form. Rising from people's selfish nature, it continually assumes new shapes and structures inside of the economical context. Because of the disguise that represents greed as a virtue, it is very hard to identify its origin in evil and in the temptation by world, flesh, and devil. Therefore, only God's law is able to recognize greed as sin. At best, human nature can only recognize the consequences of this sin. For this reason Luther stressed the necessity of constantly analyzing one's social and economic matrix, in order to see if love of the neighbor is being practiced or not. He held love of neighbor to be the principle by which to evaluate diverse economical conditions — salary and pricing policies, formation of monopolies, external trade, and so forth. He wanted thus to expose and denounce situations characterized by sin and injustice.[34]

According to Luther, poor people suffer the consequences of greed more intensively. This makes rulers align themselves for the interests of the mighty and the oppressors. Ultimately, nobody is concerned with opposing injustice against the poor except Christ and his real followers, that is, the believers who shelter miserable Lazarus in his poverty.[35]

Greed was for Luther one of the eschatological evidences of his era. In other words, it was a clear sign of the world's end. Using expressions like "flood," "pestilence," and "demonic possession," he illustrated this reality in economical relations. Greed should be understood in the perspective of the struggle between God's kingdom and Satan's kingdom. Greed manifests itself as the instrument of Satan's kingdom against the gospel's preaching, hearing, and living.

33. Rieth, *"Habsucht,"* pp. 126-36.
34. Rieth, *"Habsucht,"* pp. 136-41; 162-67.
35. Rieth, *"Habsucht,"* pp. 167-69.

Greed inverts all values, especially the priceless one of justice. A classic example is the Roman church with its practices in the area of doctrine and sacraments. This inversion happens through several institutions: monasticism, canonical laws, masses, indulgences, and purgatory. Thereby, humble people are exploited in a criminal way and enslaved by the abuses of bishops and priests using the office of the keys and promoting false piety in pilgrimage chapels or adoration of saints and relics. All those things, together with the position of the Roman church as an omnipresent economical power, are manifestations of an institution that considers greed a virtue.[36]

Greed as Unbelief

Greed assumed a central meaning in Luther's thought, in that he put it on the same level as unbelief. In this context, he meant unbelief in direct opposition to faith as trust in God's aid. When Luther identified greed with idolatry, as worship of wealth, it was in opposition to true adoration, the real worship of God.

The Christian tradition historically put idols and worship of idols in opposition to God and true worship of God. Luther lived in and from this tradition. Particularly in Luther's theology, the question about God and idols cannot be separated from the question about faith. His well-known explanation of the first commandment in the Large Catechism shows it very clearly:

What does "to have a god" mean, or what is God? Answer: A "god" is the term for that to which we are to look for all good and in which we are to find refuge in all need. Therefore, to have a god is nothing else than to trust and believe in that one with your whole heart. As I have often said, it is the trust and faith of the heart alone that make both God and an idol. If your faith and trust are right, then your God is the true one. Conversely, where your trust is false and wrong, there you do not have the true God. For these two belong together, faith and God. Anything on which your heart relies and depends, I say, that is really your God.[37]

36. Rieth, *"Habsucht,"* pp. 173-86.
37. BC 386,1-3; BC-T 365,1-3; BSLK 560, M386,5-25.

Luther wants to help catechetical students by quoting several examples for daily idols: great learning, intelligence, power, the respect of others, kinsfolk, and honors. Before that, however, he mentioned another idol, describing it in a more detailed way than the others. It is worthwhile to consider with attention this formulation of Luther:

> There are some who think that they have God and everything they need when they have money and property; they trust in them and boast in them so stubbornly and securely that they care for no one else. They too, have a god — mammon by name, that is, money and property — on which they set their whole heart. This is the most common idol on earth. Those who have money and property feel secure, happy, and fearless, as if they were sitting in the midst of paradise. On the other hand, those who have nothing doubt and despair as if they knew of no god at all. We will find very few who are cheerful, who do not fret and complain, if they do not have mammon. This desire for wealth clings and sticks to our nature all the way to the grave.[38]

If the right knowledge of God and his true worship depend on a correct faith, then the knowledge of idols and idolatry are also closely related to unbelief. Besides, if the subject is unbelief and idolatry in the economic sphere (the worship of mammon), Luther is necessarily addressing himself to greed. The word itself does not actually appear in this part of the Catechism, but the reference to the concept is clear.

Two supplementary quotations from writings of the years 1520 to 1532 also illustrate this opposition between greed and faith:

> Faith teaches this work [related to the Seventh Commandment] of itself. If the heart expects and puts its trust in divine favor, how can a man be greedy and anxious? Such a man is absolutely certain that he is acceptable to God: therefore, he does not cling to money; he uses his money cheerfully and freely for the benefit of his neighbor. He knows full well that he will have enough no matter how much he gives away. His God, whom he trusts, will neither lie to him nor forsake him, as it is written in Psalm 37[:25], "I have been young, and now I am old, yet have I never seen a man of faith who trusts God

---

38. BC 387,5-9; BC-T 365,5-9; BSLK 561,7-25.

(that is, a righteous man) forsaken, or his child begging bread." The Apostle calls no other sin idolatry except covetousness [*geytz*] [Col. 3:5], because this sin shows most starkly that a man does not trust God for anything, but expects more benefit from his money than from God. It is by confidence that God is truly honored or dishonored, as I have just said. In fact, in this commandment it can clearly be seen that all good works must be done in faith and proceed from faith. In this instance everyone most certainly feels that the cause of covetousness [*geytz*] is distrust, while on the other hand the cause of generosity is faith.[39]

For hating the Word of God is really hating God. This is how it works. You denounce a man for his unbelief and greed, and you hold the First Commandment up to him (Exod. 20:3): "You shall have no other gods before Me." That is, "You shall not attach your heart, your desire, and your love to anyone else but Me." And he refuses to hear that denunciation or to stand for it. He starts ranting and raving against it, until in his heart there is bitterness and venomous hatred against the Word and its preachers. That is why the text of the Ten Commandments contains the threat (Exod. 20:5): "I am a jealous God, visiting the sins of the fathers upon the children of those who hate Me." He is talking about these very same greedy bellies and Mammon-servers, for Scripture calls greed "idolatry," or the worship of idols (Eph. 5:5; Col. 3:5). And yet, as we have said, they lay claim to titles like "the greatest of saints" and "enemies of idolatry and heresy"; and they absolutely disclaim the title "haters of God." But they are convicted by their inability to hear or see the Word of God when it attacks their greed, and by their insistence that they get off without any denunciation. The more they are denounced and threatened, the more they deride and mock, doing whatever they please to spite God and everyone else. . . .

Christ is not talking here [Matt. 6:24] about this sort of concern [about neighbor and society]. This is an official concern, which must be sharply distinguished from greed. It is not concerned for its own sake but for the neighbor's sake; it does not seek its own interests (1 Cor. 13:5), but even neglects them and forgets them in order to

39. "Treatise on Good Works," LW 44:108-9; WA 6:272,6-20.

serve somebody else. Therefore it may be called a concern of love, something divine and Christian, not a concern devoted to its own advantage or to Mammon, militating against faith and love, and even interfering with the official concern. The man whose money is dear to him and who is on the lookout for his own advantage will not have much regard for his neighbor or for the office that involves his neighbor. . . .

Baptized or not, therefore, no greedy belly can be a Christian; but he has certainly lost Christ and has become a heathen. The two are intolerable to each other — being greedy or anxious and being a believer — and one has to eliminate the other.[40]

Greed destroys the fruits of faith. It destroys the good works that spring from faith and cannot be separate from faith. Such can be observed mainly in the personal relationship with possessed goods or with the goods someone wants to possess. Greed ruins the basic principle, which should determine one's attitude to goods and money in reference to oneself and others. This fundamental principle to administer the investment of goods and money is created by faith and shaped through fraternal love. Thus, according to Luther, ultimately greed can only be overcome by faith.[41]

Luther did not consider any social or professional class greedier than the others. He intended, instead, to identify and condemn greed in functions fulfilled by members of all classes (Stände). He recognized the presence of greed in peasants and in the rural nobility, as they manipulated the prices of their products in the market. Among citizens and craftsmen he exposed greed in the abusive price-fixing of products and services, in the usury to finance production and, above all, in anxiety for social climbing through abuse of economic power. Among noblemen and citizens in administrative functions, Luther identified the presence of greed when they retained material resources that were intended by princes to be for the work of schools and communities. He denounced the greed exhibited by lords and princes in their despotic abuses of power, selfish appropriation of recently secularized ecclesiastic patrimony, and in their readiness to accept tribute in exchange for

40. "The Sermon on the Mount," LW 21:190-91; 194; 201; WA 32:456,18-34; 459,21-30; 465,19-23.

41. Cf. Rieth, *"Habsucht,"* 152-62.

tolerating rather than curbing unjust practices in economy and society. In general, the Reformer condemned the manifestations of greed in all classes, when their members did not provide the necessary material support to the preaching and teaching of the gospel in communities and schools and to the social welfare, that is, when they did not support the "common chests."[42]

With his comprehensive perspective on greed, Luther reached a realistic way of observing his social context. Through his understanding of the deep corruption of human nature, he was sure that it is impossible for humankind to render the kingdom of God directly in economic life. For the same reason, on the basis of Luther's thought, one cannot justify the idea that it is possible to start from the practice of greed and selfishness in each other and come to a balance of power and to the individual possibilities of achievement and welfare in the economic sphere.

On the other hand, Luther posited faith as the opposite of greed. He was firmly convinced that greed can be opposed only by faith. Therefore, he charged believers within the church of Jesus Christ with the responsibility of assuming the gospel's exhortations in relation to the progressive establishment of the kingdom of God and the practice of justice, not transforming them into a kind of moralism or a reason to withdraw from the world, but observing them seriously as orientation and instruction to promote positive changes in the economic sphere.[43]

Conclusion

Some recent statements challenge the attempts to find in Luther's ethical-economic thinking any helpful approaches to contemporary practice. Several historians consider Luther's positions antiquated and reactionary, even in his own time. Luther is sometimes seen as naïve, someone who wanted by his own will to contain the irresistible progress of pre-capitalism. Luther is for them a medieval intellectual, trying to perpetuate medieval patterns and structures in the economic sphere.

42. Rieth, *"Habsucht,"* pp. 186-217.
43. Rieth, *"Habsucht,"* pp. 220-21.

However, my investigation of Luther's thinking on greed argues that such statements, themselves based on the nineteenth century's unrestricted faith in the material progress of human society, should be questioned.[44] Luther, as an interpreter of Holy Scripture, faced several social and economic problems of his time, in order to denounce and oppose the practice of injustice. In his way, he committed himself to the attempt at the improvement of general life conditions. He was not concerned with obstructing an irresistible pre-capitalistic development.

Luther's position was deeply realistic, in no way skeptical or negative; that the world was coming to its end was not necessarily medieval. Especially in our times, people are increasingly challenged to abandon the concept of a "modern world," the world characterized by unrestricted consumption, an extremely unfair and unequal distribution of goods, and an irreversible devastation of nature. Luther's economic ethics, therefore, may in fact be quite helpful to all those who foresee the consequences of this "modern world" and are concerned to find an alternative way, a more modest and wiser way, a way that does not threaten nature and future generations.

44. Rieth, *"Habsucht,"* pp. 35-36.

Luther on Marriage

SCOTT HENDRIX

For a man who did not marry until he was 41, Martin Luther had a lot to say about matrimony.[1] It was obviously a personal issue for him as it was for all priests, monks, and nuns who had vowed to live a celibate

---

1. In spite of the large body of literature now available on marriage in the Reformation, there are surprisingly few studies of Luther and marriage. Five direct treatments are: Siegmund Baranowski, *Luthers Lehre von der Ehe* (Münster: Heinrich Schoningh, 1913); Paul Althaus, *The Ethics of Martin Luther,* trans. Robert C. Schultz (Philadelphia: Fortress, 1972), pp. 83-100; Lyndal Roper, "Luther: Sex, Marriage and Motherhood," *History Today* 33 (December 1983): 33-38; Susan M. Johnson, "Luther's Reformation and (Un)holy Matrimony," *Journal of Family History* 17 (1992): 271-88; Pamela Biel, "Let the Fiancees Beware: Luther, the Lawyers and Betrothal in Sixteenth-Century Saxony," in Bruce Gordon, ed., *Protestant History and Identity in Sixteenth-Century Europe* (Aldershot, U.K. & Brookfield, Vt.: Scolar Press, 1996), vol. 2, pp. 121-41. Some of the following general works contain material on Luther: Waldemar Kawerau, *Die Reformation und die Ehe: Ein Beitrag zur Kulturgeschichte des sechzehnten Jahrhunderts* (Halle, 1892); Steven Ozment, *When Fathers Ruled: Family Life in Reformation Europe* (Cambridge, Mass. & London: Harvard University Press, 1983); Eric Josef Carlson, *Marriage and the English Reformation* (Oxford: Blackwell, 1994); Joel F. Harrington, *Reordering Marriage and Society in Reformation Germany* (Cambridge: Cambridge University Press, 1995); John Witte, Jr., *From Sacrament to Contract: Marriage, Religion, and Law in the Western Tradition* (Louisville: Westminster/John Knox, 1997); H. J. Selderhuis, *Marriage and Divorce in the Thought of Martin Bucer,* trans. John Vriend and Lyle D. Bierma (Kirksville, Mo.: Thomas Jefferson University Press, 1999); Steven Ozment, *Flesh and Spirit: Private Life in Early Modern Germany* (New York: Viking Penguin, 1999).

This article first appeared in *Lutheran Quarterly* 14 (2000): 335-50, under the same title.

life and then decided to leave that life and take a spouse. It was also a practical issue for the reformers, and most of them at some point offered recommendations about when and how to marry and under what circumstances marriages could be dissolved. These matters were no longer regulated by the canon law of the Roman church once bishops and their courts ceased to have jurisdiction over marital matters in evangelical lands. Marriage quickly became a theological issue as well. In one sense marriage was demoted because it ceased to be a sacrament; but in another sense its status was elevated because it was deemed equal to or superior to celibacy. Reformers, therefore, had to forge a new theology of marriage that took account of both changes, and in light of that new theology they had to reformulate the relationship of Christians to the matrimonial estate.

Martin Luther was in the forefront of this reformation of marriage. He was well acquainted with the way in which his culture subjected marriage and women to ridicule, and like many of his colleagues he believed married life to be in a state of decline. In 1522 he wrote:

> What we would speak most of is the fact that the estate of marriage has universally fallen into such awful disrepute. There are many pagan books which treat of nothing but the depravity of womankind and the unhappiness of the estate of marriage, such that some have thought that even if wisdom itself were a woman one should not marry.[2]

Luther is referring to the literature of classical antiquity, which sometimes disparaged women as it debated the merits of marriage for men. Some of this literature found its way into the German Reformation through collections of aphorisms like the *Sprichwörter* of Sebastian Franck (d. 1542), a chronicler and independently minded thinker usually classified as a radical reformer.[3] Authors like Franck agreed that marriage in sixteenth-century Germany was in a sad state. He described the situation as out of control, with "rampant divorce and desertion . . . where one partner abandons the other in emergencies just when they need each other the most."[4] One Lutheran pastor, Johann

2. WA 10/2:292,22-26; LW 45:36.
3. Sebastian Franck, *Sprichworter* (Frankfurt: Egenolff, 1541).
4. Franck, *Sprichworter*, vol. 2, pp. 204v-205.

Freder (d. 1562), feared that the aphorisms collected by Franck only made matters worse, and he composed a rebuttal entitled *A Dialogue in Honor of Marriage* (1545).[5] According to Freder, throughout the ages the devil has attacked God's good order of marriage by disparaging women and thereby discouraging men from entering the estate of matrimony. His *Dialogue* therefore tried to persuade men to marry by defending the honor of women and marriage against the slander that he found in the aphorisms of old. Martin Luther agreed with Freder and wrote a preface for the publication of his *Dialogue* in 1545, one year before the reformer's death.[6]

The Reformer of Marriage

Long before that, however, Luther had campaigned for a positive reformation of marriage once his view of it began to change. In 1519, Luther still regarded marriage as a sacrament, a notion that was based in part on Augustine's thought which was influential throughout the Middle Ages.[7] According to Augustine (d. 430), marriage was a sacred bond because it could not be dissolved except by the death of a spouse.[8] The sacramental character of marriage meant for Luther, as it did for Augustine, that the sin of lust involved in sexual intercourse, though a mortal sin outside marriage, was rendered inoffensive in marriage. In this early sermon Luther also accepted the other goods or benefits of marriage that had been enumerated by teachers of the church in the Augustinian tradition. One of these was the notion of marriage as a covenant of fidelity in which spouses promised to be faithful to each

5. For a discussion of Freder's dialogue and its background, see Scott H. Hendrix, "Christianizing Domestic Relations: Women and Marriage in Johann Freder's Dialogus dem Ehestand zu Ehren," *Sixteenth Century Journal* 23 (1992): 251-66.

6. WA 54:168-75.

7. WA 2:168,13-29; LW 44:10 (*A Sermon on the Estate of Marriage* 1519). Luther knew the Augustinian view of marriage well. In his Genesis lectures (1535-1545), he still says that "Augustine learnedly enumerates three benefits in marriage: trust, children, and its sacramental character." WA 42:477,33-34; LW 2:301.

8. Augustine's views are contained in a number of different treatises, excerpts from which have been collected by Elizabeth Clark, ed., *St. Augustine on Marriage and Sexuality* (Washington, D.C.: Catholic University of America Press, 1996). For the sacramental quality as stated in his treatise *The Good of Marriage*, see Clark, pp. 55-56.

other. The third benefit was the production of children, which for Luther also included raising children to serve and honor God.[9] Luther never discarded all of this Augustinian heritage. In a wedding sermon from the year 1531, he reaffirms the ancient teaching that "marriage is praiseworthy because of children, loyalty, and love."[10]

From this statement, however, it is clear that love has replaced sacrament as a chief feature of marriage for Luther. This change is already registered in *The Babylonian Captivity of the Church* (1520), Luther's revision of the sacraments which appeared a year after the sermon of 1519. Recognizing that no divine promise or divinely instituted sign was attached to marriage, Luther rejected its sacramental character and the biblical argument for it from Ephesians 5:31-32 which he had accepted the year before.[11] He also anticipates several points that will be treated at length in his first complete treatise on marriage in 1522. First, he attacks impediments to marriage that have been established above and beyond Scripture by the confessional manuals and canon law of the church. He also considers which conditions, such as sexual impotence, might annul a marriage already contracted. Finally, he reflects on the uncertainty around divorce: "As to divorce, it is still a question for debate whether it is allowable. For my part, I so greatly detest divorce that I should prefer bigamy to it; but whether it is allowable, I do not venture to decide."[12] Although Luther had decided that marriage was not a sacrament, he was only beginning to clarify the positive meaning of marriage and to deal with the practical issues connected to it. By this time he was convinced of one thing, however. The compulsory celibacy of the priesthood should be abolished. Luther believed it had led to the fall of many a priest and to the decline of the priesthood in general. In place of compulsory celibacy, Luther wanted to "restore freedom to everybody and leave every man free to marry or not to marry."[13]

In addition to his fear that marriage was in a general state of decline, the devastating effect of compulsory celibacy on the priesthood was an important impetus for Luther's reformation of marriage. Al-

9. WA 2:168,38–170,16; LW 44:10-13.

10. WA 34:52,5-6 (*Eine Hochzeitpredigt uber den Spruch Hebr.*, 13,4).

11. WA 6:550,22–551,18; LW 36:92-93. Cf. WA 2:168,23-29; LW 44:10.

12. WA 6:559,20-22; LW 36:105.

13. WA 6:441,11-12; LW 44:176 (*To the Christian Nobility of the German Nation* 1520). Cf. WA 8:543,32–544,10; LW 36:206 (*The Misuse of the Mass*, 1521).

though celibacy was an issue mainly for those who had chosen the religious life (i.e., had become priests, monks, or nuns), Luther's argument that marriage was superior to celibacy raised the status of marriage for laity as well even though it was no longer regarded as a sacrament. Luther states this most clearly in his exposition of 1 Corinthians 7 (1523), a text that had long served to support the superiority of celibacy because Paul wished that all Christians were unmarried as he was (v. 7) and because he admonished engaged persons that those who refrained from marriage did better than those who married (v. 29). Luther read the text differently, however. From the statement that each person has a particular gift from God (v. 7), Luther concludes that marriage is just as much a gift of God as chastity and that furthermore chastity is a very special gift reserved for only a few.[14] He does not stop there, however. He argues that marriage and not celibacy is the "most religious state of all," the "real religious order," because "nothing should be called religious except that inner life of faith in the heart, where the Spirit rules."[15] In Luther's eyes, marriage as instituted by God "drives and helps along toward the Spirit and faith and . . . it must consist almost entirely of faith if it is to prosper."[16] The monastic and clerical orders which had traditionally been called religious Luther now labels secular because, in spite of their intention to foster a life of devotion, they seem mainly concerned with providing their members with a comfortable and secure bodily existence.[17]

Luther's reinterpretation of 1 Corinthians 7 was revolutionary and should be set alongside his argument for the priesthood of all believers in his *Address to the Christian Nobility.* Just as the concept of the universal priesthood elevated lay Christians to the spiritual status that had been reserved for clergy, the designation of marriage as the truly religious order elevates it to the spiritual status that had been reserved for the celibate members of the priesthood and monastic orders. The point of both redefinitions was to place all Christians, lay and clerical, in the same spiritual relationship to God even though the forms of their life might differ. Remaining unmarried, even for those few who received

14. WA 12:104,19-33; 105,5-13; LW 28:16-17 (*1 Corinthians 7*).
15. WA 12:105,17-26; LW 28:17.
16. WA 12:107,13-16; LW 28:19.
17. WA 12:106,8-15; LW 28:18.

the gift of chastity, did not qualify them for a spiritual or religious status higher than that of the Christians who married. By 1523, in fact, Luther seemed to rank the married life over celibacy.

In this light one should read Luther's definitive treatise on marriage, *The Estate of Marriage (Vom ehelichen Leben)*, which was published at the end of 1522.[18] Luther calls this treatise a sermon, and it was probably based on sermons preached by Luther in parishes near Wittenberg in April and May of 1522. By this time, Luther was ready to offer a theology of marriage that would replace the sacramental view and to provide his own answers to questions about who could marry and who could leave a marriage.

The Estate of Marriage is divided into three parts: (1) who can marry; (2) who can divorce and for what reasons; and (3) how to live a Christian and godly life in the estate of marriage. In greater detail than the *Babylonian Captivity*, Part One rejects the restrictions of canon law on marriage which had accumulated during the Middle Ages and which in Luther's opinion had become so confusing that Christian people were completely bewildered by them. To clarify the matter, Luther establishes marriage as a divinely willed ordinance on the basis of Genesis 1:26-28, which describes how God created human beings male and female and bid them be fruitful and multiply. Since this ordinance of creation applies in principle to everyone, the burden of proof should be on those who decide not to marry instead of on those who do. In fact, says Luther, God has exempted only three kinds of people from marriage: the sexually impotent, men who have been castrated, and men and women who are able to abstain from sexual intercourse and therefore remain celibate without succumbing to temptation. The latter are "rare, not one in a thousand, for they are a special miracle of God."[19] In all other cases, men and women should marry and fulfill God's created purpose.

As a general rule, Luther relaxes the many impediments to a valid marriage set up by canon law, retaining only those with specific biblical precedents like, for example, the limits on marrying blood relations in Leviticus 18. The point of such impediments had been to define a clear Christian practice of marriage among the recently baptized pagans of

18. WA 10/2:275-304; LW 45:11-49.
19. WA 10/2:276,9-277,10; LW 45:21.

medieval Europe.[20] Over the centuries, however, the restrictions had become tighter and more profuse, although they could be circumvented by the payment of fines, a practice that Luther roundly condemned. The impediment of unbelief is an important case in point. Christians were prohibited from marrying Muslims, Jews, or heretics. In rejecting this impediment, Luther makes his famous declaration about the secular nature of marriage:

> Know therefore that marriage is an outward, bodily thing, like any other worldly undertaking. Just as I may eat, drink, sleep, walk, ride with, buy from, speak to, and deal with a heathen, Jew, Turk, or heretic, so I may also marry and continue in wedlock with him. Pay no attention to the precepts of those fools who forbid it. You will find plenty of Christians — and indeed the greater part of them — who are worse in their secret unbelief than any Jew, heathen, Turk, or heretic. A heathen is just as much a person — God's good creation — as St. Peter, St. Paul, and St. Lucy, not to speak of slack and spurious Christians.[21]

Although Luther endorses marriage between Christians and non-Christians and even calls marriage a worldly thing, he is not trying to secularize marriage in the sense of separating it from God or religion.[22] It is no longer a sacrament, to be sure, but marriage is intended by God for most people and, as we have seen, it is the genuinely religious form of life. Luther recognizes that marriage belongs to creation and not to redemption, and consequently Christians can marry outside the faith.

This new theology of marriage becomes clearer as the treatise proceeds. Part Two discusses grounds for divorce, of which Luther accepts three: impotence, adultery, and the refusal of sexual intercourse (the conjugal debt or duty) by one of the spouses. Luther seems to have resolved his uncertainty about divorce, and it may look as if his accep-

20. A summary of this context is given by Richard Fletcher, *The Barbarian Conversion: From Paganism to Christianity* (New York: Henry Holt, 1998), pp. 280-84.

21. WA 10/2:283,8-16; LW 45:25.

22. Paul Althaus is correct on this point and supplies additional texts. See *The Ethics of Martin Luther,* pp. 89-90. In contrast, too much emphasis is laid upon the social and secular nature of marriage by John Witte, Jr., *From Sacrament to Contract,* p. 51: "The Lutheran reformers regarded marriage as a social estate of the earthly kingdom alone."

tance of divorce derives from a less religious view of marriage. The denial of a sacramental quality to marriage does open the way for divorce since, as a sacrament, marriage could never be dissolved even if the spouses separated. Most Protestants on the continent of Europe did accept some grounds for divorce because they found it more humane to allow separated spouses to remarry than to force a spouse to live alone when he or she had been deserted or betrayed by a former partner.[23] Petitions for divorce were litigated in the new marriage courts that sprang up in Protestant towns and territories to replace the episcopal courts that had possessed jurisdiction in marital matters. Nevertheless, the availability of divorce did not mean that it became easy to obtain one. During the twenty-three-year period of Calvin's ministry in Geneva (1541-1564), only twenty-six divorces were granted for adultery and only a few more for other causes.[24]

Like other reformers, Luther is also reluctant to recommend divorce even when it is allowed. In *The Estate of Marriage*, Luther questions whether Christians should make use of divorce, at least in the case of adultery. The basis for his reluctance is the model of two kingdoms and two governments, which Luther is beginning to use as a means of deciding issues of evangelical ethics.[25] In this case, Luther argues that God gave two kinds of commandments: (1) spiritual ones that teach righteousness in the sight of God and establish a spiritual government under which Christians are supposed to live; and (2) worldly commandments for those who do not live up to the spiritual commandments. In the case of adultery, Jesus has interpreted the law of Moses in such a way as to allow divorce and remarriage on grounds of adultery. But, says Luther, people who obeyed the spiritual commandments of God did not send their spouses away and never made use of certificates of divorce. Accordingly, the permission to divorce on grounds of adultery does not apply to Christians either, who are supposed to live in the spiritual gov-

23. On divorce in the Protestant Reformation see Thomas M. Safley, *Let No Man Put Asunder: The Control of Marriage in the German Southwest: A Comparative Study,* 1550-1600 (Kirksville, Mo.: SCJ Publishers, 1984); Roderick Phillips, *Putting Asunder: A History of Divorce in Western Society* (Cambridge: Cambridge University Press, 1988); Robert M. Kingdon, *Adultery and Divorce in Calvin's Geneva* (Cambridge, Mass. & London: Harvard University Press, 1995).

24. Kingdon, *Adultery and Divorce in Calvin's Geneva,* p. 176.

25. See WA 11:249,24–253,16; LW 45:88-93 (*Temporal Authority* 1523).

ernment. If there are believers who already live with their wives in an unchristian fashion, then they should be permitted to divorce in order to demonstrate that they were not really Christians in the first place.[26]

This intricate argument reveals Luther's conviction that even though marriage itself is not a specifically Christian estate, nevertheless Christians should conduct themselves in marriage in a special way. Introducing the final section of the treatise Luther says: "In the third part, in order that we may say something about the estate of marriage which will be conducive toward the soul's salvation, we shall now consider how to live a Christian and godly life in that estate."[27] The first requirement is that Christians respect both sexes as the work of God and give no ear to "pagan" books that disparage women and married life.[28] Christians should "recognize" the estate of marriage, that is, see it in a special way, "find therein delight, love and joy without end," because they "firmly believe that God himself instituted it, brought husband and wife together, and ordained that they should beget children and care for them."[29] Christian faith looks upon all the insignificant and distasteful duties of family life "in the Spirit and is aware that they are all adorned with divine approval as with the costliest gold and jewels."[30] At this point Luther makes his oft-quoted assertion that God with all the angels and creatures is smiling at a father washing diapers not because the task is menial but because the father is acting in true Christian faith.[31] The point of Luther's comment is sometimes missed. Luther means not only to commend the daily duties of parenthood in general but to commend specifically the Christian attitude toward these duties which recognizes them as God's own work possessing a divine blessing.

26. WA 10/2:288,10-22; LW 45:31. Interpreting Matt. 5:32 in the early 1530s, Luther takes the same position in the case of adultery: "To those who really want to be Christians we would give this advice. The two partners should be admonished and urged to stay together." WA 32:379,27-29; LW 21:96.
27. WA 10/2:292,8-10; LW 41:35.
28. In rebutting the "pagan" argument that women are a necessary evil in a household, Luther says: "These are the words of blind heathen, who are ignorant of the fact that man and woman are God's creation. They blaspheme his work, as if man and woman just came into being spontaneously! I imagine that if women were to write books they would say exactly the same thing about men." WA 10/2:293,7-11; LW 45:36.
29. WA 10/2:294,25-29; LW 45:38.
30. WA 10/2:295,27-296,2; LW 45:39.
31. WA 10/2:296,27-297,4; LW 45:40.

Luther has more to say about the benefits and duties of marriage, but in principle his theology of marriage is set by the time this treatise is published in 1522. Marriage is not a sacrament, but it is a holy estate ordained and instituted by God. It is superior to celibacy and is the genuinely religious life. It is not only for Christians, but Christians should live in marriage in a special way, recognizing it as a gift and institution of God. Christian spouses should regard both sexes with respect and take upon themselves the burdens and joys of bearing and raising children. Under certain conditions divorce is permitted, but Christian spouses will try to forgive injury and bear with the weaker partner before petitioning for the marriage to be dissolved. Sexual pleasure is not forbidden, but Luther does retain the traditional notion that intercourse is never without sin. "God excuses it by his grace because the estate of marriage is his work, and he preserves in and through the sin all that good which he has implanted and blessed in marriage."[32]

The Married Reformer

Luther was quite aware that he was developing this new theology as a single person. In 1522 he hesitates to name all the benefits of a happy marriage "lest somebody shut me up by saying that I am speaking about something I have not experienced."[33] Three years passed before the monk Luther took his own advice and tested his theology personally in the reality of wedlock. Luther was candid about his reasons for marrying Katharina von Bora (1499-1552) without much fanfare in June of 1525.[34] From the letter that he sends to Nicholas von Amsdorf be-

32. WA 10/2:304,6-12; LW 45:49.

33. WA 10/2:299,8-10; LW 45:43.

34. The 500th anniversary of the birth of Katharina von Bora in 1999 was marked by the appearance of new works on her even though the sources available for reconstructing her life and thought remain slim. See, e.g., Martin Treu, *Katharina von Bora* (Wittenberg: Drei Kastanien Verlag, 1995). Martin Treu, "Die Frau an Luthers Seite: Katharina von Bora — Leben und Werk," *Luther* 70 (1999): 10-29; English version: "Katharina von Bora, the Woman at Luther's Side," *Lutheran Quarterly* 13 (1999): 157-78. Jeanette C. Smith, "Katharina von Bora through Five Centuries: A Historiography," *Sixteenth Century Journal* 30 (1999): 745-74.

tween the exchange of vows and the public banquet celebrating the marriage, one can see that Luther meant to practice what he had been preaching. In addition to satisfying his father's wish for grandchildren, Luther declared: "I also wanted to confirm what I have taught by practicing it; for I find so many timid people in spite of such great light from the gospel. God has willed and brought about this step. For I feel neither passionate love nor burning for my spouse, but I cherish her."[35] The recovery of the gospel had revealed that marriage was better than celibacy and that it was also intended by God for most people; Luther wanted not only to teach that insight but also to demonstrate it in his own life.

The remark that he did not love Katharina with passion *(amo)* but cherished her *(diligo)* should not be taken to mean that Luther entered upon a loveless marriage for the sake of illustrating a point. The verb cherish *(diligo)* is a strong affirmation of love that goes deeper than passion, and it describes both the nature of the Luther marriage insofar as we can know it[36] and the great benefit of marriage which Luther stated both before and after his marriage. In the wedding sermon from 1531 Luther said:

> The ancient doctors have rightly preached that marriage is praiseworthy because of children, loyalty, and love. But the physical benefit is also a precious thing and justly extolled as the chief virtue of marriage, namely, that spouses can rely upon each other and with confidence entrust everything they have on earth to each other, so that it is as safe with one's spouse as with oneself.[37]

---

35. Letter to Nicholas von Amsdorf, June 21, 1525, in WA BR 3:541,4-8; LW 49:117. In Latin the last sentence reads: "Ego enim nec amo nec aestuo, sed diligo uxorem."

36. See Treu, "Katharina von Bora: The Woman at Luther's Side," pp. 170-74; Heinrich Bornkamm, *Luther in Mid-Career, 1521-1530,* trans. E. Theodore Bachmann (Philadelphia: Fortress, 1983), pp. 401-15; Martin Brecht, *Martin Luther,* vol. 2 (Stuttgart: Calwer, 1986), pp. 196-203 and vol. 3, trans. James L. Schaaf (Minneapolis: Fortress, 1993), pp. 235-40; Heinrich Boehmer, "Luthers Ehe," *Lutherjahrbuch* 7 (1925): 40-76.

37. WA 34:52,5-9. Cf. the context of Luther's 1522 comment about his lack of experience: "I will not mention the other advantages and delights implicit in a marriage that goes well — that husband and wife cherish one another, become one, serve one another, and other attendant blessings — lest somebody should shut me up by saying that I am speaking about something I have not experienced." WA 10/2:299,5-10; LW 45:43.

Luther's expressions of affection and appreciation for his wife are legendary. "I would not give up my Katy for France or for Venice . . . because God gave her to me and gave me to her."[38] At table in 1537 Luther said jokingly while looking at a painting of his wife: "I think I'll have a husband added to that painting, send it to Mantua [to the church council called to meet there], and inquire whether they prefer marriage [to celibacy]."[39] The report continues: "Then he began to speak in praise of marriage, the divine institution from which everything proceeds and without which the whole world would have remained empty and all creatures would have been meaningless and of no account, since they were created for the sake of man."[40] Referring to the name of Eve as the mother of all living (Gen. 3:20), Luther adds: "Here you have the ornament that distinguishes woman, namely, that she is the fount of all living beings."[41]

Luther's own family life, therefore, seems to reflect his teaching about the benefits and duties of marriage, including the bearing and raising of children with its many joys and sorrows. Martin and Katharina had six children, two of whom predeceased them: Hans (b. 1526), Elizabeth (b. 1527) who died at eight months, Magdalene (b. 1529) who died at thirteen years of age, Martin (b. 1531), Paul (b. 1533), and Margaretha (b. 1534). Luther's comments about his children express emotions ranging from the heights of playfulness to the depths of grief. In June 1530, only days before the Augsburg Confession was read in the presence of Emperor Charles V, Luther took time to write a letter to his four-year-old son from the Coburg. Describing an imaginary garden that was a children's paradise, Luther encouraged his son to behave, study, and pray so that he and his friends could be admitted to the garden together.[42] Luther wrote this letter only two weeks after his own father Hans died. When word reached him at the Coburg, Luther reacted to the news:

> This death has certainly thrown me into sadness, thinking not only [of the bonds] of nature, but also of the very kind love [my father

38. WA TR 1:17,10-12 (no. 49; 1531); LW 54:7-8.
39. WA TR 3:378,9-11 (no. 3528; 1537); LW 54:222.
40. WA TR 3:378,12-14 (no. 3528; 1537); LW 54:223.
41. WA TR 3:378,18-19 (no. 3528; 1537); LW 54:223.
42. Letter to Hans Luther, around June 19, 1530, in WA Br 5:377-78; LW 49:321-24.

had for me]; for through him my Creator has given me all that I am and have. Even though it does comfort me . . . that [my father], strong in faith in Christ, had gently fallen asleep, yet the pity of heart and the memory of the most loving dealings with him have shaken me in the innermost parts of my being, so that seldom if ever have I despised death as much as I do now.[43]

Twelve years later, when his daughter Magdalena died, Luther wrestled with all the emotions of grief and remarked in wonder: "I am joyful in spirit but I am sad according to the flesh. The flesh doesn't take kindly to this. The separation [caused by death] troubles me above measure. It's strange to know that she is surely at peace and that she is well off there, very well off, and yet to grieve so much."[44]

During his years as a spouse and a parent Luther continued to write positively about marriage, although by 1530 he described himself as plagued by marriage matters, a complaint similar to one in 1524 when he said this one topic kept him busier than the evangelical movement as a whole.[45] The 1530 complaint came at the beginning of a treatise in which Luther deals with marital issues that reflect typical changes advocated by sixteenth-century reformers.[46] In view of the fact that secret engagements had been the cause of so many controversies, Luther argues that engagements must be public "because marriage is a public estate which is to be entered into and recognized publicly before the church."[47] Furthermore, engagements are to be freely contracted and not forced by parents, for "God has created man and woman so that they are to come together with pleasure, willingly and gladly with all their hearts."[48] In cases of divorce and desertion, Luther recommends as he did before that it is better to reconcile the spouses when possible than to grant a divorce, although divorce is possible in cases of adultery. Luther is actually harder on deserters than he is on adulterers. "It can happen to all of us

---

43. Letter to Philip Melanchthon, June 5, 1530, in WA Br 5:351,20-27; LW 49:318-19.

44. WA TR 193:12-15 (no. 5498; 1542); LW 54:432.

45. WA 15:163,7-11; LW 45:385 (*That Parents Should neither Compel nor Hinder the Marriage of Their Children, and That Children Should Not Become Engaged Without Their Parents' Consent* 1524).

46. WA 30/3:205,3-11; LW 46:265 (*On Marriage Matters* 1530).

47. WA 30/3:207,15-16; LW 46:268.

48. WA 30/3:236,9-11; LW 46:304.

that we fall, and who is without sin," he asks, but a man who deserts wife and children is a villain "who shows contempt for matrimony and the laws of the city" and should be punished as such.[49]

"Such and similar mischief," says Luther, "all results from the fact that no one has either preached or heard what marriage is. No one has looked upon marriage as a work or estate which God has commanded and placed under worldly authority."[50] This statement does illustrate a slight shift, if there is any at all, in the older Luther's view of marriage. More stress than ever is placed upon marriage as a worldly estate belonging to the temporal kingdom, and it is up to secular authorities to deal with marital issues. Against the confusion that prevailed prior to the Reformation when the church attempted to control and regulate marriage, Luther says he is "toiling to see that the two authorities or realms, the temporal and the spiritual, are kept distinct and separate from each other and that each is specifically instructed and restricted to its own task."[51] Nevertheless, Luther continues to insist that marriage is a divinely willed estate and that Christians are to live in marriage in a special way. Luther's remarks on divorce illustrate his two-kingdom approach to marriage. On the one hand, matters of divorce should be left to the civil government because marriage is a secular and outward thing. On the other, the words of Christ in Matthew 5:32 apply only to Christians, that is, to the spiritual kingdom, because Christ is "functioning as a preacher, to instruct consciences about using the divorce law properly, rather than wickedly and capriciously, contrary to God's commandment."[52] By distinguishing so sharply between kingdoms in matters of marriage and divorce, Luther makes explicit the position he had begun to formulate already in 1522.

Although the estate of marriage belongs to the temporal kingdom, the married reformer reiterates that it is one of the "holy orders and true religious institutions established by God,"[53] and he describes it in glowing terms despite the fact that it has been affected by sin. In his lectures on Genesis (1535-1545) Luther extols the trust that exists between spouses and remarks that the "world has nothing more beautiful

---

49. WA 30/3:242,2-3, 32-35, 243,6-7; LW 46:312, 313.
50. WA 30/3:243,18-20; LW 46:314.
51. WA 30/3:206,6-9; LW 46:266.
52. WA 32:377,3-7; LW 21:93 (*Sermon on the Mount* 1532).
53. WA26:504,30-31; LW 37:364 (*Confession concerning Christ's Supper* 1528).

than this union of hearts between spouses."[54] Because of sin, however, a person can fall and a spouse should anticipate this possibility and be all the more ready to forgive. "Thus love will remain, and harmony will not be disturbed. For nothing has happened that was not anticipated, and love is readiest to forgive. This is indeed a rare gift; but you, because you are a Christian, should remember that this ought to be your attitude."[55] This attitude is necessary because marriage, like all of God's creation, has been contaminated by sin. Before the fall, marriage was a genuine partnership and Adam recognized that it came from God. "But now this institution and command are all the more necessary, since sin has weakened and corrupted the flesh. Therefore this comfort stands invincible against all the doctrines of demons (1 Tim. 4:1), namely, that marriage is a divine kind of life because it was established by God himself."[56]

Conclusion

Luther's statements on some relational issues will not find a positive echo in our day, and other issues of interest are not addressed by him. For example, Luther does not emphasize the integrity of the single life precisely because his agenda is to recapture the dignity of marriage from the false exaltation of celibacy as a more perfect life. When it is not used "to deny the aid and grace of Christ," however, Luther affirms "it is entirely possible to live in a state of virginity, widowhood, and chastity without these blasphemous abominations."[57] A discordant note is sounded by the reformer's tendency to confine women to the domestic sphere. Amid the pangs and dangers of childbirth, Luther advises women to trust joyfully in God's will and let God have his way. "Should it mean your death, then depart happily, for you will die in a noble deed and in subservience to God."[58] This advice and his sharp

54. WA 42:477,35-36; LW 2:301.
55. WA 42:478,4-8; LW2:302.
56. WA 42:100,40–101,2; LW1:134. Luther suggests that the patriarchal model of the wife subjected to the husband is a result of the law given after sin. WA 42:103,31-33; LW 2:137-38.
57. WA 26:509,5-8; LW 37:371.
58. WA 10/2:296,18-21; LW 45:40.

criticism of couples who do not want children[59] reflect not only the patriarchal culture of sixteenth-century Germany but also the tenuous and perilous circumstances of the early modern family in which the death of spouses and children posed a constant threat. Luther did not pretend to offer solutions to all the issues of marital life. Like other reformers, however, he did attempt to recover the dignity of marriage by emphasizing the divine intention behind it and proposing a specifically Christian appropriation of married life. The following passage from his 1531 wedding sermon captures this intention in a particularly vivid way:

> God's Word is actually inscribed on one's spouse. When a man looks at his wife as if she were the only woman on earth, and when a woman looks at her husband as if he were the only man on earth; yes, if no king or queen, not even the sun itself sparkles any more brightly and lights up your eyes more than your own husband or wife, then right there you are face to face with God speaking. God promises to you your wife or husband, actually gives your spouse to you, saying: "The man shall be yours; the woman shall be yours. I am pleased beyond measure! Creatures earthly and heavenly are jumping for joy." For there is no jewelry more precious than God's Word; through it you come to regard your spouse as a gift of God and, as long as you do that, you will have no regrets.[60]

59. WA 42:89,22-30; LW 1:118.
60. WA 34:52,12-21.

Luther on the Turks and Islam

GREGORY J. MILLER

During the reign of Sultan Sulaiman the Magnificent (r. 1520-1566) the Ottoman Empire reached its greatest geographical extent and the height of its military power. Under Sulaiman's leadership the Ottomans conquered Christian strongholds in the East, overran Hungary, terrorized Austria, and even besieged Vienna (1529). As far away as England people feared the rising wave of Ottoman Imperialism. Throughout Europe the "Turk" became a catchword for popular fear and anxiety.

The Ottoman advance was especially disturbing to people in Germany. This was partially due to Hapsburg propaganda that exaggerated the Turkish threat in an effort to gain support for imperial ambitions in eastern Europe. However, when the military power of Hungary (the "bulwark of Christendom") was destroyed at the battle of Mohacs in 1526, even opponents of the Hapsburgs were convinced that central Europe was in grave danger. A Turkish presence in neighboring Hungary was simply too close for comfort.

To a large degree, the Turkish threat was so terrifying because many Germans understood the conflict between the Hapsburg and Ottoman Empires to be a struggle not between two political powers but between the forces of Christendom and that of its archenemy, Islam. In the most severe terms used, it was a struggle between Christ and

This article first appeared in *Lutheran Quarterly* 14 (2000): 79-97, under the same title.

antichrist, between God and the devil. The Turkish advance into south-
eastern and central Europe was understood not simply as a military
threat, but also as a spiritual one. The salvation of individual Christians and the survival of Christianity itself were at stake. A mere military response was therefore insufficient; this spiritual enemy must also
be fought with spiritual weapons.

Martin Luther and his early followers were particularly important
in shaping these views. Luther himself was especially interested in the
Turks. Luther's knowledge of Islam was considerable compared to
most of his contemporaries. He had read the Qur'an (albeit in a poor
Latin translation) and was familiar with the two most widely circulated
medieval sources on Islam, Nicholas of Cusa and Ricoldo de Monte
Croce. He kept abreast of developments through oral reports, letters,
and pamphlet literature. Like many of his contemporaries, Luther
wrote pamphlets concerning the Turks and discussed developments
both at table and in correspondence. Luther published three primary
tracts concerning the Turks, *Vom Kriege wider die Türken* (Of the War
Against the Turks) in 1529, *Heerpredigt wider den Türken* (Military Sermon Against the Turks) in 1530, and *Vermahnung zum Gebet wider den
Türken* (Admonition to Prayer Against the Turks) in 1541. In addition,
in 1543 he wrote a preface to Georg von Muhlbach's *Libellus de ritu et
moribus Turcorum* (Concerning the Rites and Customs of the Turks) and
an introduction to Theodor Bibliander's Latin edition of the Qur'an,
and he published a translation of the medieval tract *Verlegung des
Alcoran Bruder Richardi, Prediger Ordens* (Refutation of the Qur'an by
Brother Richard of the Order of Preachers) in 1542. These writings are
the basis for the following summary of important aspects of Luther's
view of the Turks and their religion, Islam.

Luther's Depiction of the Religion of the Turks

Luther's primary interest in the Turks was in responding to the Ottoman advance and understanding the place of the Ottomans in eschatology. However, Luther also demonstrated considerable interest in the
religion of the Turks. For Luther, as for his contemporaries, the Turks
and the "Mohammedan faith" (the terms Islam and Muslim were not
yet used) were synonymous. Luther knew of the ethnic difference be-

tween Turks and Arabs, but assumed the Turks to be representative Muslims. Luther's discussions of Islam were not systematic or thorough. He primarily compared the religion of the Turks with Christianity, concentrating on differences or areas that were considered to be particularly important to Christians.

Luther viewed Islam as fundamentally a religion of works-righteousness.[1] For Luther, Islam is so strongly stamped by "works" that every works-righteousness within or without Christianity could be characterized as "Turkish." This Lutheran understanding of Islamic soteriology led to some interesting interpretations of other aspects of Muslim life. Luther relegated the *shahadah* (the Muslim Confession of Faith: There is no God but God and Muhammad is His Prophet) to a minor status within Islamic life. It was a device of the devil, he wrote.[2] Instead, Luther highlighted various rituals (for example, circumcision, frequent washings, avoidance of pork) by which the Turks "in vain" attempted to earn the favor of God. In sharp contrast to most medieval Christian writings on Islam, Luther demonstrated a complete lack of interest in the person and biography of Muhammad. Biographical materials on Muhammad were available, but Luther deliberately chose to focus on the rituals and doctrine of the Turks.[3]

For Luther, the foundation of all Christian orthodoxy was a correct understanding of the person and work of Jesus.[4] Because of the Muslim denial of the divinity of Christ, the denial of his death, and the exaltation of Muhammad over Christ, all of Islam was deemed categorically false.[5] In contrast to medieval writers, Luther avoided

1. See especially Luther's preface to George of Hungary's *Libellus de ritu et moribus Turcorum,* WA 30/II:205-8; LW 46:183.

2. WA 30/II:128.

3. Luther stated specifically that he was not concerned with Muhammad's biography or personality, but only with his teaching. "Personalia, quae dicunt de Mahomet, me non movent, aber die lehre der Turcken mussen wir angreiffen." WATR 5:221 (no. 5536).

4. WA 30/II:186. According to the third article of the *Confessio Augustana,* the correct understanding of the person and work of Christ was the chief differentiator between true and false religion.

5. Luther believed Muslim Christology to consist of the following (chiefly negative) doctrines: (1) Jesus was without sin, (2) but nothing more than a prophet, (3) Jesus is not God's son or true God, (4) Jesus is not the world's savior, (5) Jesus did not die on the cross, and (6) Muhammad is higher than Jesus because his office is still in force. Luther responded with a categorical rejection of Islam. WA 30/II:122ff.; LW 46:176ff.

designating the faith of the Turks as heresy.[6] For him, it was worse. If Jesus is not the Son, God is not the Father. According to Luther, Muslims worship a different God than Christians; they worship the devil himself.[7]

At times Luther grudgingly did praise the Turks for their piety. However, this was done primarily as an attack against Roman Catholicism. In demonstrating the religious "superiority" of the Turks over the Papists, Luther wanted to highlight not only the meaninglessness of works-righteousness, but also the fact that Roman Catholics did not succeed even at what they claimed to honor. According to Luther, the discipline of the Turks would shame any Papist so much that Luther thought no one would remain in his faith if he were to spend just three days with the Turks.[8] In the end, however, Luther always used the same argument: no matter how spiritual it looks, without Christ they are damned. Miracles are no evidence of authenticity, for satanic power is great and can appear as an "angel of light."[9] The Lutheran attack on the genuineness of Muslim spirituality was not only in order to protect people from converting to Islam (this was believed to be a very real danger), but also and most importantly to prove the vanity of any works-righteousness, be it the rigorous discipline of the Turks or the comparatively shameful hypocrisy of the Papists.

As early as 1529, Luther lamented the fact that he had no accurate Latin translation of the Qur'an. About this time the Zurich reformer Theodor Bibliander initiated his study of the Arabic Qur'an, with the intention of publishing an accurate Latin edition. By 1542 Bibliander had completed an edition based on Robert of Ketton's medieval translation. Although Bibliander was able to secure the services of the Basel printer Oporinus, a subsequent controversy concerning the danger that the publication of the Qur'an might cause the Christian commu-

---

6. Islam was something essentially different than Christianity, "faith created from Jewish, Christian, and Heathen faiths." From Christians they took praise of Mary, Christ, the Apostles, and other saints; from Jews they took the prohibition of wine, fasting during certain times of the year, washings like the Nazarites, and eating off of the ground. WA 30/II:122-23; LW 46:176-78.

7. The "Tu(e)rcken Gott (das ist der Teu(e)ffel)." WA 30/II:116; LW 46:170.

8. WA 30/II:206.

9. WA 30/II:188.

nity jeopardized the entire project.[10] All printed copies were seized and Oporinus was jailed briefly by the Basel magistrates during the fall of 1542. It took a concerted effort of support from several Protestant leaders, including Bibliander, Bucer, Melanchthon, and most importantly Luther (who added an additional apologetic introduction to the publication) before the printing was allowed to continue.

Luther's interpretation of the Qur'an is illustrative of much of early Protestant thought. He translated "Qur'an" to mean "Summation or Collection of God's Commands." This highlights Luther's understanding of the Qur'an to be fundamentally a collection of laws, a book not on a par with the Bible, but similar to the Papal Decretals.[11] Furthermore, these laws were not morally good or even neutral; the Qur'an is a "foul, shameful book."[12] For Luther, the Qur'an contains only human wisdom without God's word and spirit. Muhammad's "law teaches nothing other than what human reason can easily bear. What he found in the gospel that was too difficult or lofty to believe he left out, particularly that Christ is God and that he has saved us through his death."[13] Luther supported the publication of the Qur'an in Latin because he considered the public knowledge of the hideousness of the Qur'an to be the greatest weapon against Islam. This would help preachers better to preach the gruesomeness of the Turks and help people to have courage to fight.[14]

Luther's Depiction of Turkish Society

"When I consider history," Melanchthon wrote, "I find that there has been no nation that has practiced more blasphemy of God, brutality, shameful fornication, and every kind of wild and chaotic living than

10. Concerning the controversy see especially Henry Clark's "The Publication of the Qur'an in Latin: A Reformation Dilemma," *Sixteenth Century Journal* 15 (1984): 11-12 and WA 53:563-65.

11. In figure 1, for example, the Decretals and the Qur'an are equated in the banners of the demonically powered siege of the true Church by a combined army of Turks and Papists.

12. WA 30/II:121-22; LW 46:176-77.

13. WA 30/II:165-67.

14. Luther's introduction to Bibliander's Qur'an, WA 53:565.

Figure 1. Papal Decrees and the Koran: A Woodcut by Matthias Gerung

the Turks."[15] In most of the literature of the early Lutherans, the Turks were considered not simply evil, cruel, and barbarous, but the very epitome of these characteristics. In Luther's language, the Turks were the devil incarnate: inhumanly violent, treacherous, demonically lascivious.[16] The Turks were displayed as grotesque slaughterers of children, beasts who even ripped unborn babies from their mothers' wombs. The image of a Turk impaling a Christian child became so common as to achieve almost iconic status in the publications of the period.[17] Turkish violence was especially frightening because it was directed specifically at Christians. In fact, the *raison d-être* for the Turks was to extirpate Christianity. They were portrayed as enjoying nothing more than the indiscriminate killing of all who call themselves Christians, "For he [the Turk] is the enemy of the Christian name."[18]

Lasciviousness was another chief characteristic of the Turks. This critique of the Islamic morality was based primarily on views of polygamy, the treatment of women, and rapine practiced in the Turkish raids on Christian territory. It was common knowledge that Muhammad permitted multiple wives, which Luther understood to be a sure sign of sexual perversity. Permissive divorce particularly bothered him. It was reported that women were bought and sold like cattle, mistreated and despised. The ability of the man to break the marital bond whenever he chose was considered a blasphemy to the marital estate. Luther went so far as to declare that there is no true marriage with the Turks.

Turkish religious toleration was also a subject of long polemical discourses. "Sometimes the Turks are praised because they allow one to believe what they will," Luther stated, "but this is false." In Turkey no one

---

15. They not only destroy the true teaching and worship but also all good morals and discipline. They do whatever they desire with the people and subject them to cruel slavery. M. Luther and P. Melanchthon, *Zwen trostbrieve geschriben an der Durchleuchtigen und hochgebornen Fürsten und Herrn Joachim Churfürste und Marckgraven zu Brandenburger vom Türken zuge* (Nürnberg, 1532), p. 4b.

16. WA 30/II:162.

17. See figure 2. The text reads: O Lord God in the highest throne/Look upon this great misery/That the Turkish raging tyrant/Has done in Vienna forest/Wretchedly murdering virgins and wives/Cutting children in half/Impaling them on posts./O our shepherd Jesus Christ/You who are gracious and merciful/Turn your wrath away from the people/Save us out of the hand of the Turks.

18. This was a common designation for the Turks. WA 30/II:170. Concerning the single-mindedness of Turkish attacks, see WA 30/II:172.

can publicly confess Christ, evangelize, or preach against Muhammad. "What kind of freedom of faith is this since one cannot preach Christ? Yet one must confess him, for our salvation is based in that same confession." Without preaching, a person lacks the bread of the soul and will easily fall prey to the enticements and temptations of the Turks.[19]

A similar argument was made concerning the spiritual threat posed to Turkish captives. Freedom of the soul could not be separated from freedom of the body. If the Turks captured an individual, he or she was in serious eternal danger. Children were especially at risk. They did not know how to defend themselves spiritually and were easy prey for the Turks. Luther recommended that soldiers prepare for the possibility of capture by memorizing the Catechism, especially the Ten Commandments, the Lord's Prayer, and the Creed, especially the second article concerning the divinity of Christ.[20]

In *Heerpredigt wider den Türken* Luther offered counsel to those who might be captured: be patient in your imprisonment (this may be God's will), serve your master well, do not commit suicide, suffer your bondage as a cross. Luther concluded that since biblical evidence demands that slaves be obedient to their masters, if Christians disobeyed their Turkish lords, they shamed the name of Christ and only encouraged the Turks in their faith.[21] However, "if the [captive] Christians are a true, obedient, pious, humble, diligent people, this will shame the Turkish faith and perhaps convert many."[22] Even women could participate in this missionary work by submitting to their Turkish masters at bed and table for Christ's sake. They were not to think that they were damned for doing so: "the soul can do nothing about what the enemy does to the body."[23] Citing the biblical examples of Joseph and Daniel, Luther suggested that any Turkish conversions would not take place through professional missionaries, scripture, or preaching, but only through the example of Christian captives.[24]

19. WA 30/II:120-21; LW 46:174-75.
20. WA 30/II:186.
21. WA 30/II:194.
22. WA 30/II:195.
23. WA 51:621; LW 43:239.
24. WA 30/II:192-95. For a complete treatment of Luther's interest in the evangelization of the Turks see Walter Holsten, *Christentum und nichtchristliche Religion nach der Auffassung Luthers* (Gütersloh: C. Bertelsmann, 1932).

There was one important qualification to this absolute obedience. Captives were to resist the command to fight against Christians, even to the point of death. Cooperation with the Turkish army would put an individual on the wrong side of the eschatological battle and would damn them with the rest of the devil's minions.[25]

Luther's Understanding of the Spiritual Nature of the Turkish Threat

From a modern perspective, Luther and his contemporaries should not have been overly concerned about the Ottoman Turks. The sixteenth-century Turkish military realistically could not have attacked beyond Vienna; the long march, the limited campaign season, and the difficulty of supply hampered even attacks into Austria. Yet, the danger to Christendom was believed to be both real and serious. The Turks were characterized as the "Veyndt des namen Christi" (enemy of the Christian name) and "Werkzeug" (tool) of the devil. They intended to silence Christian worship and replace Christ with the devilish Muhammad, as they had already done in the Eastern lands. In a letter to Amsdorf (19 October 1529) Luther reported that the news of the Turkish siege of Vienna actually made him physically ill.[26]

However, if the Turks were the tool of the devil, and if they were threatening to destroy both the material and spiritual life in Christendom, why does God not stop them? It was clear to Luther that the seemingly unstoppable Ottoman advance was not due to any innate Turkish advantages or even Satan's assistance. Rather, God was permitting the continued Ottoman victories because of the internal failings of Christendom. Turkish success was permitted by God both to punish a corrupt Christendom and to drive it to repentance.

Since the enemy had a fundamental demonic aspect, it is only natural that spiritual warfare was a recommended response against the Ottoman advance. Pastors and preachers were to call the people to earnest repentance and prayer as the Old Testament prophets had

25. WA 30/II:196-97.
26. WA Br 5:163.

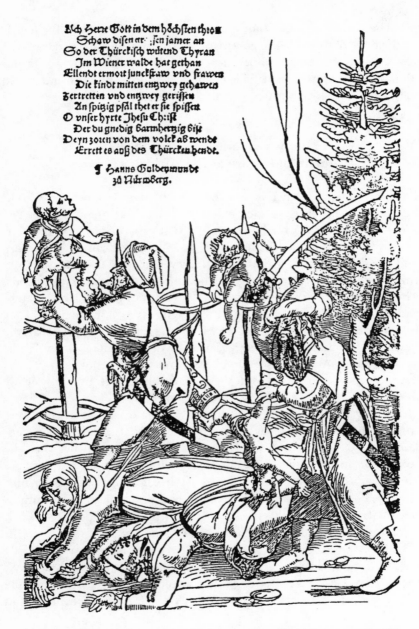

Figure 2. The Turkish Army in the Vienna Woods with a poem by Hans Goldenmunde (translated in footnote 17)

done; only by this can one take the scourge from God's hand.[27] Luther denounced processions, masses, and the long insincere prayers of the monks; these things are only "monkey business." The truly powerful prayers are frequent and short sighs with one or two words: "Oh, help us dear Father God."[28] Even children could participate in this spiritual defense against the Turks, as Luther made clear in the 1541/42 hymn he designated as a children's song: *Erhalt uns Herr bey deinem Wort* (Lord Keep Us Steadfast in Thy Word). The first verse of the original version of this well-known hymn stated: "Lord keep us steadfast in thy word/and curb the Papist and Turkish murdering/ Who desire to thrust Jesus Christ your Son from off your throne."[29] In response to prayer like this, combined with genuine conversion, Luther believed that God would end the threat. Like the Old Testament destruction of Assyria and Babylon, this victory would not come through force of arms, but by God's judgment of thunder, lightning, and hellish fire.[30] The victory would be divine, miraculous, and definitive.

Luther's Disavowal of the Crusade

Despite Luther's reliance on spiritual weapons against Islam, he also advocated a military response. However, the Lutheran military response to Islam differed significantly from the sixteenth-century Roman Catholic continuation of the medieval crusading ideal. This was primarily due to the ramifications of Luther's unequivocal denunciation of the traditional crusade as an appropriate response to Islam.

Luther's criticism of the crusade began early on. German response to the 1517 announcement of Papal-Imperial plans for a crusade was generally not favorable. Anti-clericalism was strong, and some were concerned that the war would never become reality. Many considered the Turks to be simply a pretext for the Roman "extortion" of money from Germans. Luther shared these concerns, and many lauded his

27. WA 30/II:117; LW 46:171-72.
28. WA 30/II:118-20; LW 46:172-73.
29. WA 35:467-68; LW 53:304-5.
30. WA 30/II:171.

1518 statement that fighting against the Turk is fighting against the punishment of God.[31]

Luther later developed the important criticism that the crusade was a blasphemous confusion of the heavenly and earthly kingdoms. Christians as Christians were not to lead or even participate in battle. Scripture commanded believers not to resist evil; fighting against the Turks would be a protest against martyrdom. Furthermore, ecclesiastical attempts at military leadership angered God and were a prime cause of defeat in battle (for example, the loss at the Hungarian battle of Mohacs).[32] Clergy were to preach and pray, not to bear arms and fight. According to Luther, soldiers even had a right to protest this kind of a church-led crusade through disobedience: "If I were a soldier and saw in the battlefield a priest's banner or cross, even if it were the very crucifix, I would run away as though the very devil were chasing me!"[33]

Related to this argument was the criticism that Christ, not the emperor or secular rulers, was the defender of the church.[34] The emperor was neither "the head of Christianity" nor the "the defender of the Gospel or the faith." To rely on the emperor was looking to man for salvation, and that is an abomination to God. In essence, there was no religious justification for any military action — be it against false Christians, heretics, or even Turks. "There are Turks, Jews, heathens, and all too many non-Christians, both with public false teaching and with outrageously shameful life. Let the Turks believe and live as they will, just as one allows the papacy and other false Christians to live. The Emperor's sword has nothing to do with faith — it belongs to corporal, earthly things."[35] Spiritual

31. WA 1:535; LW 31:92.
32. WA 30/II:114; LW 46:167.
33. WA 30/II:115; LW 46:168.
34. WA 30/II:130; LW 46:185.
35. WA 30/II:131; LW 46:186 and WA 30/II:143; LW 46:198. According to Luther's colleague Justus Jonas: "Although the Turks are non-Christians, there would not be sufficient cause to make war on them if they kept the peace. . . . [No ruler had a mandate from God] to start a war against non-Christians on purely religious grounds. . . . We can kill non-Christians with our fists — but we cannot make Christians of them with our fists — we cannot, in this way, put faith and the Holy Spirit into their hearts." Quoted in John W. Bohnstedt, "The Infidel Scourge of God: The Turkish Menace as seen by German Pamphleteers of the Reformation Era," in *Transactions of the American Philosophical Society*, n.s., 58, no. 9 (1968): 33.

enemies must be fought with spiritual weapons alone. No crusade or holy war was permissible.

Luther's argument was quickly criticized by Roman Catholic theologians but was highly influential.[36] Some understood Luther to be advocating pacifism and declaring that lordship over the body was not intimately related to lordship over the soul. Luther had not intended his disavowal of the crusade to go this far, however. In place of the crusade Luther saw a spiritual eschatological battle. However, military action was still necessary because Christians were not only citizens of heaven, but also citizens of an earthly kingdom. War against the Turks was justified *(a jus bellum)* on the basis of God's dual political commands: governments must preserve peace and order, Christian subjects must obey established authority. Luther was deeply concerned with the Turkish problem and not just a shrewd negotiator of Protestant liberties in exchange for aid against the Turks, as some scholars have argued.[37]

Since Luther's early statements concerning the Turks had been misinterpreted in such a way as to discount the Ottoman threat, he then wrote *Vom Kriege wider die Türken* and *Heerpredigt wider den Türken* as a clarion call to earnest action. Do not underestimate the Turks as we Germans are inclined to do, Luther stated. Even after the withdrawal of the Turks from Vienna, Luther admonished the Germans not to go back to sleep. Action is needed, not complacency. The entire purpose for the *Heerpredigt* was to admonish the "fist"; by means of the Turks the devil seeks not only to rule the political world but also to destroy Christ's kingdom and his saints.[38] Evangelical pastors were not to permit anyone to teach that the Turk is not to be resisted because revenge is prohibited for the Christian. Rather, people should be taught that the authorities have been given the sword and power to punish all murderers and robbers, including the Turks.[39]

If called upon to give material or physical support to the military

36. Cuspinianus, Eppendorf, Eck, Anderbach, and Cochleus wrote criticisms of Luther's response to the Turks.

37. See for example, Kenneth M. Setton, "Lutheranism and the Turkish Peril," *Balkan Studies* 3 (1962): 133-68.

38. WA 30/II:160-61.

39. *Unterricht der Visitatoren,* WA 26:236-40; LW 40:305-6. In *Unterricht der Visitatoren* the Turkish issue was considered important enough to warrant a separate section.

Figure 3. A Woodcut for Revelation 20, Depicting the Turkish Army
near Vienna, by Matthias Gerung

effort against the Turks, Christian subjects should give willingly. In the *Heerpredigt,* Luther warned:

> If you hold back and refuse to pay or to ride [in battle], look out — the Turk will teach you when he comes in your land and does to you like what was done at Vienna [1529]. Namely, he won't demand taxes or military service from you, but instead attack your house and home, take your livestock and provisions, money and goods, stab you to death (if you are so lucky), shame or strangle your wife and daughter before your eyes, hack your children to death and impale them on the fenceposts. And, what is worst of all, you must suffer all this with a wicked, troubled conscience as a damned unchristian who has been disobedient to God and his government.[40]

If you do not pay now, you certainly will pay later. If commanded, men and even women should fight even to the death, sacrificing their own homes if necessary. They can fight in good conscience, certain that they are killing God's enemy and someone condemned to hell.[41]

After the Turks failed at Vienna in 1529, some Protestants who did not share Luther's intense eschatological urgency became more inclined to use the Turks as a bargaining tool to force an internal settlement of the German religious situation. It was no coincidence that most Imperial acts from 1532 to 1545 that reconfirmed the Religious Peace of Nuremberg were influenced by Turkish pressure in the Balkans.[42] While it is clear that Ottoman imperialism did play a role in the development of legal guarantees for Protestants, it did not do so to the extent that some historians claim. For the most part, the Lutheran princes and cities decided questions of imperial aid against the Turks according to the good of the empire and not their particular interests. In fact, when asked to give his definitive expert advice for Johann Friedrich in 1538 as to how much should be demanded by Protestants in return for military assistance against the Turks, Luther made his position very clear:

40. WA 30/II:181.
41. WA 30/II:173.
42. Stephen Fischer-Galati, *Ottoman Imperialism and German Protestantism, 1521-1555* (Cambridge, Mass.: Harvard University Press, 1972), p. 95.

The Turks are a punishment from God on Germany against which there is no defense.

King Ferdinand will most likely not have much luck in the war against the Turks. However, whatever is not merely in the interest of Ferdinand but also concerns the Fatherland: you are responsible for this help against the Turks, even if it is to be feared that after a victory over the Turks the Protestants would be attacked.[43]

Despite his pessimism about the outcome of military action against the Ottoman Empire, Luther remained convinced that it was his duty to battle the Turkish enemy to the bitter end.

Luther's Understanding of the Eschatological Role of Islam

Comparing the contemporary condition of the world to Scripture, it was clear to Luther that he was living in the last days. "For the scripture is completely fulfilled: so many signs have been seen and so great a light of the Gospel has shown forth, yet there is such great wickedness in the world as never before; things could never get any worse, the world must come to an end."[44]

The Turks played an important role in his interpretation of the eschaton. Because the end of the world is near, the devil rages with his two weapons: the antichrist (the pope) and the Turks. "The Turks are certainly the last and most furious raging of the devil against Christ . . . after the Turk comes the judgment and hell."[45]

Luther interpreted the prophetic book of Daniel as specifically speaking concerning the Turks. The four beasts of chapter 7 were interpreted historically to represent the four kingdoms of Assyria-Babylon, Medo-Persia, the Greeks, and the Romans.[46] The ten horns represent the ten provinces of the Roman Empire: France, Italy, Spain, Africa, Germany, England, Hungary, Greece, Asia, and Egypt. The Turks en-

---

43. Quoted in Carl Göllner, *Turcica: Die Türkenfrage in der Öffentlichen Meinung Europas im 16. Jahrhundert,* vol. 3 (Bucharest: Editura Academei, 1978), p. 193.

44. WA 30/II:172.

45. WA 30/II:162.

46. The following discussion is taken primarily from *Heerpredigt,* WA 30/II:165-71.

tered the interpretation in verse 8: Muhammad and his faith was the little horn that arose in the midst of the ten horns. The eyes of the horn are Muhammad's Qur'an with which he rules. "In whose law there is no divine eye, but mere human reason without God's word and spirit." The mouth that speaks blasphemous things is Muhammad exalting himself over Christ. The statement that the little horn will oppress and rule over the saints was clearly true of the Turks: "For no people are more the enemies of the Turks than the Christians; the Turks fight against no one with such bloodthirstiness as against Christians."

The book of Revelation also offered valuable insights on the contemporary situation. In Luther's analysis, Muhammad and the Turks appeared prominently in several portions of St. John's prophecy. Marginal comments of the *Deutsche Bibel* stated that Muhammad was the second woe (chapter 9:13-21) between Arius and the pope.[47] The most direct reference to the Turks in the book of Revelation was in relation to Gog and Magog in chapter 20. Luther understood Gog/Magog to be the biblical designation for the Turks, as had been established by a separately published translation of Ezekiel 38 and 39.[48] Revelation 20 declares that after 1000 years the devil will be loosed to make war on the saints. He will gather Gog and Magog to besiege the city of God's people, but they will be destroyed by fire from heaven and cast into eternal damnation (20:7-10).[49] Both Daniel and Revelation were interpreted to prophesy that the Turks would be allowed dominion for a time, but then would be destroyed from on high. The Last Judgment would follow immediately after the defeat of the Turks. This strong connection between eschatology and the Turks is reflected clearly in the closing prayer of *Vom Kriege wider die Türken*: "So help us, dear Lord Jesus Christ, and come down from heaven with the Last Judgment. Strike both the Turks and the Pope to the ground together with all tyrants and the godless. Deliver us from all sin and evil, Amen."[50]

---

47. WA DB 7:409; LW 35:404-5.

48. WA 30/II:220-35.

49. See figure 3. This illustration accompanied Revelation 20 in the 1530 Luther Bible. The "City of God" in the illustration bears significant resemblance to Vienna. See Andrew Gow, *The Red Jews* (Leiden: E. J. Brill, 1995).

50. WA 30/II:148; LW 46:205.

Conclusion

Although the period of intense contact was brief, the Ottoman advance into central Europe in the early sixteenth century formed an important chapter in the history of Christian-Islamic relations. While continuities with the medieval period remained, the theological orientation of Luther and his colleagues did cause important alterations in the interpretation of the Turks and Islam. Attacks on Muhammad became less important than differences in theology. Islam was seen less as a Christian heresy and more as a "works-based" religion similar to Judaism. Luther's absolute rejection of the crusade as an appropriate response to Islam was an important factor in the closing of a chapter in the history of Christian-Islamic relations. Perhaps the most important long-term consequence of Luther's view of Islam, however, was that an eschatological interpretation of Islam was built into the very foundation of Protestantism. A close identification of Christian-Islamic conflict with an eschatological confrontation between God and the devil has remained very influential among some Protestant groups. When they are threatened by Islam, some Christians still see contemporary events forecast in the biblical prophecies of Daniel and Revelation. Coexistence is not possible with this kind of cosmic enemy. Rather, they see God as directing events toward the ultimate eschatological confrontation and the absolute and final destruction of Islam.

FOR FURTHER REFERENCE

Bohnstedt, John W. "The Infidel Scourge of God: The Turkish Menace as Seen by German Pamphleteers of the Reformation Era." *Transactions of the American Philosophical Society* NS 58-9 (1968).

Clark, Henry. "The Publication of the Koran in Latin: A Reformation Dilemma." *Sixteenth Century Journal* 15 (1984): 3-12.

Fischer-Galati, Stephen A. *Ottoman Imperialism and German Protestantism, 1521-1555*. Cambridge, Mass.: Harvard University Press, 1972.

Göllner, Carl. *Turcica: Die Türkenfrage in der Öffentlichen Meinung Europas im 16. Jahrhundert.* Vol. III. Bucharest: Editura Academiei, 1978.

Holsten, Walter. *Christentum und nichtchristliche Religion nach der Auffassung Luthers.* Gütersloh: C. Bertelsmann, 1932.

Lamparter, Helmut. *Luthers Stellung zum Türkenkrieg.* München: Evangelische Verlag Albert Lempp, 1940.

Mau, Rudolf. "Luthers Stellung zu den Türken." In Helmar Junghans, ed., *Leben und Werk Martin Luthers von 1526 bis 1546*. Göttingen: Vandenhoeck und Ruprecht, 1983, pp. 647-62.

Rajashekar, J. Paul. "Luther and Islam: An Asian Perspective." *Luther Jahrbuch* (1990), pp. 174-91.

Setton, Kenneth M. "Lutheranism and the Turkish Peril." *Balkan Studies* 3 (1962): 133-68.

Luther and Christ's Church

Luther on the Reform of Worship

HELMAR JUNGHANS

The reform of worship that Luther set in motion and that culminated in Wittenberg in 1525 is principally an event in the history of liturgy at the beginning of the Reformation in the sixteenth century. However, its importance is by no means limited to those interested in church history. In fact, research into Luther's reform of worship conducted between the two world wars had manifold consequences for the structuring of worship.[1] After the Second World War, several theologians developed the outline of a Lutheran doctrine of worship based upon a critical use of Luther.[2] This decade-long engagement with Luther's comments on worship affected the design of the "Agenda for Evangeli-

---

1. See, for example, Karl Holl, "Was können wir für die Neugestaltung unseres evangelischen Gottesdienstes von Luther lernen?" *Luther-Jahrbuch* 6 (1924): 3-21; Friedrich Gebhardt, "Die musikalischen Grundlagen zu Luthers Deutscher Messe," *Luther-Jahrbuch* 10 (1928): 56-169; Marie Louise Henry, "Luthers bleibende Bedeutung für die Gestaltung des Gottesdienstes: Bericht über einen Vortrag von Hauptpastor D. Knolle, Hamburg," *Luther* 23 (1941): 77-82.

2. See Vilmos Vajta, *Luther on Worship* (Philadelphia: Fortress, 1958).

This article, translated from the German by Timothy J. Wengert, was originally published as "Luthers Gottesdienstreform — Konzept oder Verlegenheit?" in *Herausforderung: Gottesdienst*, vol. 1 of *Liturgische Studien und Forschungen* (Leipzig: Evangelische Verlagsanstalt, 1998), pp. 77-92. Depending upon the context, the word *Gottesdienst* has been translated worship, worship service, divine worship, or liturgy. The English version of this article first appeared in *Lutheran Quarterly* 13 (1999): 315-33, under the same title.

cal Lutheran Churches and Congregations," published in 1955 and then enacted in individual territorial churches.[3] This agenda in its reworked form continues to define our worship today. Thus, whoever wrestles with the question of worship in Luther's thought is also shaping the prerequisites for a better understanding and a deeper experience of evangelical Lutheran worship.

Luther's reform of worship has attracted attention in the twentieth century even outside Lutheran circles. After the Second World War Roman Catholic liturgiologists have also directed their attention to Luther's reform of worship. This, too, happened not only out of purely historical interests but also to promote liturgical reform that came to fruition during the Second Vatican Council. The Jesuit, Hans Bernhard Meyer (b. 1924), produced a dissertation in Innsbruck, "Luther and the Mass: A Liturgical Investigation of the Relation of Luther to the Mass of the Late Middle Ages."[4] Not only did this work arise in cooperation with Lutheran liturgical specialists, but in many instances it adjudged Luther's work in a positive light and as worthy of imitation.

Thus, knowledge of Luther's design for worship will remain a live possibility by virtue of countless publications[5] and through the enactment of worship forms also shaped by him. At all times, however, engagement with his writings, sermons, letters, and comments at table can themselves also deepen our understanding. Whereas those who would study the initial development of worship in the New Testament must deplore the extremely fragmentary nature of the sources,[6] anyone working on this theme always must wrestle with the dilemma of which sources to choose, given the variety.

The theme with which this essay will deal places in the foreground

3. Cf. Frieder Schulz, "Der Gottesdienst bei Luther," in *Leben und Werk Martin Luthers von 1526 bis 1546: Festgabe zu seinem 500. Geburtstag,* ed. Helmar Junghans, 2 vols. (Berlin: Evangelische Verlagsanstalt, 1983), vol. 1, p. 297; vol. 2, pp. 811-13.

4. Hans Bernhard Meyer, *Luther und die Messe: Eine liturgiewissenschaftliche Untersuchung über das Verhältnis Luthers zum Meßwesen des späten Mittelalters* (Paderborn: Bonifacius, 1965). See also the literature given in Schulz, "Der Gottesdienst bei Luther," vol. 1, p. 297; vol. 2, p. 813.

5. On the continuing publications, see the yearly "Lutherbibliographie" in *Luther-Jahrbuch* under the subsection "k) Gottesdienst, Gebet, Kirchenlied, Musik," where in 1995 alone forty-two titles are listed.

6. See, for example, from the same volume in which this essay originally appeared, Werner Vogler, "Mahlfeier oder Synagoge?" in *Herausforderung: Gottesdienst,* p. 64.

this question: Did Luther carefully conceive the reform of worship in Wittenberg or did he simply create a provisional form under the pressure of the moment? Those who desire to answer this question should first be clear what concept for the structure and essence of worship they themselves have. Rudolf Stählin (b. 1911) saw worship as "having grown out of a single tree, enduring throughout the centuries, with many boughs — new sprouts and withered branches — in all complexity and yet a single whole."[7]

This view, based upon an intellectual-historical perspective, can concentrate upon the formation of the trunk, that is, on the development of the "correct" form of worship. However, it seems to me more helpful both for understanding what developed in the past and for providing an orientation in the present to bring in more fully the historical context of Luther's reform of worship.

The theme of this essay is divided into two parts. The first deals with Luther's overall concept of worship, and the second with its realization. Then, we will consider the question of whether Luther's reform of worship proceeded from some overall conception of liturgy or was only a temporary solution of the moment.

Luther's Concept of Worship

We begin with something of seemingly secondary importance. Luther spoke of the mass *under the papacy,* not of a Roman and certainly not of a catholic mass. He pronounced judgment on the mass prior to the Reformation, that is, concretely on the late medieval mass in Germany. Keeping this historical situation in mind protects the reader from getting caught too quickly in later confessional struggles and judgments. How much Luther's criticism still applies to the Roman mass that the Council of Trent constructed, or to the mass celebrated in the Roman Catholic Church since the Vatican II Council, is a completely separate question.

7. Rudolf Stählin, "Die Geschichte des christlichen Gottesdienstes von der Urkirche bis zur Gegenwart," in *Leiturgia: Handbuch des evangelischen Gottesdienstes,* ed. K. F. Müller and W. Blankenburg, vol. 1, *Geschichte und Lehre des evangelischen Gottesdienstes* (Kassel: Stauda, 1954), p. 2.

The Word of God instead of Human Accretions

And, indeed, the greatest and most useful art is to know what really and essentially belongs to the mass, and what is added and foreign to it. For where there is no clear distinction, the eyes and the heart are easily misled by such sham into a false impression and delusion. Then what men have contrived is considered the mass; and what the mass [really] is, is never experienced, to say nothing of deriving benefit from it. Thus alas! It is happening in our times. For I fear every day more than a thousand masses are said, of which perhaps not one is a real mass. O dear Christians, to have many masses is not to have the mass. There is more to it than that.[8]

Luther knew what he was talking about. He had prepared himself very carefully for his ordination as a priest. He worked through the exposition of the mass by Gabriel Biel (1410-1495), the *Canonis misse expositio*,[9] which made his heart bleed.[10] After his first mass on 2 May 1507, he celebrated the mass as priest regularly and with great earnestness. With the publication in 1520 of the tract *A Treatise on the New Testament, That Is, The Holy Mass,* he developed the fundamental principles or rules — in a certain sense an overall concept — which are supposed to hold true for a mass, that is, for proper Christian worship.

From the very beginning, Luther's criticism of contemporary theology, church, and piety grew out of the fact that he viewed them from the perspective of the Scripture. He also employed this approach with the mass. He developed this basic principle: "Now the nearer our Masses are to the first Mass of Christ, the better they undoubtedly are; and the further from Christ's Mass, the more dangerous."[11]

On this basis, Luther saw that in Christ's Words of Institution "lies the whole Mass, its nature, work, profit, and benefit."[12] From this insight he derived his basic understanding of what worship itself really is.

---

8. LW 35:81-82; WA 6:355,13-20.

9. Gabriel Biel, *Canonis misse expositio*, ed. Heiko A. Oberman and William J. Courtenay, 4 vols. (Wiesbaden: Steiner, 1963-67); *Registerband*, ed. Wilfrid Werbeck (Wiesbaden: Steiner, 1976).

10. LW 54:264; WA TR 3:564,5-6, no. 3722.

11. LW 35:81; WA 6:355,3-4.

12. LW 35:82; WA 6:355,34.

At the same time he possessed a yardstick with which to measure the value of individual parts of worship.

Already in the earliest lectures on the Psalms from 1513 to 1515 Luther's concept of the basic structure for how God and humanity relate was clear. The God who speaks works through his Word to each individual person, for whom there remains only hearing and obeying. In this relation God is the active partner, the individual is the passive one.[13] Now in 1519, Luther stressed this for worship as well. For him worship is above all the gathering of the community in which God serves the assembled people.

Because the Word proceeding from God — above all, his promise (the gospel) — is the decisive thing, this Word must be made known. This demand, however, stood completely opposed to the praxis in the late medieval mass, where the notion had taken root that the priest *silently* prayed the Canon of the Mass. That Canon consisted of the offering up of the gifts and prayers for the church, prayers for the living, remembrance of the saints, petition for the acceptance of the offered elements, petition for the transubstantiation of the elements, the transubstantiation itself (Words of Institution), remembrance of Christ's work of salvation, petition for the acceptance of the unbloodied sacrifice, petition that we may be united with Christ's sacrifice, remembrance of the dead, petition for communion with the saints, blessing, and praise.

Over against this perspective, Luther stressed his conviction that God's Word must be made known. How in the world could anyone know what the mass is, if the words, on which the mass stands or falls, remain unknown? At the same time, Luther demanded that these words should also be understandable. Thus, he desired that the words be spoken out loud and no longer in Latin but in German.[14]

Luther was not only concerned that the Words of Institution be heard. He also wanted their content to be understood. For this reason, they had to be explained in the worship service itself. For the sermon is nothing less than an explanation of Christ's words. "What is the whole gospel but an explanation of this testament?"[15] For Luther, the procla-

13. See Helmar Junghans, *Der junge Luther und die Humanisten* (Weimar: Böhlau, 1984), pp. 274-87, esp. 282-83.

14. LW 35:90; WA 6:362,26-35.

15. LW 35:106; WA 6:374,3-4.

mation of the Word, the sermon, logically belonged to the indispensable makeup of a worship service.

By bringing the proclamation of God's Word into worship as a central piece, all human additions suddenly appeared in a critical light. In view of the many liturgical regulations and customs that had become a part of the late medieval mass, Luther wrote in 1520, "When Christ himself first instituted this sacrament and held the first mass, there was no tonsure, no chasuble, no singing, no pageantry, but only thanksgiving to God and the use of the sacrament."[16]

From this observation Luther developed an entire list of very critical comments concerning the structure of the late medieval mass. However, did this principle ("God's Word instead of human accretions") also mean for him that human additions had no place at all in the worship service or that they were totally arbitrary?

Christ's Testament instead of the Priest's Sacrificial Offering

By keeping in mind the fact that the Lord's Supper has to do with Christ's testament, Luther considerably deepened the central truth that in the mass the action proceeds from God. Now, the testator determines who will get the estate. The heir, on the contrary, *receives* the estate.[17]

With this explanation, Luther underscored the basic structure of worship: the action proceeds from God, not from human beings. Christ distributes his body and blood with the help of bread and wine, but each person receives these gifts. From this orientation arose Luther's fundamental critique of the late medieval mass.

This notion shaped the late medieval mass: that the priest presents the elements of the Lord's Supper as an offering to God and thereby demands from God the fruits of the mass for the participants at the mass and for those absent — living and dead — for whom the mass was endowed. This notion made possible masses without the participation of the congregation. At the end of the Middle Ages endowments of masses multiplied in order to reduce the punishment in purgatory. Fre-

16. LW 35:81; WA 6:354,28-31.
17. LW 35:85-87; WA 6:357,10-359,29.

quently altars were endowed at which the "altarists" read masses for particular persons in exchange for a living or a cash payment. The Castle Church in Wittenberg (dedicated in 1503 and completed in 1509) included nineteen side altars, at which — including the high altar — nearly 9000 masses were sung or read in 1519 alone.[18]

These notions also lifted the priest above the parishioners, since he was granted the ability to change bread and wine into the body and blood of Christ and thereby to effect something before God. Biel wrote about this in his explanation of the mass. The priest's dignity surpassed not only that of all earthly authority but also the dignity of the angels and the Mother of God herself, despite the fact that she was called upon to intercede with her Son.[19] As a result of these convictions, it appears that it is still impossible in 1995 to ordain women to a priesthood arising out of such a tradition.[20]

The change in elements brought about by the priest was to a certain extent understood as a magical act, in which the Words of Institution assumed the function of a magic formula. Some feared that the Words of Institution would be learned by the laity and then used by them to effect this very change. To prevent this, they were kept secret and spoken only in silence.[21]

Because Luther set forth Christ as the active one, priests could not bring a sacrifice to God but could only aid him in the distribution of the Testament. For this they needed no higher spiritual quality than that of any baptized Christian.

Faith instead of "Good Works"

The decisive reality of worship is God's action. God acts without human beings entreating him. God instigates matters and bestows a promise through his Word. Human beings are the recipients, who accept this Word with thanksgiving and trust him, that is, believe him.

18. See Helmar Junghans, *Martin Luther und Wittenberg* (München: Koehler & Amelang, 1996), pp. 45, 51-52.

19. Gabriel Biel, *Canonis misse expositio,* lectio 4 BC 1:31-33.

20. On the declaration of 28 October 1995, see "Glaubenskongregation bekräftigt Nein zur Priesterweihe von Frauen," *Herder-Korrespondenz* 49 (1995): 680.

21. See Meyer, *Luther und die Messe,* pp. 214-37.

They are incapable of climbing up into heaven and moving God to be gracious. Instead, God must make the first move, that is, through his Word make a particular promise that human beings grasp with firm faith, so that the Holy Spirit then follows.[22]

Luther led the fight against the sacrificial character of the late medieval mass on the basis of pastoral responsibility. He attacked it because it gave Christians a false sense of security and thereby became their undoing. With this he struck down all attempts to earn God's grace through so-called good works — which his contemporaries understood much more as particular acts of piety than as works of love for the neighbor. In the Smalcald Articles of 1537 he held firm to the central article that faith in Jesus Christ alone justifies and from that perspective developed a thoroughgoing critique of the late medieval mass.

> The Mass in the papacy must be regarded as the greatest and most horrible abomination because it runs into direct and violent conflict with this fundamental article. Yet, above and beyond all others, it has been the supreme and most precious of the papal idolatries, for it is held that this sacrifice or work of the Mass (even when offered by an evil scoundrel) delivers men from their sins, both here in this life and yonder in purgatory, although in reality this can and must be done by the Lamb of God alone, as has been stated above. There is to be no concession or compromise in this article either, for the first article does not permit it. . . .
>
> Besides, this dragon's tail[23] — that is, the Mass — has brought forth a brood of vermin and the poison of manifold idolatries.
>
> The first is purgatory. They were so occupied with requiem Masses, with vigils,[24] with the weekly, monthly, and yearly celebrations of requiems,[25] with the common week,[26] with All Souls' Day,[27]

22. LW 35:82-83; WA 6:356,3-19.

23. An expression borrowed from Revelation 12:3-4 and repeatedly used by Luther.

24. Luther here probably has in mind vigils celebrated on the eve of a particular mass for the dead.

25. Masses for the dead celebrated on seventh and thirtieth day after the death and on its anniversary.

26. The week after the Feast of St. Michael and All Angels (29 September), during which countless masses for the dead were read.

27. 2 November.

and with soul-baths[28] that the Mass was used almost exclusively for the dead although Christ instituted the sacrament for the living alone. . . .

The second is a consequence of this: evil spirits have introduced the knavery of appearing as spirits of the departed and, with unspeakable lies and cunning, of demanding Masses, vigils, pilgrimages, and other alms. . . .

The third are pilgrimages. Masses, forgiveness of sins, and God's grace were sought here, too, for Masses dominated everything. . . .

The fourth are fraternities. Here monasteries, chapters, and vicars have obligated themselves to transfer (by legal and open sale) all Masses, good works, etc. for the benefit of the living and the dead. . . .

The fifth are relics. In this connection so many manifest lies and so much nonsense has been invented about the bones of dogs and horses that even the devil has laughed at such knavery. Even if there were some good in them, relics should long since have been condemned. . . .

The sixth place belongs to the precious indulgences, which are granted to the living and the dead (for money) and by which the pope sells the merits of Christ together with the superabundant merits of all the saints and the entire church.[29]

Luther's Implementation of Liturgical Reform

All who truly want to understand Luther must not limit themselves merely to his dogmatic pronouncements but must at the same time consider his actual behavior. This is particularly true for his order of worship.

28. Baths endowed on behalf of the poor and indigent for the purpose of reducing the deceased's punishment for sin.

29. Smalcald Articles II.ii.I, 11, 12, 18, 21, 24, in BC 301-6; BC-T 293-96 (WA 50:200,7-26; 204,24–209,11; BSLK 416,7-17; 419,18–424,3).

Evangelical Reform of Worship apart from Luther

Luther was not in a hurry to draw immediate consequences from his insights into the essence of worship and thereby reform the mass. This first began rather while he was in hiding at the Wartburg. The professor of theology, Andrew Bodenstein von Karlstadt (1486-1541), sparked the discussion of a new form of the mass when he published a series of theses on 19 July 1521. In them he labeled as sinful distributing only the bread at the Lord's Supper.[30] To be sure, Luther rejected this assertion in a letter dated 1 August. However, he left no doubt that he held the practice of offering the chalice to be scripturally sound and, hence, better. He even proffered the following declaration: "But I also will never say another private Mass in all eternity."[31] With these words he drew a practical consequence from his concept of worship.

The Wittenbergers felt this validated their point of view. Some private masses were discontinued. Beginning on 29 September 1521 Philip Melanchthon (1497-1560) and several students participated in celebrations of the mass in private houses during which both bread and wine were distributed. Luther's fellow Augustinian, Gabriel Zwilling (ca. 1487-1558), celebrated masses using both kinds in the Augustinians' Chapel of the Holy Spirit — that is, until the prior, Konrad Helt (d. 1548), forbade it. On Christmas Day in the Castle Church, Karlstadt began to celebrate the Lord's Supper distributing both kinds and handing the chalice to the communicants.[32] On 24 January 1522 the Wittenberg City Council passed a new decree ordering church life, despite the fact that Elector Frederick the Wise (1463-1525; ruler from 1486) had prohibited any changes. In it the council laid down that paintings and altars must be reduced to three. Immediately thereafter they cited the basic principle formulated by Luther: "Thus the mass should not be celebrated in any other way than the way Christ instituted it in the Last Supper." A few liturgical portions were left in, but the Canon of the Mass was excised because it did not conform to the Scripture. The communicants were allowed to receive the host and put

---

30. Martin Brecht, *Martin Luther,* vol. 2: *Shaping and Defining the Reformation: 1521-1532,* trans. James L. Schaaf (Minneapolis: Augsburg Fortress, 1990), p. 26.

31. LW 48:28; WA Br 2:372,73 [no. 424].

32. Brecht, *Shaping and Defining the Reformation,* pp. 26, 34.

it in their mouths and to take the chalice in their hands and drink out of it.[33]

With this the City Council had gathered into an order the various things about which Luther had voiced his approval. Did not Luther have reason to rejoice over this success, that Wittenberg had realized his idea of true Christian worship? Not in the least! Instead, he came out decisively against it, and not only because the electoral chancellery stood helplessly opposed to the activities in Wittenberg or because the Imperial Governing Council threatened punishment against these innovations. Luther objected much more because things had proceeded in a false direction. He demanded the following: from the inside to the outside, not the other way around. That is to say, God's Word must first work faith in the heart before this faith can express itself outwardly in new forms of worship. It is wrong to change externals before the proper faith is present, "For the Word created heaven and earth and all things [Ps. 33:6]; the Word must do this thing, and not we poor sinners. In short, I will preach it, teach it, write it, but I will constrain no man by force, for faith must come freely without compulsion."[34] Here Luther expressed his protest against the promulgation of too many liturgical and church orders too fast. It was a protest he maintained his whole life long.

Concern for the Weak in Faith

Luther's criticism of the Wittenbergers' behavior was shaped in large measure by concern for the weak in faith, as Paul had urged in Romans 8:7-13. In his first sermon delivered after his return from the Wartburg at the Wittenberg city church on 9 March 1522, he reproached his listeners in this way: "And here, dear friends, one must not insist upon his rights, but must see what may be useful and helpful to his brother, as Paul says, . . . 'All things are lawful for me, but not all things are helpful' [1 Cor. 6:12]."[35]

In that Luther raised this comment of Paul to a criterion for the

33. MLStA 2:527,20-528,5.
34. LW 51:77; WA 10/III: 18,8-12/25-30.
35. LW 51:72; WA 10/III: 5,6-10/20-24.

structure of the liturgy, the congregational connection to worship became an integral, constitutive part of every liturgy. How he took this into account may be shown on the basis of several examples.

In *Receiving Both Kinds in the Sacrament*, published in April 1522, Luther justified his rescinding certain innovations in Wittenberg and once again offering only the host in the mass. He expressly emphasized that the innovations — offering the cup to the laity — were appropriate. Nevertheless he complained that "there are not enough people who are qualified to do it."[36] At the same time, he affirmed that he did not wish to stand in the way of anyone who celebrated the Lord's Supper using both kinds, as long as it did not occur in the presence of those who were weak in faith. The danger was too great that they would participate in the Supper and then afterwards confess this as a sin or absent themselves from the Lord's Supper altogether.[37]

Luther demanded that out of love consideration be taken for the consciences of the weak for a certain period of time until the gospel had been more fully proclaimed.[38]

Excising Unscriptural Elements

Proposals for a new pattern for the liturgy came not only from Wittenberg. In other places, too, pastors and preachers undertook changes in the mass and introduced new orders of worship. For example, Thomas Müntzer (c. 1489-1525) did so in Allstadt in 1523. As a result, beginning on 18 July 1523, the pastor in Zwickau, Nicholas Hausmann (1478/79-1538), begged Luther for liturgical advice. On 4 December 1523 Luther was able to send him the *Formula missae et communionis pro ecclesia Wittenbergensi* (The Form of Mass and Communion for the Church of Wittenberg), in which Luther still preserved Latin as the language of the liturgy.

It is customary to cite the title without mention of Wittenberg. This was already begun in both German translations of this writing, which were published in Wittenberg and Nuremberg beginning in 1524.

36. LW 36:249; WA 10/II: 24,10.
37. LW 36:256; WA 10/II: 30,28-31,3.
38. LW 36:256; WA 10/II: 31,6-8.

With this omission it became easy to forget that Luther was not publishing a master proposal for an evangelical form of worship. Instead, he was reporting on the state of liturgical reform in Wittenberg in 1523. That other congregations used Wittenberg as their model was their decision.

Luther criticized the Canon of the Mass and the priests' claims to a monopoly over the Sacrament implied therein. He reported that everything which had the least echo of sacrifice had been excised, including the Canon.[39] However, Luther by no means removed everything that went beyond what the New Testament reported about the institution of the Lord's Supper. On the contrary, he referred instead to 1 Thessalonians 5:12 and announced that "In the meanwhile we shall prove all things and hold fast what is good."[40] Included in this "proving" was the fact that Luther acquainted himself with the form of worship used in the early church, using especially the "Rationale divinorum officiorum" that William Durandus, bishop of Mende (1230/31-1291), wrote sometime before 1291 and since 1459 was available in print.[41] Thus, Luther could describe how the various liturgical elements had been introduced into the worship service[42] and pass judgment for himself on the later, spurious additions to the liturgy.

In comparison to 1522, a change had been introduced into the distribution of the Lord's Supper, because now the communicants were also offered the cup. Luther justified this based on the fact that in Wittenberg the gospel had been impressed upon the people for two years, so that the weak had now experienced sufficient forbearance. Now it was important not to strengthen the intransigent by continuing to tolerate the weak.[43]

Luther stuck to this line of argument. Later, in 1527-28, while developing *Instruction by the Visitors for the Pastors in Electoral Saxony* as the standard for constructing an evangelical church, he took account of the fact that in the previous years the evangelical message had been proclaimed with varying degrees of clarity. Thus, he took pains not only to insure adherence to the evangelical teaching regarding the

39. LW 53:21-22; WA 12: 207,14–208,1.
40. LW 53:22; WA 12:208,6-7.
41. See MLStA 1:366.
42. LW 53:20-21; WA 12: 205,23–207,9.
43. LW 53:34-35; WA 12:217,6-16.

Lord's Supper but also to maintain the possibility that those insufficiently instructed might for a time receive only the host.[44] Luther's conviction, that the structure of the liturgy must take into account the spiritual condition of the worshipers, deserves special attention.

Inclusion of the Singing Congregation

During the Middle Ages, two developments squeezed the congregation out of active participation in the celebration of the liturgy. What belonged to the official liturgy of the mass was to be prayed by the priest himself, since choral singing was no longer viewed as possessing full authority. Those pieces left the choir were so artfully constructed that the congregation could no longer participate in them.[45]

Already in the *Formula missae et communionis pro ecclesia Wittenbergensi* of 1523, Luther expressed the desire for many German songs that could be sung by the congregation during worship. He complained that qualified poets and musicians were lacking, who could create useful, Christian, and spiritual hymns.[46] The next year Luther and others brought out German songs that were enthusiastically received by congregations and spread rapidly throughout Germany. As Luther introduced a German mass in 1525 in Wittenberg, the situation regarding congregational songs differed radically from before.

Luther used these hymns. He constructed a completely sung worship service that incorporated the congregation. The priest sang the prayer of the day (collect), the Epistle lesson, the Gospel, the Words of Institution, the post-communion prayer, and the final blessing. The congregation sang an opening hymn, the Kyrie, a hymn between the readings, the Creed, and hymns during the distribution of the Lord's Supper.[47]

Luther did not anticipate choral singing in the German Mass of 1525, which was thought of as the worship service for regular Sundays. Choral singing had its place in the Latin Mass used on festival days. In the Ger-

44. LW 40:290-91; WA 26:214,1-216,6, especially 214,37-215,14.
45. Meyer, *Luther und die Messe*, pp. 36, 48-49, 75-76.
46. LW 53:36; WA 12: 218,15-23.
47. Schulz, "Der Gottesdienst bei Luther," 300.

man Mass of 1525 Luther involved the congregation in an active way to an extent that was unknown in the Middle Ages. Despite this, a development emerged through time parallel to what had occurred in the Middle Ages. To the extent that church music blossomed, the choir took over congregational singing. Church musicians and theologians chose for the congregation what they considered to be the most valuable songs and thereby overwhelmed the congregation to some extent. This made the congregation's full, personal participation in worship difficult. Some found little joy in these (for them) extremely difficult church hymns and became alienated from the worship service. Moreover, it could also happen that in some places church music became separated from worship and developed independent forms for its performance.

Consideration for the Various Groups in a Congregation

The agenda, *The German Mass and Order of Worship*, first rolled off the presses in the early part of 1526. Luther's discussion there of those who earnestly want to be Christians is generally well known and often cited.[48] His comments — that such people could gather separately in a house, that they would not need many songs or much in the way of an order of worship — are interpreted as a denigration of the liturgy and a lack of understanding for or interest in it. They are even used as justification for not attending worship. In this way it is not always kept in mind that Luther here is thinking of a community of Christians that practices intensive, communal spiritual care for one another and brotherly and sisterly exhortation according to Matthew 10:15-17. Luther had to admit that the people for such a community were neither available nor exactly lining up to join.

Thus, these remarks prove less Luther's disparagement of the liturgy than much more the necessity of it for all who want to be Christians and do not yet live in an inner, spiritual community.

Luther did not orient the pattern of the worship exclusively toward the spiritual experiences of the participants. Instead, he also considered their spiritual receptivity. That cannot be otherwise if the goal of worship is communicating the content of the gospel.

48. LW 53:63-64; WA 19:75,3-23.

Although Luther introduced a German Mass in Wittenberg in 1525, he did not want to abolish the Latin Mass completely, for in Wittenberg there was a Latin school and a large number of students. Latin was the language of almost all the universities in Europe. People who were familiar with Latin worship could speak with people in other lands and thereby serve Christ.[49]

Furthermore, in the Wittenberg of 1525 there were still other worship services designated for particular groups. Thus, at five or six o'clock in the morning on Sundays there was a service of preaching intended especially for the household servants.[50] This was necessary because the maids and menservants could not come to a later worship service on account of their household chores. Here the time for worship was accommodated to a particular group so that they could hear the Word of God. Then, too, on weekday mornings and evenings there were worship opportunities for the schoolchildren.[51]

The worship offerings in Wittenberg in 1525 were thus extremely varied. The receptivity of the worshipers was seriously taken into consideration. Moreover, there were also differences with respect to the texts. In the weekday services, parts of the catechism were read and explained on Mondays and Tuesdays; Wednesdays, selections related to love and good deeds from Matthew's Gospel; and Saturdays, selections from John's Gospel, which overwhelmingly taught faith.[52]

Luther on Worship: Slapdash, Arbitrary, or Free?

From the time of his sojourn at the Wartburg, Luther had felt under pressure to formulate a new order of worship — by 1525 finally even by the elector, John the Steadfast (1468-1532; ruler from 1525). Luther stressed that the Wittenberg order of worship dare not be universally binding and thereby made into a law.[53] One can assemble even more of his comments which leave the impression that, with respect to the or-

49. LW 53:62-63; WA 19:74,11-13.
50. LW 53:68; WA 19: 78,27-79,4.
51. LW 53:68-69; WA 19:80,1-24.
52. LW 53:68; WA 19:79,17-80,3.
53. LW 53:62; WA 19:72,3-73,6.

der of worship, Luther found himself in dire straits and willy-nilly concocted a provisional order.

This view, however, overlooks how intensively Luther had for years wrestled with the form and essence of the liturgy and with the reform of the late medieval mass, and how he had in fact developed an overall concept for worship. This concept grew out of his confrontation with the late medieval mass, but it is for that very reason not simply a rejection of the late medieval mass. Luther carefully examined the actual parts of the liturgy with the help of Scripture in order to celebrate a service of divine worship according to the Word of God.

Regarding the melodies used in the liturgy, he saw to it that the intonation of the melodies matched that of the text — just as he had learned from the humanists in Erfurt. Before completing his work, Luther turned for advice to the musical director at the Castle Torgau, Konrad Ruppsch (c. 1475-1530), and Johann Walther (1496-1570), who in 1526 had become the cantor of the city church in Torgau.[54] Therefore, Luther certainly did not undertake the reform of the liturgy out of "confusion caused by uncertainty," to use the dictionary's definition of *Verlegenheit.*[55]

However, did he not approach the liturgical texts and practices with too little understanding for their meaning? And did he not view the pattern of the worship service as something completely arbitrary? Did he not finally say

> We however take the middle course and say: There is to be neither commanding nor forbidding, neither to the right nor to the left. We are neither papistic nor Karlstadtian, but free and Christian, in that we elevate or do not elevate the sacrament, how, where, when, as long as it pleases us, as God has given us the liberty to do. Just as we are free to remain outside of marriage or to enter into marriage, to eat meat or not, to wear the chasuble or not, to have the cowl or tonsure

54. Brecht, *Shaping and Defining the Reformation,* p. 254.

55. *Brockhaus Enzyklopädie,* 19th ed., vol. 28, *Deutsches Worterbuch: Reh-Zz,* ed. Gunther Drosdowski (Mannheim: Brockhaus, 1995), p. 368a. Translator: The German reads, "Verwirrung verursachten Unsicherheit." In the heading of this section, the word "Verlegenheit" is rendered slapdash. In a letter to the translator dated 9 March 1999, Prof. Junghans wrote concerning the use of this term: "The theme of 'Verlegenheit' was assigned to me. The idea was to ask whether Luther had introduced liturgical reform pragmatically, without an underlying concept."

or not. In this respect we are lords and will put up with no commandment, teaching, or prohibition. We have also done both here in Wittenberg. For in the cloister we observed mass without chasuble, without elevation, in the most plain and simple way which Karlstadt extols [as following] Christ's example. On the other hand, in the parish church we still have the chasuble, alb, altar, and elevate [the host] as long as it pleases us.[56]

Behind these statements in no way stands the conviction that what happens in the worship service is completely arbitrary. Instead, Luther is protesting against attributing to human additions in worship the appearance of divine regulations. He simply dismisses arguing over externals in the worship service: for example whether the liturgical garb should or must be red, white, or black. For from such things arise fights and divisions, but without improving the mass itself.[57] However, he does not do this because it appears arbitrary to him. At the end of his order for the German Mass, he states what is decisive. "In short, this or any other order shall be so used that whenever it becomes an abuse, it shall be straightway abolished and replaced by another." And this change is not up to the arbitrary choice of any old person; instead it has a substantive basis. "For the orders must serve for the promotion of faith and love and not be to the detriment of faith. As soon as they fail to do this, they are invalid, dead and gone."[58]

Here Luther touches upon a central problem of liturgical texts and practices. They are symbols for proceedings that can lose the acceptance of many worshipers. They are then dead, despite the correctness of their actions and their weighty content, and no longer fulfill their purpose in divine worship.

For this reason there can never be a "correct" worship service. Even when the concept of the worship is the proper one, there is not for that concept a single pattern of worship that alone is the correct one. Thus, Luther never wanted to work out the "correct" worship service. Instead, he shaped it on the basis of his conception of worship, using the liturgical tradition for his Wittenberg congregation at a particular time. He

56. LW 40:130; WA 18:112,33–113,5. Cf. also WA 5:401,15-19 *(Operationes in Psalmos)* and LW 36:250; WA 10/II:24,25-27.

57. LW 35:80-81; WA 6:355,4-9.

58. LW 53:90; WA 19:113,4-10.

did not act in a slapdash manner, and he viewed liturgical texts and practices as anything but arbitrary. Rather, in Christian freedom and out of pastoral concern for his flock, he took up into the new form what appeared to him would further faith and love in the Wittenberg of his time. Luther's concept of worship poses this question to us: Do our evangelical, Lutheran orders of worship further faith and love among our congregational members?

In our day, liturgical efforts sometimes tend toward an ecumenical liturgy that allows the most churches possible to participate. For common worship services such efforts are doubtless worthwhile. However, as a rule such efforts tend to correspond to the counter-reformation structure of the mass. For Pope Pius V (1504-1572; pope from 1566) allowed the Council of Trent to implement a new pattern for the mass with the intention of strict uniformity. The "Missale Romanum" promulgated by him in 1570 was, apart from a few exceptions, to be the binding norm for the entire Western Church.[59]

Even in his later years Luther represented a different conviction. Thus, he thought it best that in territory of the Freiberg superintendent the customary ceremonies be maintained even six years after the introduction of the Reformation. For he feared that efforts toward uniformity would raise liturgical decisions to the level of articles of faith and lead to controversy. He could well imagine that with agreement in the chief things (that is, in the content of the proclamation) differences in external ceremonies would lead to enrichment and that the many voices would, as in music, result in a beautiful harmony.[60]

More important than uniformity for Luther was having a liturgy that furthered faith and love in congregations of a particular cultural context, according to their spiritual condition. At the same time, it was important for him that this liturgy matched his concept of worship. In this way, Lutheran liturgy always remains faced with this never-ending task: to use the liturgical tradition so that in the worship service God himself can act upon and serve current congregations in an easily accessible, enlivening way.

59. Josef Andreas Jungmann, "Messe," in *Lexikon für Theologie und Kirche,* 2nd ed. (Freiburg: Herder, 1962), 7:326.

60. WA Br 10:259,5–260,17 (no. 3846): Luther's answer to Superintendent Caspar Zeuner in Freiberg, dated 9 February 1543.

Luther on the Psalter

CARL AXEL AURELIUS

"... as if they were put there just for his sake."

Throughout the whole world, the Psalms are prayed daily in Christian congregations. It has been so since the beginning. No other book of prayers is used so diligently and is so highly beloved as the Psalter. How did this come about? The explanation can perhaps be found in the fact that the Psalms are uniquely up-to-date and of general validity. In his *Preface to the Psalter,* Luther points to this fact:

> Hence it is that the Psalter is the book of all saints; and everyone, in whatever situation he may be, finds in that situation psalms and words that fit his case, that suit him as if they were put there just for his sake, so that he could not put it better himself, or find or wish for anything better.[1]

Church history provides many examples of such an experience; for example, Augustine read the Psalter at Cassiciacum. In the *Confessions* he mentions among other items how the fourth Psalm completely changed the situation and the mood in which he then found himself:

1. LW 35:256; WA DB 10/1:103,22ff.

Translated by Wilhelm Linss. This article first appeared in *Lutheran Quarterly* 14 (2000): 193-205, under the same title.

What cries did I send up to you, my God, when I read the psalms of David, those canticles of faith, those songs of devotion, which exclude a boastful mind. I wish that they [my opponents] had been somewhere near me at that time, so that without me knowing it they could see my face and hear my voice as I read Psalm 4 in that time of meditation and witness what that psalm wrought within me, "When I called upon you, you heard me, O God of my justice! when I was in distress, you have enlarged me. Have mercy on me, and hear my prayer." . . . I shook with fear, and at the same time I grew ardent with hope and exultation in your mercy, O Father.[2]

In our own time, there are the letters of Bonhoeffer from his prison cell and especially the letter to his parents of May 15, 1943. He says, "I read the Psalms every day, as I have done for years; I know them and love them more than any other book."[3] In this letter he relates that it has become clear to him what the Bible and Luther mean by *Anfechtung* (Temptation) — a restlessness of the heart that quite without tangible psychical or physical cause suddenly disturbs the peace and the balance that support a person: "It feels like an invasion from outside, like evil powers trying to rob one of what is most vital."[4] In this connection, he quotes Psalm 13 in which the question is raised "that threatens to dominate everything here: 'How long, O Lord?'"

A third and last example from history is less well known. It is taken from the diary of a Swedish warrior, First Lieutenant Lyth. He participated in the devastating northern war, at the beginning of the eighteenth century. Like tens of thousands of others, he was a prisoner of war in Siberia after the defeat near Poltava and the capitulation near Perevolotjna. When the message of the death of the Swedish King Carl XII arrived in Siberia, he wrote the following lines:

We were sitting in our prison huts in this Siberian Babel and were weeping our hearts out when we thought of the unhappy death of our king and of our Swedish Zion. All our joy here was at an end, and

2. *The Confessions of St. Augustine,* trans. John K. Ryan (Garden City, N.Y.: Doubleday/Image Books, 1960), p. 210.

3. Dietrich Bonhoeffer, *Letters and Papers from Prison,* ed. E. Bethge (New York: Macmillan, 1971), p. 40.

4. Bonhoeffer, *Letters and Papers from Prison,* p. 39.

yet we had to hear often in our heartrending sadness from those who kept us prisoners: You dear Swedes, sing a song of your Zion and of where your king is. In this way we were often reviled and mocked in our great sorrow by our enemies; this was the comfort which we got to hear from them in our weeping. O misery! O distress! How should we with our fearful and wounded heart sing the song of our Lord in a foreign land?[5]

The passage in the diary of Lt. Lyth is nothing but a paraphrase of Ps. 137:

1. By the rivers of Babylon — there we sat down and there we wept when we remembered Zion.
2. On the willows there we hung up our harps.
3. For there our captors asked us for songs, and our tormentors asked for mirth saying, "Sing us one of the songs of Zion!"
4. How could we sing the Lord's song in a foreign land?

The Lieutenant was able to recognize in the words of the Psalm the personal and national catastrophe. In the words of the Psalm he was able to give expression to his and the others' "fearful and wounded heart."

Augustine, Bonhoeffer, and Lt. Lyth, Psalm 4, Psalm 13, and Psalm 137 — three examples of the aptness of Luther's statement that each can find in the Psalter "psalms and words . . . that suit him as if they were put there just for his sake." And in saying this, Luther speaks out of his own experience.

"In the meantime I had returned to the book of Psalms . . ."

Throughout his life Luther prayed and worked with the Psalter. In his old age, Luther tells in a preface to the edition of his Latin works of his so-called reformatory breakthrough when his unrest and fear changed into clarity and joy. There he says at the beginning, "I began a second

5. *Joachim Mathiae Lyths dagbok* (Stockholm: 1986), p. 89.

time to interpret the Psalter."[6] These words merit underlining, but maybe not because of the old debate over the dating of this event but rather as marking the horizon of understanding that represents the background of the event. In struggling with the words of God's righteousness in Romans 1:17, the Psalms are highly appropriate, not only as something with which Luther lived but also because at that very time he was occupied with the Psalter. The significance of reading the Psalter for the so-called reformatory breakthrough has already been emphasized, for example, by Heinrich Boehmer and Erich Vogelsang, starting with Luther's first great interpretation of the Psalter, the *Dictata super Psalterium*.[7] But perhaps something could be added.

By approaching the Latin preface with Luther's other great commentary on the Psalter (the *Operationes in psalmos*) in mind, one can make quite a few discoveries. Here one finds immediately things that connect directly to the late report on the breakthrough. Consider particularly the interpretation of Psalm 5:9: *Domine, deduc me in iusticia tua propter inimicos meos, dirige in conspectu tuo viam meam* (Lead me, O Lord, in your righteousness because of my enemies; direct my way in your sight [Ps. 5:8 NRSV]). The interpretation of the passage appears to be a short *model* for the Latin preface. The wording is similar; allusions and references are the same: Isaiah 61:10; Habakkuk 2:4; Augustine's *De spiritu et litera*, etc. Listen to some lines of the interpretation of this passage of the Psalter:

> We have to get used to the little word righteousness so that we have and retain its correct understanding and thus are enabled to understand God's righteousness: not the one by which God himself is righteous and condemns the godless, as it is ordinarily understood; but (as St. Augustine says, in his little book *On the Spirit and Letter*) the righteousness of God by which God clothes the human being when he makes him or her righteous, namely God's goodness and mercy, or God's grace which makes righteous, and through which we also are considered pious and righteous before God. St. Paul says of it in Rom. 1:17, "For in it (the gospel) the righteousness of God is revealed through faith for faith; as it is written (Hab. 2:4), 'The one

6. LW 34:337; WA 54:185,12.

7. See also James S. Preus, *From Shadow to Promise* (Cambridge, Mass.: Harvard University Press, 1969).

who is righteous will live by faith.'" . . . But the righteousness of God is called our righteousness because it is given to us, purely by God's grace and goodness, as a work of God which he works in us, like the word of God which he speaks in us and like the power of God which he works and exercises in us, and much more.[8]

Following Sigfried Raeder, one might say that the concept of "righteousness" here takes a meaning that is distinguished from the usual Western sense where it expresses the relationship to a norm and stands in immediate relationship to being rather than to doing. In pointing to Ludwig Köhler's and Gerhard von Rad's Old Testament theologies among others, Raeder states that by God's "righteousness" (sedaka) in the Old Testament "deeds, i.e. demonstrations of salvation" are meant — so that it is "not a juristic but a community-related concept." Therefore, the term is the expression of an "I-Thou relation" and not of an "I-norm relation."[9] According to Raeder, Luther came to this understanding of the term "God's righteousness" in his reformatory breakthrough.

I am not so exegetically trained as to be able to evaluate Raeder's terminological presentation, but I can state that the conclusion he draws is in complete agreement with fundamental trains of thought in Luther's understanding of the Psalter, especially in the pervasive theme that consists of the contrasting pair *abandonment and community*. That is, more correctly, the experience of being abandoned or of being in community. According to Luther, the Psalms are to be understood not as a discourse *concerning* God but rather as an address *to* God in various human situations that also bring to expression very different "affective" responses.

In this regard, Psalm 5 is no exception. According to Luther, the Psalm is an expression for what a person feels when assailed as a result of false proclamation. The Psalm provides a view into the struggle that is raging — for the Word, for faith and hope. When seen in the context of the Psalter, justification can hardly be understood as the basic idea in a theoretical system. It has a much larger context and is concerned

---

8. WA 5:144.

9. Siegfried Raeder, *Grammatica theologica. Studien zu Luthers Operationes in Psalmos* (Tübingen: Mohr, 1977), pp. 121f.

with the total existence of the human being, notably also with the questions of suffering and abandonment.

"There you look into the hearts . . ."

At the same time, the Psalms possess a general validity and reach deep inside the person. Normally when a person attempts to create something that suits many people, the result is superficial and vague. According to Luther, the remarkable thing about the Psalms is that here it is precisely the other way around. They are of general validity, always timely, and at the same time expose the feelings and thoughts in our innermost self. The Psalms let us see into the heart, that is, into the center of personality where both thoughts and feelings have their residence.

> What is the greatest thing in the Psalter but this earnest speaking amid these storm winds of every kind? Where does one find finer words of joy than in the psalms of praise and thanksgiving? There you look into the hearts of all the saints, as into fair and pleasant gardens, yes, as into heaven itself. . . . On the other hand, where do you find deeper, more sorrowful, more pitiful words of sadness than in the psalms of lamentation? There again you look into the hearts of all the saints, as into death, yes, as into hell itself.[10]

In this way, Luther says, the prayers of the Psalter are distinguished from all legends of martyrs, stories of saints, and books of examples that now have gained the upper hand. His observation is correct. At the end of the Middle Ages, it had come about that the prayers of the Psalter, still recited daily, were supplanted for the most part by another kind of prayer. In his preface to the *Personal Prayer Book,* the same critique can be found in an even more developed form.

> Among the many harmful books and doctrines which are misleading and deceiving Christians and give rise to countless false beliefs, I regard the personal prayer books as by no means the least objectionable. They drub into the minds of simple people such a wretched

10. LW 35:255f.; WA DB 10/1:103,7ff.

counting up of sins and going to confession, such un-Christian tom-
foolery about prayers to God and his saints! Moreover, these books
are puffed up with promises of indulgences and come out with deco-
rations in red ink and pretty titles; one is called *Hortulus animae,* another *Paradisus animae,* and so on. These books need a basic and thorough reformation if not total extermination. And I would also make
the same judgment about those passionals or books of legends into
which the devil has tossed his own additions.[11]

The legends draw an image of speechless people. We do not hear
them speak; we do not look into their hearts. Instead, their *deeds* are
represented and praised as worthy of imitation. This results in people
being misled to seek comfort where there is none, which in turn leads
to despair or hypocrisy. Thus the communion of saints is dissolved.
The good model is not lacking, but the word by which people can call
on God in the variety of life situations is missing. The Psalter gives this.
The various Psalms reflect the condition of the heart, the thoughts
and emotions that gain the upper hand in various situations. The
movement between sadness and joy, lament and praise, reflect nothing
but the course of the Christian life:

> For those who are tempted must at various times be comforted so
> that they may endure. Therefore joyous Psalms and Psalms of la-
> ment are mixed with each other in different order, so that this mix-
> ture of various Psalms and this confused order, as one thinks, is an
> example and an image of Christian life, which is exercised under
> many afflictions of the world and comforts of God.[12]

In his *Personal Prayer Book,* Luther attempts to deal with the imbal-
ance that had come about because of the Psalms' being superseded by
the books of examples and other books of this kind. The prayer book
consists mainly of instruction and assistance in prayer in the form of
an interpretation of the commandments, the creed, and the Lord's
Prayer. In addition, about ten Psalms are added.

In this connection it is worth mentioning that already this prayer
book hints at ideas characteristic of Luther, namely, that the Lord's

11. LW 43:11f.; WA 10/2:375,3ff.
12. WA 5:287,16ff.

Prayer comprehends all the prayers in the Psalter, indeed every true prayer. This idea is found also, for example, in Dietrich Bonhoeffer with direct reference to Luther:

> All prayers of Holy Writ are summarized in the Lord's Prayer. They are taken up into its immeasurable breadth. They are not made superfluous by the Lord's Prayer but they are the inexhaustible riches of the Lord's Prayer just as the Lord's Prayer is their crown and unity. Luther says of the Psalter, "It is so permeated by the Lord's Prayer and the Lord's Prayer by the Psalter that one can understand very well one from the other and that they happily harmonize."[13]

Bonhoeffer also helps illustrate what it means in our time to contrast the Psalms with the books of examples and legends. I am thinking of his meditative prayer, "similar to the Psalter," *Who am I?*[14] First we encounter the perspective of the surface, the perspective where the books of examples remain stuck, "serene and happy and solid like a lord of the manor in his castle." Then follows the perspective that lets us look under the surface, the perspective of the Psalms, "Or am I only that which I know of myself? Restless, longing, ill, like a bird in the cage, struggling for the breath of life, as if someone were strangling my throat." And then finally, that which alone can quiet the restlessness, "Who am I? Lonesome questioning mocks me. Whoever I am, you know me, I am yours, O God!"

But can such a poem indeed be characterized as a prayer, a prayer that is "similar to the Psalter"? Certainly it can, if one considers Luther's understanding of prayer in general and the prayer of the Psalter in particular. At the 1997 Luther Congress in Heidelberg, Gerhard Ebeling lectured on Luther and prayer. There he stated among other things, "Luther expands the literal meaning of 'prayer' to the entire meditative occupation with the Word of God."[15] In this connection, Ebeling quoted Luther's words in the Church Postil (Gospel for the Sunday after Christmas),

---

13. Dietrich Bonhoeffer, *Das Gebetbuch der Bibel. Eine Einfuhrung in die Psalmen* (1940) in *Gesammelte Schriften* 3 (München: Kaiser, 1987), p. 547.

14. Bonhoeffer, *Letters and Papers from Prison*, p. 347.

15. Gerhard Ebeling, "Beten als Wahrnehmen der Wirklichkeit des Menschen, wie Luther es lehrte und lebte," *Luther-Jahrbuch* 66 (1999): 165.

"Prayer," too, is understood to be not only oral prayer, but everything the soul does in God's Word — hearing, speaking, composing, meditating, etc. Quite a few psalms are recited as prayers and yet in them scarcely three verses offer petitions; the other verses say and teach something; they punish sin, they invite us to talk with God, with ourselves, and with people.[16]

Lament and Praise

The prayer of Bonhoeffer demonstrates a clear similarity with certain Psalms. Take, for example, Psalms 6 and 13, which begin with lament and then change into praise. In Luther's interpretation, this point of transition in the midst of the Psalms becomes meaningful, "What a completely different emotion this is."[17] Thus there is order, a model so to speak, in the midst of the disorder of the Psalms. The saddened person is comforted, and affliction and lament change into joy and gratitude. But what takes place? How is it to be understood when the praying individual at first laments the deep affliction and then immediately bursts out in praise? What is Luther's comment on this?

The first parts of Psalms 6 and 13 indeed provide insight into the situation of the assailed person, into the emotion — or better still, movement — of his senses. We become aware of the thoughts and feelings that eddy in his or her interior. They all attest that here the most difficult of battles has to be waged, the battle with death and hell. In distinction from what applies to lighter suffering (expressed in other Psalms) here all enemies disappear from the scene, and the person under assault (angefochten) experiences him or herself as opposed by God. In God's wrath God rejects the person for eternity. The words show and describe existence from the point of view of the one assailed, a condition where comfort is not to be found anywhere. Like the mystics, Luther speaks of this condition as a "darkness." What he means by this expression is shown by the two words of the Bible that he quotes here together: Genesis 1:2 and Romans 8:26. Obviously here the darkness of chaos, which "covered the face of the deep," is meant. The Spirit which

16. LW 52:139; WA 10/1:435,8ff.
17. WA 5:387,37.

at that time "swept over the face of the waters" is the Spirit that becomes now effective in the person under assault and "intercedes with sighs too deep for words." The Spirit brings it about that prayers — to be sure in the form of lament — rise to God in the one under assault. Luther, in other words, understands this sole sign of life not as a result of a last-ditch effort of the one under assault but as evidence for the fact that the Spirit lives and prays in the person. Also, the Spirit is operative in the intercessions of the faithful for the person concerned. In this way the person can overcome the assault until it is over. Such a change happens for Luther only through a word from outside, "*non tamen nisi per verbum dei et Ihesum Christum* (not in any other way but through the Word of God and through Jesus Christ)."[18]

In this way Luther explains the sudden transition in the Psalms from lament to praise. To summarize, Luther reads out of the Psalms an act of creation that, like the first creation, takes place *ex nihilo* and through the Word. Creation and salvation move closer to each other, almost become one and the same. The creative Word is the Word of God's mercy, that is, Jesus Christ. He comes to the person who now interprets the situation completely differently. Luther can say that for the person praying God has changed. Now he or she can again hope for everything good from God:

> But now since you have become my Lord and my God, so turn now to me, not only in order to hear me but also in order to hear me favorably and to do nothing else except to save and preserve me so that I may have a most merciful God in the place of a wrathful judge (*ut sic pro irato iudice clementissimum deum habeam*).[19]

God appears quite different to the praying person, and his or her entire conception of reality is changed. The real enemy, the devil, becomes manifest again; he uses, finally, false proclamation to keep the person under assault in order to bring that person to despair.

In Luther's interpretation, the overcoming of temptation, as it is reflected in the Psalter, becomes a thoroughly *creative* and *salvific drama* with a *trinitarian character*: the prayer of the Spirit, the arrival of the Son, the mercy of the Father. This transition — from darkness to light,

18. WA 5:216,2.
19. WA 5:388,19ff.

from death to life — is illuminated by the Psalms through the change of emotions they express. The pattern that appears is but the pattern of Good Friday and Easter and the pattern of baptism.

"The Use of the Gospel . . ."

It has been asserted that the Psalms in Luther's translation communicate an "atmosphere of loneliness" that makes any talk of church impossible. Luther appears, so to speak, as a destroyer of churches. For example, Werner Elert paints such a picture.

> This impression is given by the initial evangelical insight. We have developed it in the background of "fear," conscience, the Law, the wrath of God. . . . The judged person stands before God completely alone and lost. And this loneliness, this total feeling of abandonment, is essential to the experiencing of judgment.[20]

Elert does not deny that Luther certainly speaks of the church against this background; but basically he considers such speaking as impossible.

> Luther, it is true, did not absolutely destroy the church as a supraindividual unity; but he spiritualized it in such a way that when one pursues these thoughts to their logical conclusion, it is eliminated as a formative force of history.[21]

But how then can Luther assert that the Psalms let us see "the holy Christian Church painted in living color and shape,"[22] that they also — perhaps even especially — mediate an "atmosphere of community"? The answer to this may be traced in the preceding. For Luther, loneliness is far removed from any ideal. The experience of loneliness belongs to affliction and especially to assault (Anfechtung). In this loneliness is

20. Werner Elert, *The Structure of Lutheranism,* trans. Walter A. Hansen (Saint Louis: Concordia, 1962), vol. 1, p. 257 (with corrections).
21. Elert, *The Structure of Lutheranism,* p. 258. Elert naturally does not deny that Luther develops an ecclesiology, but "from a completely different side" that obviously has nothing to do with the Psalms.
22. LW 35:256; WA DB 10/1:105,5f.

found the sting of suffering and assault. In the Psalms this experience is made clear more dramatically than elsewhere. But as far as I can see, this is not an "evangelical starting point." In this way of thinking the theology of the cross *(theologia crucis)* runs the danger of becoming a principle by which it becomes possible to interpret reality in the same way the theologians of glory *(theologia gloriae)* do. The cross can appear only in the light of the resurrection as a symbol of salvation. "Evangelical starting point" means here not the emotions but to begin speaking, that is, prayer. The gospel is concerned with the answer to prayer, with the overcoming of temptation by a word from the outside that throws a completely new light on reality — as well as on suffering. The suffering and assaulted person is enabled to endure and to keep up courage for living by believing in God's mercy. This is how the trinitarian, creative, and salvific action of God looks in Luther's interpretation.

To the suffering person the situation appears no longer as hopeless because the Word differs from what the person sees and feels and from which he or she draws conclusions. The Word *contradicts and rejects the experienced reality*. You are not alone even if you perceive it to be so. When Luther wants to make clear this change of perspective that is brought about by the Word, he sometimes uses the story of Elisha and his servant, for example, in *A Sermon on Preparing to Die* from the year 1519. Luther quotes Psalm 32:8, "My eyes will constantly be upon you lest you perish." He continues:

> If God looks upon you, all the angels, saints, and all creatures will fix their eyes upon you. And if you remain in that faith, all of them will uphold you with their hands. And when your soul leaves your body, they will be on hand to receive it, and you cannot perish. This is borne out in the person of Elisha, who according to II Kings 6[:16-17] said to his servant, "Fear not, for those who are with us are more than those who are with them." This he said although enemies had surrounded them and they could see nothing but these. The Lord opened the eyes of the young man, and they were surrounded by a huge mass of horses and chariots of fire.[23]

The Psalms let us look into "the heart of all the saints," says Luther. But is it not only the praise that shows us the saints and gives us a

---

23. LW 42:112; WA 2:695,34ff.

picture of the church "painted in living color"? No, the Psalter accomplishes this in its entirety, all the Psalms, including the ones containing questions, laments, or protests, for the simple reason that they are sincere prayer where people turn to God in all the manifold situations of life, in all kinds of emotional states, with feelings and thoughts of every kind in the heart. And each sincere prayer testifies to the presence of God through the Holy Spirit.

In many cases, the praying individual speaks *contrary to his or her own heart,* feeling completely abandoned by people and by God, *nevertheless* calling to God. This may be the most outstanding feature of the Psalter, which Luther explains by reference to the presence of the Holy Spirit.

The contrast between Christian and non-Christian therefore becomes a question of what is important, whether one prays or not, whether one turns to God or away from God. Therefore Luther also can say, "What else . . . is faith but pure prayer?"[24]

Accordingly, for Luther every sincere prayer is an important *nota ecclesiae,* a mark of "the communion of all believers," just like the address of God through the proclaimed Word. Both testify that humans live *in the Word and from the Word.* Both attest how "the Father gives the Son to love the world in the Son and through the Spirit to draw the world back to God."[25] In this manner the triune God gathers and leads his people in the midst of what is hidden. The prayer and the address of God are "certain signs" for every questioning person — not least for the anxious one — that all this actually takes place.[26]

Thus it is not "the atmosphere of loneliness" but rather "the devotion of the community" that characterizes the Psalter in Luther's interpretation. And, against this backdrop, it is not difficult to discern one crucial consequence for Luther's purpose in the stormy years following 1520. It becomes clear when considering his *pastoral concern.* He is intentionally concerned with enabling the people to live in and from the Word. He translates the biblical texts. He writes model sermons. He teaches about prayer and issues prayer books and catechisms. He works with orders of services and orders for schools. He writes hymns.

---

24. WA 8:360,26ff.
25. Olov Hartman, "Treenigheten I dogm och mystik," in *Vår Lösen* (1976): 521.
26. LW 41:148; 164; WA 50:628,29ff.; 641,20ff.

Regarding this last-mentioned item, he prefers to start with the Psalter. Luther's letter to his friend Spalatin is well known. It contains some lines that explain the motivations for this undertaking by Luther: *quo verbum dei vel cantu inter populos maneat* (so that the Word of God may also remain among the people in song).[27] This motivation may — as far as I understand it — also be advantageously applied to the entire work of the Reformation in its various branches: "that God's Word may remain among the people." According to Luther, this is the decisive point, and therefore the Psalter is his "little Bible," so important for himself and for the reforming work he did.[28]

27. LW 49:68-70; WA Br 3:220 (no. 698).
28. LW 35:254; WA DB 10/1:99,24f.

Martin Luther's Reformation of Spirituality

SCOTT HENDRIX

Nobody would be more surprised than Martin Luther (1483-1546) himself to see an essay that discussed his view of spirituality.[1] Although it had been around for centuries,[2] the word *spiritualitas* was not commonly used by Luther, and it would be extraordinary to find him treating spirituality as a quality that belonged to him or to anyone else. Nevertheless, one can find a number of studies that bring together Luther and the words spiritual and spirituality. These works indicate several different ways in which one can define spirituality and write about its relationship to Luther.

In 1983 the Roman Catholic scholar, Jared Wicks, published a book titled *Luther and His Spiritual Legacy*,[3] most of which was an English translation of Wicks's article about Luther in the *Dictionnaire de Spiri-*

---

1. This essay was originally delivered as a lecture at the 1998 Martin Luther Colloquium on "Luther and Spirituality" at the Lutheran Theological Seminary in Gettysburg. It has been revised for publication.

2. Aimé Solignac, "L'apparition du mot 'spiritualitas' au moyen âge," *Archivum Latinitatis Medii Aevi*, vol. 44-45 (Leiden: E. J. Brill, 1985), pp. 185-206. Solignac finds the first occurrence of the Latin term in a letter written by Pelagius (c. 400) and traces the further usage of *spiritualitas*, which is rather sparse, into the fourteenth century. Thanks to my colleague Paul Rorem for bringing this essay to my attention.

3. Jared Wicks, S.J., *Luther and His Spiritual Legacy* (Wilmington, Del.: Michael Glazier, 1983).

This article first appeared in *Lutheran Quarterly* 13 (1999): 249-70, under the same title.

tualité.[4] Wicks defined Luther's spiritual legacy as those writings that speak to people about "living the Christian life" and lead them to "fuller Christian authenticity."[5] Eric Gritsch recently published a collection of Luther texts under the subtitle "Faith in Christ and the Gospel — Selected Spiritual Writings."[6] This appealing collection includes a wide range of texts set in the framework of a Roman Catholic ecumenical appreciation of the reformer. In this context the term spiritual also seems to define writings of Luther that provide a guide to Christian living in contrast to the polemical works of the reformer or to his treatments of political and social issues. The German scholar Robert Stupperich produced a study of Luther's inner religious journey to which he gave the title "Luther's Itio Spiritualis" or "Luther's Spiritual Journey."[7] What used to be described under the heading of Luther's early theological development or his Reformation discovery is here personalized to the extent that Luther's inner religious development becomes the main object of attention. One should also not forget Regin Prenter's classic study of Luther's teaching about the Holy Spirit, entitled *Spiritus Creator,* which Prenter introduces with the following statement: "The concept of the Holy Spirit completely dominates Luther's theology."[8]

These works demonstrate that one can take several approaches to the theme of spirituality and Luther. One can investigate Luther's views of prayer and personal devotion, study the Catechisms, and explore his treatises on the Christian life. Or one can study Luther's own religious development and assess its importance for the Reformation and for the churches that emerged from it. Finally, one could examine the place of the Holy Spirit in Luther's theology and relate it, as Prenter did, to the centrality of faith in Christ, to justification, and to word and sacrament. My purpose is closest to the first of these op-

4. Jared Wicks, S.J., "Luther (Martin)," *Dictionnaire de Spiritualité* 9:1206-43.

5. Wicks, *Luther and His Spiritual Legacy,* p. 7.

6. *Martin Luther: Faith in Christ and the Gospel — Selected Spiritual Writings,* ed. E. W. Gritsch (Hyde Park, N.Y.: New City Press, 1996).

7. Robert Stupperich, "Luther's Itio Spiritualis," in *The Bible, the Reformation, and the Church: Essays in Honour of James Atkinson,* ed. W. P. Stephens (Sheffield: Sheffield Academic Press, 1995), pp. 246-57.

8. Regin Prenter, *Spiritus Creator: Luther's Concept of the Holy Spirit,* trans. J. M. Jensen (Philadelphia: Muhlenberg Press, 1953), p. ix.

tions but not identical with any of them. If spirituality is taken in the sense of piety or living the Christian life,[9] then I am convinced that Luther initiated a reformation of spirituality; or, to say it another way: the Reformation which Luther initiated was also intended to be a Reformation of spirituality. Luther did not just write about living more devotionally as a Christian in the same way he might have done if there had been no Reformation. Instead, once the Reformation was underway, Luther and the evangelical movement proposed to change the actual pattern of Christian living, and they urged that pattern upon the faithful as the genuine way of being spiritual, as authentic Christian spirituality.

Spirituality and the Reformation

To find the precise meaning of spirituality for Luther and to appreciate its significance for the Reformation, it is helpful to consider one instance in which Luther uses the German equivalent of the Latin term *spiritualitas*. This German word, *Geistlichkeit,* occurs in Luther's exposition of the Gospel of John, which was constructed from sermons he delivered in Wittenberg in 1537. Even though what he says about *Geistlichkeit* is negative, his comments and their context — the first verses of John 15 — help us to understand what Luther thinks the right kind of spirituality would be. The text is verse 5: "I am the vine, you are the branches. Those who abide in me, and I in them, bear much fruit, because apart from me you can do nothing." This claim strikes Luther as exaggerated, and he asks what Christ could have meant by it:

> Is it possible that all the pious, excellent people who lived at that time among the Jews and that still exist among the Christians, accomplished nothing? . . . Is it not true that they performed, and still perform, many more works, and greater ones, than the poor, wretched, little flock which can boast of nothing but this Christ? . . . Or look at the heathen. See how well they have governed lands and

9. According to Solignac, this meaning is the first of three senses in which the term *spiritualitas* is used by medieval authors. He names this meaning the religious sense; the other senses he calls philosophical and juridical. Solignac, "L'apparition du mot 'spiritualitas' au moyen âge," p. 186.

people, established law and order, maintained peace and discipline, fostered knowledge of many kinds.[10]

Obviously they performed all these feats without Christ. How can Christ say: "Apart from me you can do nothing"?

The answer, says Luther, is to remember that Christ is speaking exclusively of his spiritual kingdom. "In this kingdom," Christ says, "you are nothing and can do nothing unless you are and remain in me."[11] Luther continues:

> All that the world undertakes, considers, and is able to do counts for nothing before God as, for instance, the meditation, the spirituality [*Geistlichkeit*], and the self-chosen worship[12] of all the Jews, Turks, and the pope's saints. . . . Nor can all monks and orders which teach and practice their works righteousness; they can never come to Christ, instill true knowledge, counsel or console consciences, deliver from the smallest sin, or bear any Christian fruit.[13]

The word here translated "spirituality," *Geistlichkeit,* refers to the religious activities of professionally religious people and in particular to religious activities which in Luther's eyes appear to be "self-chosen," that is, not commanded by God. According to Luther, his own experience in the cloister confirms that such spirituality is worth nothing in God's sight:

> For more than twenty years I was a pious monk, read mass daily, and so weakened myself with fasting and praying that I would not have been long for this life if I had continued. Yet all this taken together cannot help me in even one little crisis to be able to say before God: "All this I have done; now please consider it and be gracious to me." . . . I must now condemn it as sin committed in idolatry and unbelief; it terrifies me when I think of it.[14]

---

10. WA 45:668,34–669,4; 669,9-12; LW 24:227-28.

11. WA 45:669,19-20, 30-32; LW 24:228.

12. This phrase is an allusion to Luther's translation of a phrase in Colossians 2:23: "durch selb erwelete geistligkeyt." See WA DB 4:392,30. The verse was often used by the reformers in their critique of false piety. Thanks to Timothy Wengert for alerting me to this text.

13. WA 45:670,9-12; LW 24:229.

14. WA 45:670,15-20, 25-27; LW 24:229.

In Luther's mind, false spirituality or *Geistlichkeit* comprised the external devotions of late medieval piety — the countless masses and vigils, devotion to saints and pilgrimages to their shrines, the penitential system with its indulgences, and the entire world of monasticism. In other words, Luther rejected late medieval Christianity in its most popular forms, the practice of which he called spirituality, the external rites and devotions which he, too, believed he had mastered after twenty years of effort but which did not bring him peace and which he now rejected as the false worship of God.

This rejection is well known to students of the Reformation, but its significance can be underestimated by approaches to the Reformation that emphasize its continuity with medieval Christianity. This emphasis highlights the positive legacy of early Christianity that was preserved by the medieval church in contrast to the abuses of late medieval piety, which had to be removed by the reformers even as they claimed that positive legacy for themselves. It is true that Luther did not intend to establish a new church and that he did claim infant baptism and the Lord's Supper along with the Nicene faith as essential components of Christianity received by him and others through the medieval tradition.[15] Soon after 1517, however, if not already in that very year, Luther realized that he was engaged in more than a reclaiming of Pauline theology alongside the removal of a few religious abuses. Indeed, within four years, Luther had issued radical condemnations of the kind of Christianity practiced by most people around him as well as the kind of Christianity he had tried to practice himself. At the same time, Luther set about to install a new piety, that is, a new way of living and practicing the Christian religion.

In other words, while Luther the reformer never intended to start a new church, from the beginning he did intend to establish a new spirituality. Although his criticism of indulgences was experimental, its critique of the penitential system and of the papacy was biting enough to grab the attention of the clerical hierarchy who immediately saw the threat to their way of being Christian. The *Ninety-five Theses* were only the beginning of a campaign that within ten years abolished most of late medieval religiosity — spirituality — in the evangelical churches of Saxony. Gone were indulgences, gone were most private masses and

15. See, e.g., WA 26:147,13-26; LW 40:231-32 (*Concerning Rebaptism* 1528).

vigils, gone were pilgrimages, gone were monastic vows; for that matter gone from the cloisters were many monks and nuns, who with many priests, had left behind the celibate life for the state of holy matrimony. These rituals and institutions had dominated the spirituality of late medieval Christians, and Luther condemned them as a false *Geistlichkeit* that should be abolished.

There was continuity, of course, especially in public worship.[16] The public mass had not been abolished but revised to express and to embody the gospel; infant baptism and its liturgy were retained; the sacrament of penance was streamlined to emphasize confession and absolution in both a corporate and an individual form that was maintained or reintroduced in some places. The cycle of the Christian year was retained with its most important festivals. In spite of this continuity, however, five years later, not much was left in Wittenberg of popular late medieval religion. Even private masses and the relic collection at the All Saints Chapter, which gave stout resistance to the Reformation,[17] were dissolved by 1525. Private devotion to the saints, the use of rosaries, holy water, and similar practices continued behind closed doors in all evangelical areas. That we know from the so-called visitation records, the reports of teams of inspectors who were sent to the parishes of new evangelical churches to uncover and to root out the remnants of medieval piety.[18] Publicly, however, the practice of Christianity in Wittenberg had noticeably changed.

From our standpoint in a more ecumenical environment it is difficult to recapture how radical Luther's reformation of spirituality was. We can grasp it better, however, if we contrast it with the most popular and influential work on spirituality to come out of the sixteenth century, the *Spiritual Exercises* of Ignatius Loyola (c. 1491-1556), founder of the Society of Jesus. The *Spiritual Exercises* arose gradually from Loyola's

16. For an elaboration of this continuity and discontinuity in rituals that involved marriage, baptism, the churching of women, penance, the Lord's Supper, and dying, see Susan C. Karant-Nunn, *The Reformation of Ritual: An Interpretation of Early Modern Germany* (London and New York: Routledge, 1997).

17. Helmar Junghans, *Martin Luther und Wittenberg* (München & Berlin: Koehler & Amelang, 1996), pp. 100-105.

18. For a sample of such practices, see Ernst Walter Zeeden, *Katholische Überlieferungen in den lutherischen Kirchenordnungen des 16. Jahrhunderts* (Münster: Aschendorff, 1959), pp. 83-86.

own journey into the practice of Christian life.[19] The *Exercises*, however, were not intended to replace the already established forms of Christian piety, but to supplement them in order to help Jesuits prepare themselves and others to attain their goal of teaching Christianity. By this term, "teaching Christianity," they meant instructing people on how to live more serious Christian lives, or to guide, as John O'Malley says, "the formation of the good Christian."[20]

At the end of the *Spiritual Exercises* stands one of its most famous sections: "Rules for Thinking, Judging, and Feeling with the Church." These rules present a forceful reassertion of late medieval piety against the perception that reformers were abolishing the traditional forms of devotion. In fact, Ignatius had been suspected of wanting to do the same thing. For that reason perhaps, after advocating obedience to the church and weekly confession and reception of the sacrament, Ignatius explicitly upholds the following: frequent attendance at mass; long prayers inside and outside the church; holding virginity and continence higher than marriage; vows of obedience, poverty, and chastity and "vows to perform other works of supererogation which conduce to perfection"; prayer to the saints and veneration of their relics; pilgrimages, indulgences for jubilees and crusades, the lighting of candles in churches; precepts of fasting and abstinence; images and their veneration.[21] In other words, the *Exercises* reaffirm the entire late medieval system of external devotion, the hard scaffolding of medieval spirituality that Luther was trying to demolish because it was, in his words, "sin committed in idolatry and unbelief." Although the *Exercises* as a whole aimed at the reordering of interior attitudes and the seeking of God's will for one's life,[22] these aims were still pursued in the context of traditional piety.

---

19. For the English text of the *Exercises* and of Ignatius' *Autobiography* and for a thorough introduction to both, see *Ignatius of Loyola: The Spiritual Exercises and Selected Works*, ed. George E. Ganss, S.J., Classics of Western Spirituality (New York and Mahwah, N.J.: Paulist Press, 1991), pp. 9-214. For an analysis of the *Exercises* and a convincing interpretation of the origin and ministry of the Society of Jesus, see John W. O'Malley, *The First Jesuits* (Cambridge, Mass. and London: Harvard University Press, 1993), pp. 24-90, especially pp. 37-50.

20. O'Malley, *The First Jesuits*, p. 87.

21. Ignatius Loyola, *Spiritual Exercises*, ed. Ganss, pp. 211-12.

22. Ignatius Loyola, *Spiritual Exercises*, ed. Ganss, p. 121; O'Malley, *The First Jesuits*, p. 49.

Spirituality as Connectedness to Christ

What did Luther want to put in place of that traditional piety? What was the new spirituality, the new piety, the new landscape of an evangelical life? Luther painted this new landscape with the same textual brush that caused him to reject self-chosen *Geistlichkeit* — the exposition of John 15 (1537). He called that new landscape the spiritual kingdom and "God's own realm." It was, he said, "to baptize, to preach the gospel, to administer the sacrament, to console and strengthen timid and grieving consciences, to terrify and punish the wicked with excommunication, to perform works of love and mercy, and to endure the cross."[23]

This passage is one of many summaries of the evangelical life that occur in Luther's works, and it is set in the framework of what is often called his doctrine of two kingdoms. Mere mention of the two kingdoms evokes notions of a secular piety, an emphasis on the goodness and integrity of God's creation and on the legitimacy of secular callings for Christians. Both are indeed affirmed by Luther, especially the legitimacy of Christian life outside religious vocations, a point he also makes in his 1537 exposition of John 15. Against the external piety of the monastic life, which he judges to be done apart from Christ, Luther sets the actions of all Christians and calls them good fruit "even if it were something more menial than when a farm hand loads and hauls manure." Luther's main point, however, is not that all useful work done by anyone is good in God's eyes, but that a great difference obtains between what Christians do and what "a heathen or someone else — apart from Christ — does, even if the work is completely identical. For the works of the heathen do not spring and grow from Christ the vine. Therefore they cannot be called Christian fruit. But since the works of Christians proceed from faith in Christ, they are all true and useful fruit."[24]

In other words, Luther is making a point that is seldom emphasized when the language of two kingdoms appears. Luther is arguing that Christian life, that is, life in the spiritual kingdom under the government of Christ, is different from the life of non-Christians, not be-

23. WA 45:669,30-36; LW 24:228.
24. WA 45:672,15-26; LW 24:231-32.

cause Christian life is manifestly and voluntarily religious, but because Christians, by virtue of baptism and faith, are tied to Christ just as branches are connected to the vine and receive their life from it. Luther does not call this connection spirituality, but if we apply the term to his writings in a positive sense, then we can safely say that for Luther spirituality is what makes life in the kingdom of Christ different from life in the world. That difference is the connectedness of Christians to Christ, which they have not chosen but instead received.

He does not call it spirituality in the exposition of John, but in 1537 and fourteen years earlier in exactly the same context Luther does use the term spiritual life *(vita spiritualis; geistliches Leben)* for the essence of what it means to be Christian. Luther rejects the church's regulation of external matters as essential to the Christian life. Fasting, festivals, vestments, other external matters — none of those things is Christ, he says, and without Christ none of those externals brings faith, the Spirit, or anything else that belongs to the spiritual life. "It [the spiritual life] comes from Christ alone *(ex solo Christo),* not from your fasting, not from your cowl, not from your monastery, nor from any of those things ever established by popes, councils, or monasteries."[25]

The spiritual life comes out of Christ alone — *ex solo Christo* — and consists of an intimate connection to Christ. In 1537 Luther expresses this connection forcefully, stringing together several different metaphors: "Christ and Christians become one loaf and one body," he writes, "so that Christians can bear good fruit — not their own fruit but that of Christ. For when Christians baptize, preach, console, exhort, work, and suffer, they do these things not as children of Adam, but Christ does it in them. The lips and tongues with which they proclaim and confess God's Word are not theirs; they are the lips and tongue of Christ. The hands with which they toil and serve their neighbors are the hands and members of Christ, who . . . is in them, and they are in Christ."[26] This emphatic statement of the connection between Christ and the Christian — and others like it — testify to Luther's conviction that life in Christ is a new reality in which the baptized and the justified participate. The spiritual life in Christ is for Luther not just a possibility but in some sense a present reality.

25. WA Br 3:211,74-82 (Latin); 3:216,92-217,103 (German).
26. WA 45:667,32-668,3; LW 24:226.

The exact nature of this reality plays a significant role in the current debate over the views of the Finnish school of Luther research. These scholars argue that justification for Luther entails a real union between the believer and Christ which approximates the Orthodox view of salvation as divinization *(theosis)* or becoming like God.[27] A full discussion of this debate is not possible here, but it does help to sharpen the issue of the nature of Christian spirituality (the *vita spiritualis*) for Luther. The Finnish theologians have reacted in general against the tendency of much Luther scholarship to interpret the reformer's view of justification mainly in a forensic way that minimizes the change which happens in justification and that minimizes the difference between the person before and the Christian after baptism. The same forensic view of justification emphasizes Luther's contention that the baptized believer remains a sinner and is therefore *simul iustus et peccator.* In terms of spirituality, the same view might argue that the *vita spiritualis,* the new life in Christ, is for Luther mostly eschatological, a union more to be hoped for than to be enjoyed in the present. The new reality of justification and Christian spirituality would then be located more in God's new evaluation of believers than in the believers themselves.

Against this view the Finnish scholars hold up, among other passages, Luther's use of terms related to the notion of divinization, and they point to passages, like the one quoted above, that depict the connection of the believer to Christ in metaphorical but very graphic terms.[28] What do these metaphors say about the spiritual life in Christ

---

27. This school, composed of Tuomo Mannermaa and former students, began to take shape in the 1980s through their publications and a series of symposia in Europe. It became increasingly visible to American scholars at the international congresses for Luther research held at St. Paul in 1993 and at Heidelberg in 1997. Some representative essays and bibliography are available in *Union with Christ: The New Finnish Interpretation of Luther,* ed. C. Braaten and R. Jenson (Grand Rapids and Cambridge, U.K.: Eerdmans, 1998). See also the essays from a 1992 symposium in Helsinki titled *Luther und Ontologie: Das Sein Christi im Glauben als strukturierendes Prinzip der Theologie Luthers,* ed. A. Ghiselli, K. Kopperi, and R. Vinke (Helsinki and Erlangen: Luther-Agricola-Gesellschaft and Martin-Luther-Verlag, 1993); and the Festschrift for Mannermaa, *Caritas Dei: Beiträge zum Verständnis Luthers und der gegenwärtigen Ökumene* (Helsinki: Luther-Agricola-Gesellschaft, 1997).

28. A careful analysis of Luther's use of such terms and metaphors is offered by Albrecht Beutel, "Antwort und Wort," in *Luther und Ontologie* (see note 27), pp. 70-93. Beutel notes that Luther uses the terms *deificare* and its derivatives sparingly and does not engage in speculation about the divinization of humanity (p. 76).

in light of the Finnish openness to concepts like divinization? In the first place, the fact that Luther uses such biblical, metaphorical language for the connection of Christians to Christ does not mean that Christians become Christ in the sense of losing their humanity in a union with the divine. Other theologians whose works Luther knew well explicitly limited the union of Christians with Christ the vine to the human nature of Christ. Augustine (354-430) said that humans could only be united with the *human* nature of Christ and, consequently, Christ is the vine only in his human nature.[29] Using another traditional image, Luther's Augustinian superior and spiritual mentor, Johann von Staupitz (d. 1524), described the union between Christ and the Christian as an exchange between bride and bridegroom, even projecting an exchange of properties that enabled Christ and the Christian to say that each was the other. Still, von Staupitz makes clear that this exchange is not the result of our union with the divinity of Christ but of the assumption by Christ of human nature.[30] Since Luther also emphasized the redemptive efficacy of Christ's human nature, for example in the Lord's Supper, and since the term "union" can imply a mystical identification with the divine nature alone, I prefer to speak of the believer's connectedness to Christ instead of the believer's union with Christ.

In the second place, however, these metaphors point to the reality of this connectedness and to the distinctiveness of Christian existence

29. Augustine, *In Joannis evangelium* lxxx.1, *Patrologiae cursus completus,* Series Latina, ed. J.-P. Migne (Paris, pp. 1841ff.), 35:1839: "Unius quippe naturae sunt vitis et palmites: propter quod cum esset Deus, cuius naturae non sumus, factus est homo, ut in illo esset vitis humana natura, cuius et nos homines palmites esse possemus." Hereafter cited as PL.

30. Johann von Staupitz, *Libellus de exsecutione aeternae praedestinationis,* ed. L. Graf zu Dohna and R. Wetzel, ix.56, in *Lateinische Schriften II,* vol. 14 of *Spätmittelalter und Reformation: Texte und Untersuchungen* (Berlin and New York: Walter de Gruyter, 1979), p. 144: "Contractus Christi et ecclesiae consummatus est, et talis: 'Ego accipio te in meam, accipio te mihi, accipio te in me'; et econverso ecclesia sive anima dicit Christo: 'Ego accipio te in meum, accipio te mihi, accipio te in me'; ut sic Christus dicat: 'Christianus est meus, christianus est mihi, christianus est ego'; et sponsa: 'Christus est meus, Christus est mihi, Christus est ego'"; and ix.61, p. 148: "Ex his omnibus consequens est, quod omnia quae habet Christus, verbum incarnatum, per assumptionem humanae naturae nostra fecit, ad salutem nostram omnia donavit, dicente scriptura: 'Qui proprio filio non pepercit, sed pro nobis omnibus tradidit illum, quomodo non etiam cum illo omnia nobis donavit.'"

in the world. It is difficult to believe that Luther would use such graphic metaphorical language if he were not trying to show that the *vita spiritualis* of Christians (which comes from Christ alone) is participation in a divine reality that changes them. As long as the term *theosis* or divinization is not taken to mean that the baptized believer is unencumbered by sin or that no forensic language whatsoever is appropriate, then Finnish scholarship has performed a service by calling attention again to the new reality in Christ that constitutes the heart of Luther's spirituality. Even though we remain human and continue to struggle with sin, Christ still speaks and acts through us, and this reality empowers the Christian life and makes Christians different, in Luther's eyes, from the world.

Spirituality and Luther's Theology

If the core of Luther's spirituality is connectedness to Christ in the spiritual kingdom, several more things need to be said about it in order to make its place in Luther's theology more precise and to avoid misunderstandings.

First, when Luther rejects the external forms of late medieval piety, he is not saying that Christian life or spirituality is strictly internal, but that Christianity is never a matter of mere externals. A Christian who merely goes through the motions or relies exclusively on manifest religiosity is not truly Christian. Instead, a new person has to be created internally; a new birth has to take place. Commenting on the text "the one who abides in me and I in him" (John 15:5), Luther writes,

> Christ wants to indicate that Christianity is not put on like a garment, nor does it consist in the adoption of a new manner of living, which, like monasticism and self-chosen sanctity, is concerned with works. It is a new birth brought about by God's Word and Spirit; there must be an entirely new person from the bottom of the heart. Then, when the heart is born anew in Christ, fruits will follow naturally, such as confession of the Gospel, works of love, obedience, patience, chastity, and others.[31]

31. WA 45:668,4-12; LW 24:227.

A familiar theme reappears in this text. Christian life is not a "self-chosen" *(selb erwelete)* form of holiness but emerges "naturally" from the new birth in Christ.

This natural or spontaneous flow of Christian life has both external and internal components. It takes the form of a sandwich, not a lofty illustration to be sure, but graphic and instructive nonetheless. The filling inside is the new person in Christ, but that new person is always flanked by two slices of very important bread: on one side, the proper external means through which the new internal birth takes place, namely, the Word of God in its oral and visible forms, enumerated by Luther in many places: baptism, preaching, the Lord's Supper, and office of the keys. On the other side, that other slice of bread, the external results of the new birth are the visible expression of the new person in Christ. This visible behavior was held up by Luther as part of life in God's own realm — performing works of mercy and enduring the cross.[32] Being born anew and staying rooted in Christ depend on the proper external ritual, and they generate appropriate external responses. Sandwiches can fall apart if they are not handled carefully; but so can the Christian life when it is not carefully nurtured by the assiduous use of external means and when external responses dry up.

Second, the Holy Spirit plays an essential role in Christian spirituality for Luther. The new birth and the new connectedness to Christ come only through the operation of the Holy Spirit. Luther's spirituality is indeed Christocentric, but it is not Christomonist; it neither ignores nor neglects the third person of the Trinity. Nor can the Holy Spirit place us into a new spiritual life apart from Christ, a life that looks for spiritual paths to God other than Christ. Luther writes:

> When I am baptized or converted by the Gospel, the Holy Spirit is present. He takes me as clay and makes of me a new creature, which is endowed with a different mind, heart, and thoughts, that is, with a true knowledge of God and a sincere trust in God's grace. To summarize, the very essence of my heart is renewed and changed. This makes me a new plant, one that is grafted on Christ the vine and grows from him.[33]

32. WA 45:669,35-36; LW 24:228.
33. WA 45:667,20-26; LW 24:226.

The essence of Luther's spirituality, connectedness with Christ, is a work of the Holy Spirit, who creates that connection through baptism and the word. There is no spirituality for Luther, or spiritual life in Christ, without the work of the Spirit. And there is no genuine work of the Spirit in us that does not connect us to Christ.

Third, spirituality for Luther is certainly internal as well as external, but it is not, in my historical understanding of the word, mystical. On this point I differ slightly from Bengt Hoffman, although I second the way in which Hoffman held up the internal and personal dimension of the Christian life for Luther. In a chapter on Lutheran spirituality, Hoffman wrote:

> If we define spirituality as the awareness of the presence of the Holy Spirit mediated by the risen Christ, it is clear . . . that the tradition emanating from Martin Luther contains an essential element of the inward, personal, and subjective, which is often associated with the term "spirituality."[34]

I agree with that statement, and I also agree with his assertion that certain interpretations of Luther have obscured this dimension of Luther's thought.[35] When too much emphasis is placed upon the Christ *for* us to the exclusion of the Christ *in* us, and when *simul iustus et peccator* is construed to mean that the new person in Christ looks like the same old ugly sinner without Christ, then Luther's theology is so distorted that the "riches and glory of the Christian life"[36] evaporate and there seems to be no difference, not to mention no point, in becoming Christian at all. Hoffman held up that difference, the newness

34. Bengt Hoffman, "Lutheran Spirituality," in *Spiritual Traditions for the Contemporary Church*, ed. R. Maas and G. O'Donnell (Nashville: Abingdon, 1990), p. 147.

35. Hoffman, "Lutheran Spirituality," p. 148. Although I agree with Jim Kittelson's claim that Luther "knew no unbridgeable duality, not even the currently vaunted one between mind and heart," I disagree with his criticism that Hoffman introduces such a duality into Luther's thought. See James M. Kittelson, "Contemporary Spirituality's Challenge to Sola Gratia," *Lutheran Quarterly* 9 (1995): 367-90, esp. 390, n. 43. The duality of which Hoffman speaks, "the two sides of gospel proclamation, the Christ-for-us of Lutheran orthodoxy and the Christ-in-us of Lutheran pietism," are for him "integrally related in Luther's thought." See Hoffman, "Lutheran Spirituality," p. 148.

36. WA 7:66,29-38; LW 31:368 (*Freedom of a Christian* 1520).

and integrity of the Christian life, against tendencies to overemphasize the continuing power of sin, the Christ *extra nos,* and even Luther's own worldliness. And in this vein, Hoffman dared to affirm Luther's spirituality before it became fashionable and regarded it, rightly I think, as integral to the Reformation.

Whether Luther's reformation of spirituality is also mystical, however, depends completely on how one defines mystical. Martin Bucer (1491-1551), a decidedly non-mystical reformer, could write in the same vein as Luther: "For Christ, our master and governor, lives and acts in individual Christians."[37] The German Luther scholar Reinhard Schwarz argues that "if we understand mysticism to be the inwardness of being united with God, then we find mysticism in Luther."[38] Indeed, if, as Bengt Hoffman defined it, mystical theology for Luther was the experience of God,[39] then Luther's spirituality had a significant mystical component. If, however, we adopt the stricter criterion of Bernard McGinn, Luther looks less like a mystic: "The mystical element within Christianity involves a form of immediate encounter with God whose essential purpose is to convey a loving knowledge . . . that transforms the mystic's consciousness and whole way of life."[40] The degree of Luther's mysticism, if it exists, depends therefore on how mysticism is defined; but it is clear that, while Luther retained its emphasis on the inward experience of God, medieval mysticism incorporated features that were antithetical to Luther's spirituality. It is important to be clear about these; otherwise one overlooks important discontinuities between medieval piety and Luther's spirituality.

Although it was not an explicit part of his agenda, Luther could have reformed mysticism in the same way that he reformed piety: by

37. Martin Bucer, *De regno Christi* i.8; in *Martini Buceri opera latina,* vol. 15, 1, ed. F. Wendel (Gütersloh: Bertelsmann, 1955), p. 71: "Etenim Christus, magister et gubernator noster, vivit agitque in Christianis singulis." Cf. *Melanchthon and Bucer,* ed. W. Pauck, Library of Christian Classics 19 (Philadelphia: Westminster, 1969), p. 241.

38. Reinhard Schwarz, "Martin Luther (1483-1546)," in *Grosse Mystiker, Leben und Wirken,* ed. G. Ruhbach and J. Sudbrack (München, 1984), pp. 185-202, 375-80.

39. Hoffman, "Lutheran Spirituality," p. 150. For a more elaborate treatment of this question see Bengt Hoffman, *Luther and the Mystics* (Minneapolis: Augsburg, 1976).

40. Bernard McGinn, "The Changing Shape of Late Medieval Mysticism," *Church History* 65, no. 2 (1996): 197-219. Luther's original understanding of this criterion, usually called ecstasy, is traced by David C. Steinmetz, "Religious Ecstasy in Staupitz and the Young Luther," *Sixteenth Century Journal* 11 (1980): 23-37.

recalling Christian experience to its center in Christ[41] and by extending the spiritual privilege of union with Christ to all the baptized on the basis of their membership in the spiritual kingdom. Wherever medieval mystics posited an access to God that depended on something other than faith in Christ and wherever that access seemed limited to an elite group of spiritual people, then Luther would reject that kind of mysticism just as he rejected monasticism, which, in his judgment, set certain religious practices over others on the basis of self-chosen external devotions not centered in Christ. Insofar as Luther emphasized the inner life of faith and made the internal connection with Christ the core of spiritual life, he represents continuity with the best of the Christian spiritual tradition, a continuity deservedly held up by Bengt Hoffman and others. Insofar, however, as Luther's spiritual priesthood of the baptized contradicted tendencies of mysticism, his discontinuity with that tradition is part of his reformation of spirituality.

Luther's Guestly Spirituality

This reformation is marked by the fact that Luther was more of a historian than a mystic. For him the spiritual life focuses more on the ongoing life of believers in the Spirit than of the Spirit in believers. The connectedness to Christ is not so much a state of mystical union as it is an actual journey taken with Christ. Spiritual life in the kingdom of Christ does not mean to transcend the world in ecstasy or to deny it in withdrawal, but instead to live in the world bravely, yet provisionally. In Luther's reformation of spirituality, the Christian lives in the world neither as a mystic nor as a monk, but as a guest. This image of Luther's spirituality — Christians as guests in the world — is evoked by a text from his lectures on Genesis 12:1: "Now the Lord said to Abram, 'Go from your country and your kindred and your father's house to the land that I will show you.'" For Luther, as for the author of Hebrews (11:8-12), Abraham is an example of faith because he obeyed the command of God promptly, leaving everything behind without knowing

---

41. See, for example, Paul Rorem, "Martin Luther's Christocentric Critique of Pseudo-Dionysian Spirituality," *Lutheran Quarterly* 11 (1997): 291-307.

exactly where he was going.[42] Sarah, too, says Luther, is equally praise-worthy, because she "herself leaves her native country and dear relatives as well as a household that was surely well established — all to follow an uncertain hope."[43] Sarah did not follow Abraham "merely out of wifely affection," but "she was aided by the Holy Spirit, who moved her heart so that she also, disregarding everything else, followed God when he called, since she also desired to be saved."[44] And even though Abraham, Sarah, and Lot took with them all their possessions, says Luther, yet they were still exiles because "they had these possessions as though they did not have them" in the spirit of 1 Corinthians 7:31, "dealing with the world as though they had no dealings with it."[45]

Luther then describes this faith — this guestly spirituality of Abraham and Sarah — in more detail for his readers and hearers to contemplate:

> Thus they live in the world at all times . . . and concern themselves with the affairs of the home and of the state, govern common-wealths and rear families, till fields, run businesses and perform manual labor; and yet, they are aware that they are exiles and strangers, like their ancestors. They make use of the world as an inn from which they must emigrate in a short time, and they do not attach their heart to the affairs of this life. They tend to worldly matters with their left hand, while they raise their right hand upward to the eternal homeland. No matter how they may be treated in this inn, it is satisfactory to them; for they know that eternal mansions have been prepared by the Son of God.[46]

That Christians should regard themselves as exiles or guests in the world is a commonplace in the Christian tradition. For Augustine the heavenly city of God is always on a pilgrimage through this world, and Ignatius Loyola refers to himself as "the pilgrim."[47] Luther, however,

---

42. WA 42:462,35–463,6; LW 2:281.
43. WA 42:441,7-9; LW 2:251-52.
44. WA 42:441,22-25; LW 2:252.
45. WA 42:441,36-39; LW 2:252-53.
46. WA 42:441,40–442,7; LW 2:253.
47. Augustine, *De civitate dei* xix.17 and xviii.1, PL 41:645-46 and 41:559. See Peter Brown, *Augustine of Hippo: A Biography* (Berkeley and Los Angeles: University of Califor-

has a specific guestly stance in mind. The merit of Abraham's obedience is not merely that he left behind all his worldly advantages but that he forsook the false religion of his ancestors for the true worship of God. In that obedience Luther sees a precedent for his own experience and for the Reformation as a whole:

> It is something far greater and more difficult that [Abraham] allows himself to be convinced that the religion in which he was reared by his parents was ungodly and contrary to the will of God. It is our experience, too, that it is by far the most difficult of all tasks to win those who were brought up in the papistic religion, even though it is manifestly ungodly and blasphemous. Yes, even we ourselves, who renounced the doctrine of the pope long ago, still have to struggle often and hard to overcome this wretchedness, which has been doubled by habit; for we are born hypocrites, and afterwards we are confirmed in our hypocrisy by ungodly teachers.[48]

This passage is not just the crotchety old Luther talking; nor is it the angry, anti-ecumenical outburst of a Christian who momentarily violates his own spirituality. This is the voice of a reformer, a reformer of spirituality, who sincerely believes that the old piety was a betrayal of the essence of Christianity and that the evangelical movement had recovered genuine Christian piety, called by Luther elsewhere the "spiritual life" and represented here by the journey of faith undertaken by Abraham and Sarah, living day by day as guests in the inn of the world.

It may seem to be straining the texts to relate Luther's exposition of John to his lectures on Genesis, life in the vine to life in the guesthouse, the deep-rootedness of Christians in Christ with the journey of Abraham and Sarah in faith. Luther, however, sees them together and demonstrates the connection in his comments on Genesis 12:3: "And in you all the families of the earth shall be blessed." The connection is the promise of God to Abraham and how it was fulfilled and disclosed:

> In such brief and simple words the Holy Spirit wrapped the mystery of the incarnation of the Son of God, which later the holy patriarchs

nia Press, 1969), pp. 323-24. Ignatius Loyola, *Autobiography*, ed. Ganss, pp. 87, 89, 90 et al. See O'Malley, *The First Jesuits*, p. 271.

48. WA 42:440,33-40; LW 2:251.

and prophets developed more broadly in their sermons, namely, that through the Son of God the whole world would be liberated, hell and death destroyed, the law abrogated, sins pardoned, and eternal life and salvation freely given to all who believe in him. This is the day of Christ, concerning which he preaches in John [8:56], which Abraham did not see with bodily eyes but saw in the spirit and he rejoiced.[49]

Luther's guestly spirituality, therefore, is an important commentary on his spirituality of connectedness with Christ. The stance of Christians as guests in the world points to the fact that Luther's main concern was not to scrutinize this connectedness or to narrate his experience of it in the tradition of some mystics. It was a real connectedness, no doubt about it, and it was essential for genuine Christian life in the world. It took precedence over external forms of piety and it was the source of all activity that was good in the eyes of God. Ultimately, however, it was not a static communion with God that embodied the spiritual life but a dynamic participation in the day of Christ that was already present to guests in this world and still to come in fullness at the end of the Christian's journey.

The guestly metaphor helps us to avoid two misinterpretations of Luther's abandonment of his own ancestral religion. First, it corrects an overemphasis on Luther's worldliness that one finds in the wake of his condemnation of monasticism.[50] In Luther's eyes, to be sure, Christians should not abandon the world; they affirm and participate in the world, its stewardship and its governance. Still, they do it with a certain tenuousness because they are guests and not its owners, and like guests they treat it with respect, appreciate and even enjoy it, but they do not invest it with ultimate meaning, knowing that the destiny of the world, like their own, is in the hands of God their Creator. Luther's goal was not to make Christians more worldly by yanking them out of the cloister, but to call all baptized Christians to a deeper connection with Christ, that is, a deeper spirituality, in the world.

49. WA 42:448,17-23; LW 2:261.
50. Indeed, elements of Luther's monastic training and experience remained part of his own devotional life. A good example is his advice about how to read Scripture for the study of theology by means of *oratio*, *meditatio*, and *tentatio*. This advice is contained in his preface to the 1539 Wittenberg edition of his German writings; WA 50:657-61; LW 34:283-88.

Second, it is not fair to Luther if one speaks ahistorically about his spirituality. We should not treat Luther the spiritual author as if the Reformation never happened. One can, of course, select texts from Luther's writings that make him seem like one more great commentator on the spiritual life in a long line of such venerable Christian experts. Some of those texts, such as the ones cited in this essay, can be held up as inspiring samples of Luther's Christ-centered spirituality. To do only that, however, would be to abstract Luther's spirituality from its historical context, the real struggle, in which it was forged.

Although it may seem downright unspiritual, the Reformation was a battle over spirituality, over the genuine practice of Christianity that would enable the historic trinitarian faith to take deeper root in Europe. The example of Abraham was not just an inspiring possibility to ponder; instead, leaving behind the religion of one's ancestors for new ways of living out one's connectedness to Christ — that was the daunting reality of the Reformation that led into a future known only to God. To adopt this new spirituality was itself to set out on a journey of faith that left behind the props of the old religion before the new supports were securely in place. Luther's guestly spirituality, therefore, was not a theoretical model, but a reality in his own life, just as real as his connectedness to Christ and just as real as his baptism, which launched him on the journey from this life to his destination in the life of God.

Spirituality as a New Reality

All during his journey, Luther is very much aware that the word spiritual can mean something less than the new and deep life in Christ that he envisioned as the goal of the Reformation. The word *Geistlichkeit* was negative for Luther, and the word spiritual can be the same. It can mean merely metaphorical or less than real, as Luther makes clear in his statements about baptism in the *Babylonian Captivity of the Church*. Arguing that the full significance of baptism is more than the washing away of sins, indeed, that it involves death and resurrection, Luther writes: "The sinner does not so much need to be washed as to die, in order to be wholly renewed and made another creature, and to be conformed to the death and the resurrection of Christ, with whom the person dies and rises again through baptism."[51] For believers in Christ the sacrament of baptism is shown to have an ongoing and permanent effect.

> For as long as we live, we do that which baptism signifies, that is, we die and we rise; we die, I say, not only in our desire and spiritually by renouncing the sins and vanities of the world, but we die truly, we begin to leave behind this bodily life and to lay hold on the life to come, so that there is, as they say, a real and bodily passing out of this world unto the Father.[52]

In Luther's guestly spirituality, then, the faithful are not on a spiritual journey in some metaphorical sense, not just guests in the world in a manner of speaking. No, in baptism they really die to the world — not only in their desires and spiritually, but in truth, in reality *(non solum in affectu et spiritualiter sed revera)* — they have entered a real passage from this world into the eternal life of God. Luther's spirituality is a new reality. Christians are guests in this world because they have begun to make a new home elsewhere; their journey is a real passage, and their rootedness in Christ the vine is a real, continuing, and permanent source of everlasting life.

The reality of this spirituality is why Luther judged in 1520 that the riches and glory of the Christian life were in his day unknown throughout the world.[53] This reality is why he abandoned the external piety of his ancestors for a Christian life *ex solo Christo* and embarked on a journey that attempted to reawaken believers to their deep connectedness with Christ, a journey that became a reformation of spirituality.

51. WA 6:534,24-26; LW 36:68.
52. WA 6:534,34-39; LW 36:69.
53. See note 36.